SCHUBERT'S

WINTER JOURNEY

SCHUBERT'S WINTER JOURNEY

Anatomy of an Obsession

IAN BOSTRIDGE

FABER & FABER

First published in the UK in 2015
by Faber & Faber Limited, Bloomsbury House,
74–77 Great Russell Street, London WC1B 3DA
First published in the United States by Alfred A. Knopf

Printed in Italy by L.E.G.O. S.p.A.

The right of Ian Bostridge to be identified as author of this work has been asserted
in accordance with Section 77 of the Copyright, Designs and Patents Act 1988

Grateful acknowledgment is made to the following
for permission to reprint previously published material:

David Higham Associates Ltd: Excerpt from *Summertime* by J. M. Coetzee,
copyright © 2009 by J. M. Coetzee (Vintage, London, 2010). Reprinted
by permission of David Higham Associates Ltd., London.

The Estate of Peter Porter: Excerpt from "Lament Addressed to the People"
[Klage an das Volk (Schubert)] from *Collected Poems Volume 2* by Peter Porter,
translation copyright © 1998 by Peter Porter. Reprinted by permission of Rogers,
Coleridge & White Ltd., London, administering on behalf of the author's estate.

Liveright Publishing Corporation: "1(a" from *Complete Poems: 1904–1962*
by E. E. Cummings, edited by George J. Firmage, copyright © 1958, 1986, 1991
by the Trustees for the E. E. Cummings Trust. Reprinted by permission
of Liveright Publishing Corporation.

Harvard University Press: "Those—dying then" reprinted by permission of the
publishers and the Trustees of Amherst College from *The Poems of Emily Dickinson*,
edited by Thomas H. Johnson, Cambridge, Mass.: The Belknap Press of
Harvard University Press, Copyright © 1951, 1955 by the President and Fellows
of Harvard College. Copyright © renewed 1979, 1983 by the President and
Fellows of Harvard College. Copyright © 1914, 1918, 1919, 1924, 1929, 1930,
1932, 1935, 1937, 1942, by Martha Dickinson Bianchi. Copyright © 1952, 1957,
1958, 1963, 1965, by Mary L. Hampson.

A CIP record for this book is available from the British Library

ISBN 978–0–571–28280–7

4 6 8 10 9 7 5 3

Der schönen Müllerin gewidmet

| CONTENTS |

Introduction   ix

Contents

viii

With a heart filled with endless love for those who scorned me, I . . . wandered far away. For many and many a year I sang songs. Whenever I tried to sing of love, it turned to pain. And again, when I tried to sing of pain, it turned to love.

—SCHUBERT, "My Dream," manuscript, July 3, 1822

Winterreise—*Winter Journey*—a cycle of twenty-four songs for voice and piano, was composed by Franz Schubert towards the end of his short life. He died in Vienna in 1828 aged only thirty-one.

Schubert was renowned, even in his own lifetime, as a song composer of matchless fecundity and a master of seductive melody; the *Winter Journey* apparently discombobulated his friends. One of the closest of these, Joseph von Spaun, remembered thirty years later how the cycle had been received by the Schubert circle:

For some time Schubert appeared very upset and melancholy. When I asked him what was troubling him, he would only say, "Soon you will hear and understand." One day he said to me, "Come over to Schober's today, and I will sing you a cycle of horrifying songs. I am anxious to know what you will say about them. They have cost me more effort than any of my other songs." So he sang the entire *Winter Journey* through to us in a voice full of emotion. We were utterly dumbfounded by the mournful, gloomy tone of these songs, and Schober said that only one, "The Linden Tree," had appealed to him. To this Schubert replied, "I like these songs more than all the rest, and you will come to like them as well."

Another close friend, with whom Schubert had shared digs some years before, was Johann Mayrhofer, government official and poet (Schubert set some forty-seven of his poems to music). For Mayrhofer, *Winter Journey* was an expression of personal trauma:

He had been long and seriously ill [with the syphilis he had first contracted towards the end of 1822], had gone through disheartening experiences, and life had shed its rosy colour; winter had come for him. The poet's irony, rooted in despair, appealed to him: he expressed it in cutting tones.

Spaun confounded even more dramatically the personal and the aesthetic in his account of the cycle's genesis. "There is no doubt in my mind," he wrote, "that the state of excitement in which he wrote his most beautiful songs, and especially his *Winter Journey,* contributed to his early death."

There is something profoundly mythologising about these accounts, especially Spaun's, which has something of Christ in the Garden of Gethsemane about it—the dejection, the friends who miss the point, the sense of a mystery that will only be understood after the death of its progenitor. As against the persistent legend of "poor Schubert"—unappreciated, unloved, unsuccessful in his own lifetime—it is worth remembering that he earned well from his music, was welcomed into the salons of the well-connected (if not the aristocracy), and earned critical plaudits as well as his fair share of brickbats. Schubert was probably the first great composer to operate as a freelancer outside the security and restriction of a church position or noble patronage and, allowing for a certain youthful fecklessness, he did well for himself. His music was second only to Rossini's for its popularity on Viennese programmes; it was played by most of the great instrumentalists of the day; and his fees were substantial. *Winter Journey* itself did not fall still-born from the press. Here is one contemporary review, from the *Theaterzeitung* of March 29, 1828:

Schubert's mind shows a bold sweep everywhere,
whereby he carries everyone away with him who
approaches, and he takes them through the immeasur-
able depth of the human heart into the far distance,
where premonitions of the infinite dawn upon them
longingly in a rosy radiance, but where at the same
time the shuddering bliss of an inexpressible pre-
sentiment is accompanied by the gentle pain of the
constraining present which hems in the boundaries
of human existence.

Despite the slightly windy Romantic rhetoric, the
writer has clearly perceived and engaged with what has
become the acknowledged, canonical sublimity of the
cycle; that transcendental quality which transmogri-
fies what could so easily be mistaken for a self-indulgent
parade of disappointed love lyrics. For the initiate, *Winter
Journey* is one of the great feasts of the musical calendar:
an austere one, but one almost guaranteed to touch the
ineffable as well as the heart. After the last song, "The
Hurdy-Gurdy Man," the silence is palpable, the sort
of silence that otherwise only a Bach Passion can
summon up.

Yet the very notion of the "initiate" will set some alarm
bells ringing. It's one of the reasons for writing another
book about the piece: to explain, to justify, to contextual-

ise and embroider. Piano-accompanied song is no longer part of everyday domestic life, and has lost its one-time supremacy in the concert hall. Art song, as Americans call it—what Germans know as *Lieder*—is a niche product, even within the niche that is classical music; but *Winter Journey* is incontestably a great work of art which should be as much a part of our common experience as the poetry of Shakespeare and Dante, the paintings of Van Gogh and Pablo Picasso, the novels of the Brontë sisters or Marcel Proust. It is surely remarkable that the piece lives and makes an impact in concert halls all over the world, in cultures remote from the circumstances of its origins in 1820s Vienna: I'm writing this introduction in Tokyo, where *Winter Journey* is as telling as it is in Berlin, London, or New York.

In this book I want to use each song as a platform for exploring those origins; setting the piece in its historical context, but also finding new and unexpected connections, both contemporary and long dead—literary, visual, psychological, scientific, and political. Musical analysis will inevitably play its part, but this is nothing as systematic as a guide to *Winter Journey*, of which there are plenty already out there. That I do not have the technical qualifications to analyse music in the traditional, musicological sense—I have never studied music at university or music college—has its disadvantages, but maybe advantages too. I have been heartened by Nicholas Cook's exploration of the "discrepancies between the listener's experience of music and the way in which it is described or explained in theoretical terms" (in his brilliant study *Music, Imagination and Culture*). Experiment has shown that even highly trained musicians tend not to listen to music as musical form in the technical sense; for all of us, unless we're making a special and determined effort of analysis, our encounter with music is more episodic and even cavalier, less relentlessly theoretical—even when we're listening to a piece from the great tradition that presents itself as musical argument, a Beethoven symphony for example, or a Bach fugue. Within as diffuse a structure as *Winter Journey*—a set of twenty-four songs, the first and greatest of concept albums—there may be recurring patterns or harmonic devices that deserve pointing out; but I tend to do so in what one might call a phenomenological mode, tracing the subjective and culturally loaded trajectories of listener and performer rather than cataloguing modulations, cadences, and root positions.

By gathering such a disparate mass of material I hope to illuminate, to explain, and to deepen our common response; to intensify the experience of those who already know the piece, and to reach out to those who have never heard it or heard of it. The lynchpin is always the piece itself—how do we perform it? how should we hear it?—

but by placing it within a much broader framework unfamiliar, unexpected perspectives will emerge with, I hope, their own fascination.

MY OWN WAY TO *Winter Journey* was eased by great teaching and by personal idiosyncrasy. I first came across the music of Franz Schubert and the poetry of Wilhelm Müller (who wrote the words of *Winter Journey*) at school, aged twelve or thirteen. Our miracle of a music teacher, Michael Spencer, was always getting us to do magnificently, even absurdly, ambitious musical projects. As a singer, and not an instrumentalist, I had always felt slightly outside the charmed circle, though we sang plenty enough fantastic music—Britten, Bach, Tallis, and Richard Rodney Bennett for starters. When Michael, Mr. Spencer, suggested that he (piano) and one of my classmates, Edward Osmond (clarinet), perform something called "The Shepherd on the Rock," I had no idea how brilliantly off the wall it was. Going to his house on a Saturday morning to be with the other musicians and rehearse was one of the great excitements of my life.

"Der Hirt auf dem Felsen" was one of the very last pieces Schubert composed, written at the express request of the great opera diva Anna Milder-Hauptmann, whose voice was a contemporary marvel: "a house," as one had it; "pure metal," another. The opening and concluding verses are by the poet of *Winter Journey,* Wilhelm Müller, but nothing could be further from Schubert's great song cycle than this dazzling confection of virtuoso pastoral. A shepherd stands on a rock singing into the Alpine landscape before him. His voice echoes and reechoes and he remembers his lover far away. A grieving middle section is succeeded by an excited and excitable invocation of spring. Spring will come, the shepherd will wander, and he and his girl will be reunited. It's the very opposite of *Winter Journey,* as we shall discover.

Somewhere in a box in my attic is a tape of that school performance. I haven't listened to it for a long time, but I do remember that the famous vocal challenges of the piece are unaddressed by my fragile treble. At the same time, there was something nice about reclaiming this trouser role, this travesty shepherd boy, for an actual boy's voice. Anyway, I fell in love with the music but then promptly forgot it, this first encounter with the Lieder tradition.

Step up another great teacher, this time a German master at senior school, Richard Stokes, whose deep, urgent, and infectious love of song infiltrated many, if not most, of his lessons. Imagine twenty or so fourteen- and fifteen-year-olds, in varying states of vocal health, bellowing Schubert's "Erl King" or Marlene Dietrich's "Where Have All the Flowers Gone?" in the language lab, and you get the idea. It was "The Erl King" that made me fall in love with German song, the Lied, with a passion which dominated my teenage years. It was one particular recording of it—played in our very first German lesson—which seized my imagination and my intellect: Dietrich Fischer-Dieskau, the prince of German baritones, and Gerald Moore, his English accompanist. I didn't yet speak the language, but the sound of it and the drama which piano and voice—sometimes honeyed, sometimes trembling, sometimes incarnate evil—together conveyed were utterly new to me. I got my hands on as many recordings of Fischer-Dieskau's song singing as I could, and I sang along to them, probably right through my voice change from treble to tenor: not ideal for my embryonic vocal technique, as Fischer-Dieskau was unmistakeably a baritone.

Personal idiosyncrasy played its part in my Lieder obsession too, as I used the music and the lyrics to work my way through the perils and pains of adolescence. The other Wilhelm Müller cycle, the first—*Die schöne Müllerin* (The Beautiful Miller Girl)—was perfect for someone of my very particular Romantic disposition. I thought I'd fallen in love with a girl who lived in my street, but my clumsy attentions were first unnoticed and then spurned, and in my imagination, maybe in reality, she formed a liaison with a sporty type from the local tennis club. It seemed quite natural to tramp the South London streets near her house, singing Schubert under my breath, the songs of rapture and those of the angry reject. After all, the fair maid of the mill goes off with the macho hunter, not the sensitive singing miller boy.

Winter Journey was something I got to know a little later, but I was already primed for it. I heard two great Germans sing it in London—Peter Schreier and Hermann Prey—but I somehow managed to miss my only opportunity to hear Fischer-Dieskau perform it, with Alfred Brendel, at the Royal Opera House, Covent Garden. I gave my own first public performance of *Winterreise* to thirty or so friends, teachers, and fellow students at St John's College, Oxford, in the President's Lodgings, in January 1985. People always ask me how I remember all the words; the answer is to start young. As this book is published, I shall have been singing the cycle for thirty years.

THIS BOOK IS THE RESULT of a couple of years of writing and research but also of three decades of obsessing about *Winterreise*, performing it—probably more than any other piece in my repertoire—and trying to find new ways of singing it, of presenting it, and of understanding it. As a result I have accumulated debts to friends and colleagues which are too numerous to honour in any-

thing like their entirety. I have already mentioned two
teachers who inspired me, Michael Spencer and Richard
Stokes. The pianists with whom I have performed the
piece have all contributed to this book in a crucial way.
Schubert himself, on tour in Salzburg in 1825 and writing to his brother, recognised that through both his
songwriting and his performances he had created a new
artform which required a very particular union between
singer and player: "The manner in which Vogl sings and
the way I accompany, as though we were one at such a
moment, is something quite new and unheard-of." Julius
Drake, with whom I filmed the piece and have performed
it countless times before and since, has been the most
wonderful companion on this journey of journeys, wise
friend, and extraordinary musician; Graham Johnson has
shared with me the inspirations of the moment in concert
and the unparalleled depth of his Schubertian scholarship in conversation; Leif Ove Andsnes, a wonderful and
humane solo pianist, took time out to tour and record
the cycle with me; Mitsuko Uchida likewise took me to
special places with her playing; Wenwen Du, a novice but
no novice, with her freshness of approach has recently
brought new insight; and, as I complete this book, I
look forward to a tour of *Winterreise* with the composer
Thomas Adès, who is already finding new and unexpected
things to say about the piece. Rehearsing and performing

with him as this book reached its proof stage has been a salutary and painful reminder that my verbal descriptions of what is going on in this protean music are at best provisional and at worst utterly inadequate. Ying Chang was the very first pianist I worked with on *Winterreise*, a fine historian and amateur musician, to whom I owe special thanks. At Faber & Faber and at Knopf I have had two fabled and fabulous editors, Belinda Matthews and Carol Janeway, whose faith and encouragement in this project have sustained me, and whose words of wisdom have saved me from myself. The team around them has been first-class and they deserve more than mere alphabetical listing: Peter Andersen, Lisa Baker, Lizzie Bishop, Kevin Bourke, Kate Burton, Eleanor Crow, Roméo Enriquez, Maggie Hinders, Andy Hughes, Josephine Kals, Joshua LaMorey, Peter Mendelsund, Pedro Nelson, Kate Ward, Bronagh Woods.

Peter Bloor, Phillippa Cole, Adam Gopnik, Liesl Kundert, Robert Rattray, Tamsin Shaw, Caroline Woodfield—thank you all. And a special apology to Alexander Bird, dear friend, who turns out to have been right all those years ago: Schubert is, indeed, the best.

Finally I want to thank my family: my mother, who gave me my first book of Schubert songs; my late father, who used to sing with me on long car journeys; and especially my children, Oliver and Ottilie, who put up

xx |

with my too frequent absences and whose love keeps the alienation that dominates *Winterreise* at bay. The book is dedicated to my beloved wife and best friend, Lucasta Miller. Its structure was her idea, and her profound knowledge of the 1820s means that many of the best ideas in this book are hers. Her love and companionship make everything possible.

A NOTE ON THE TRANSLATIONS

I translated Müller's poems as I went along, using the process of translation as a spur to writing each chapter. The results are a little coarse, and I have not taken a consistent approach to reconciling the demands of the literal and the poetic. Each chapter, each poem, seemed to require a different balance. Likewise, I sometimes render certain lines afresh within my text, to cast an alternative light on Müller's words. Writing the book, my admiration for Müller as a crafty and gifted poet has grown; it is difficult adequately to render the complexities and beauties of his verse.

| I |

GUTE NACHT

GOOD NIGHT

Fremd bin ich eingezogen,
Fremd zieh ich wieder aus.
Der Mai war mir gewogen
Mit manchem Blumenstrauß.
Das Mädchen sprach von Liebe,
Die Mutter gar von Eh'—
Nun ist die Welt so trübe,
Der Weg gehüllt in Schnee.

Ich kann zu meiner Reisen
Nicht wählen mit der Zeit:
Muß selbst den Weg mir weisen
In dieser Dunkelheit.
Es zieht ein Mondenschatten
Als mein Gefährte mit,
Und auf den weißen Matten
Such' ich des Wildes Tritt.

Was soll ich länger weilen,
Daß man mich trieb' hinaus?
Laß irre Hunde heulen
Vor ihres Herren Haus!
Die Liebe liebt das Wandern,—
Gott hat sie so gemacht—
Von einem zu dem andern,
Fein Liebchen, gute Nacht!

I came a stranger,
I depart a stranger.
May was good to me
With many a garland of flowers.
The girl, she talked of love,
The mother even of marriage—
Now the world is so gloomy,
The way is shrouded in snow.

I cannot choose the time
Of my journey:
Must find my own way
In this darkness.
A moon beam goes along
As my companion,
And on the white meadows
I look for tracks of deer.

Why should I hang around any longer
Waiting for someone to throw me out?
Let stray dogs howl
In front of their master's house!
Love loves to wander—
God made it that way—
From one to another—
Sweetest love, good night!

Will dich im Traum nicht stören,
Wär' schad' um deine Ruh',
Sollst meinen Tritt nicht hören—
Sacht, sacht die Türe ʒu!
Schreib' im Vorübergehen
An's Tor dir gute Nacht,
Damit du mögest sehen,
An dich hab' ich gedacht.

I won't disturb you in your dream,
It would be a shame to disturb your rest,
You oughtn't to hear my footstep—
Softly, softly the door closes!
I'll write on the gate
As I go by it—good night—
So you can see
I've thought of you.

*G*OOD NIGHT" is very often the end of the tale, isn't it? It's what we say to children when the bedtime story is finished. It has something gentle about it, and this is a gentle song, a song which, in rehearsal or in performance, I always experience as both an ending to something and also a prelude to the cycle proper. Marked down in dynamics and hushed pretty much throughout, as the wanderer creeps away from the household in which he has loved and, somehow, lost, it contains only the barest hints of the alienation and emotional extremes to come. The hints are there, though, to be registered and refracted through later songs.

I used to dread this song when I first started on my journey with *Winterreise;* or rather, I used to feel a sense of enormous relief when it came to an end. There was the fear that through inexperience, through lack of proper engagement and a lack of trust in the composer's conception, I would bore myself and, consequently (and much,

much worse), the audience. "Gute Nacht" is longer than any of the other songs in *Winterreise*, especially considering that it is moderate in tempo rather than slow: it is essentially repetitive and perhaps, ideally, rather featureless. The temptation when we hear about the wayward dogs barking in the third verse is to register some sort of dynamic change, to sing louder, with more accentuation, and mimic their barking. This should be resisted, though the resistance should doubtless be felt. That repetitive, quiet texture, carefully marked by Schubert, is crucial; crucial for the quintessentially Schubertian effect in the final verse, as the key shifts magically from minor to major. As so often in Schubert, the major seems, contrary to the commonplace notion of key mythologised in Cole Porter's "Ev'ry Time We Say Goodbye" ("and how strange the change from major to minor"), sadder than the minor. Its sadness here is partly a question of its fragility: this radiant thought of the girl, asleep and dreaming, is itself a dream. Dreams of happiness, cast in the major key, and all the more heartbreaking for it, are a recurrent aspect of this song cycle.

This is one of those songs that seem to have been going on forever at the very moment that they start. Repeated, moderately paced quavers trudge across the page and on through the song, relentless, intertwined at first with a dispiriting descending figure broken by the stabs of

| 7

accents which in Schubert's manuscript are stabs of pain.
In that same manuscript, Schubert has given the song
the tempo marking "mässig, in gehender Bewegung,"
or "moderate, at a walking pace" (literally "a going
motion")—and that walking motion, like a dying fall, is
the touchstone of the whole work: a winter journey, moving from one place to another but, in a sense, privileging
motion above all else, the need to get away, to be a wanderer in the nineteenth century's sense (the Wandering
Jew, the Flying Dutchman), on the road in the twentieth
century's (Jack Kerouac, Highway 61). Schubert himself
had already used the marking in one of his darkest settings, one of the songs of Goethe's cursed outsider, the
Harper, which begins, "I will creep from door to door";
it may also have reminded him of Beethoven's Piano
Sonata no. 26. This, the so-called "Les Adieux," has a
first movement grounded in a musical motif above which
the composer wrote "Lebewohl," a heartfelt farewell; and
its central movement is entitled "Abwesenheit," absence,
with the tempo marking "Andante espressivo (in gehender
Bewegung, doch mit viel Ausdruck)"—in walking
motion, but with much expression.

Why does the man singing these songs need to get
away? We don't really know, though it's often assumed
that we do, and that he has been rejected in love and has to
move on. The information we are given is, let us remind
ourselves, sketchy to a point—the girl talked about love,

the mother even of marriage. The phrase is repeated in
Schubert's setting, rising in pitch and expectation. Then
a great gulf opens up, a sort of depressive caesura marking the end of hope, a turn from the inside warmth of
the past to the bitterness of the landscape which we will
henceforth inhabit—"Now the world is so murky, the
way is shrouded in snow." But remember, it's not clear
what drove him out. Did he dump her? Did she dump
him? Was the mother's talk about marriage a sort of
hopeful mirage, or a nightmare vision for an itinerant
commitment-phobe? Has he been doing this his whole
life? Why is he here in this house, in this town, at this
hour? Has he been staying, visiting, dropping by? It's
nighttime. Everyone's asleep.

| 9

Part of the key to this lies in the poet Wilhelm Müller's
immersion in things Byronic (he published major essays
on the poet of *Childe Harold* and *Don Juan* in German in
the 1820s) and what we might call the Byronic method of
absence, something Byron himself had taken and developed from Walter Scott (the poet of *Marmion* who later
morphed into the historical novelist of *Ivanhoe*). Müller's
protagonist is, like a Byronic hero, wrapped in an aura of
mystery ("I came a stranger, a stranger I depart" is how
he introduces himself); a tragic figure the roots of whose
predicament are never satisfactorily revealed. As he says
himself (significantly, much later in the cycle, when the
poet's imprecision has done its work), almost mocking

this Byronic model, "Habe ja doch nichts begangen, daß
ich Menschen sollte scheu'n" (I haven't done anything
that means I ought to shun human company). It's almost
a question—"Have I? You tell me. . . ." This mystery
was at the core of the Byron cult itself, a cult which fed
the poetry. He was a poet associated with his own poetic
voice in an unprecedented way. "It is difficult," one
reader, Annabella Milbanke, wrote in 1814 (she married Byron a year later), "it is difficult to believe that he
could have known these beings so thoroughly but from
introspection." Byron lived out the mythology of his own
poetic narratives—fragmented narratives, like that of
Winterreise—by becoming an exile, a wanderer, cast out
for a dark and mysterious crime (which turned out, some
decades later, to have been incest with his own half-sister).

Yet there's no suggestion of a terribly dark crime
in *Winterreise:* our wanderer is no Manfred or Ancient
Mariner. There's also no hint that at the time he wrote it
the happily married Wilhelm Müller was living out the
experiences of his protagonist (though an earlier love
affair, in Brussels at the end of the Napoleonic Wars,
may have provided useful material). His earlier life, or
indeed Schubert's, are a different matter, as we shall see;
but it's only as a sort of allegory about German political
alienation in the post-Napoleonic, Metternich-dominated
period that the cycle can relate to Müller's own circum-

stances when he wrote the poems. That's hardly plausible
as a mainstream reading of the poems, though it is one we
shall be exploring later. It is, in fact, a very domestic predicament that yields this existential angst, one rooted in
a Biedermeier setting, a world away from the melodrama
of Scott's *Marmion* or Byron's *Manfred*. This is, no doubt,
why Müller's verse so appealed to the great deflator of
Romantic excess, Heinrich Heine. It is also, this ordinari-
ness, surely, the source of the cycle's originality and of
its power. Yet that Byronically inspired absence of a clear
narrative mise-en-scène, the stinginess with information,
is a vital part of the way we become implicated in our
protagonist's fate, a piece of poetical legerdemain. We are
drawn in by an obsessively confessional soul, apparently
an emotional exhibitionist, who won't give us the facts;
but this allows us to supply the facts of our own lives, and
make him our mirror. At the same time the great waves of
unattached subjectivity in these poems, unconstrained by
plot or even character (we know so little, from a conventional point of view, about this man), the infinite depths,
suggest precisely why Müller, of all Schubert's contemporaries, so cried out for his poems to be set to music:

> I can neither play nor sing, yet when I write verses, I
> sing and play after all. If I could produce the melodies,
> my songs would be more pleasing than they are now.

> But courage! perhaps there is a kindred spirit some-
> where who will hear the tunes behind the words and
> give them back to me.

He wrote this in his diary in 1815, on his twenty-first
birthday. When, in 1822, the composer Bernhard Josef
Klein published settings of six of Müller's poems, the latter

thanked him in these words:

> For indeed my songs lead but half a life, a paper
> existence of black-and-white, until music breathes life
> into them, or at least calls it forth and awakens it if it is
> already dormant in them.

The irony is that Müller never heard Schubert's settings
of either his earlier poetic cycle, *Die schöne Müllerin,* or of
Winterreise—though he surely heard earlier settings by
other, less fabled composers.

SCHUBERT'S EARLIEST TRIUMPHS in songwriting, some
fourteen years before the completion of *Winterreise,* were
settings of the greatest German writer of his, or probably any, age, Johann Wolfgang von Goethe. "Erlkönig"
and "Gretchen am Spinnrade" (Gretchen at the Spinning
Wheel) couldn't be more emotionally different at first

sight; yet the method Schubert brings to bear on both is essentially the same, and utterly new in song. In one, a boy is carried through the forest by his father on horse-back, terrified by the demonic whisperings of the faery Erl King. The father attempts to soothe, to distract his son, but at the end of the journey, and of the song, the boy is dead. Goethe wrote the poem as a ballad to open a court entertainment about fishermen, a *Singspiel,* at Weimar in 1782. It aspires, at least superficially, to a sort of artless rusticity. It took the adolescent composer Schubert to tease out its psychological depths. "Gretchen am Spinn-rade," by contrast, is a patent masterpiece of psychological realism and erotic intensity which forms part of Goethe's most famous achievement in verse, *Faust.* Sitting alone at her spinning wheel, Gretchen unravels her obsession with Faust, describing him and her feelings for him with an increasing abandon which can end, as she puts it herself, only in a death for which she longs, the double death, as we sense, of both sexual climax and extinction.

These were, and remain, two very famous poems in the German literary canon, and Schubert invented for them—it's so natural that it almost seems more a matter of discovery than of invention—a musical language which is so powerful that it subsumes them, takes them over, embraces them in a way which it is difficult, once heard, to un-imagine.

In both, a flexible musical figure is used as an analogy for the central material image which Schubert has selected from the poem. With "Erlkönig" it's hammering repeated octaves (murderous for the pianist's right hand on a modern piano); for Gretchen, a repetitive semiquaver arabesque. The technique is so familiar, so taken for granted, that it's worth analysing it just a little (especially as it is the basis of so much in *Winterreise,* in many, though not all, of its songs). It's no use describing it as realism, as if a musical sound can directly represent, or even evoke, something in the material world. The pounding octaves in "Erlkönig" *are* the pounding hooves, the arabesques in "Gretchen" *are* the motion of the spinning wheel (they are many other things too—the heartbeat of the rider, the obsessive thought processes of the spinner). And of course, pounding octaves could not, reasonably or believably, be a spinning wheel, or an arabesque a horse at full tilt. The images work by association, reinforcing each other, and creating an integrated poetic sound world. They animate, in both cases, the whole song, and subtle changes are used to shift perspective (from father to son to Erl King) or emotional temperature (tempo and key changes crank up the hysteria in "Gretchen"). Music and poem fuse and we are carried through on one great arc: broken midpoint for Gretchen, as the thought of Faust's kiss causes her to stop spinning and gradually set to work again; and at the end of "Erlkönig" as the father reaches home. The sense of psychological depth achieved by such a rich and relentless undertaking—Schubert never lets go of the musical or poetic logic—is palpable, and it is difficult to go back to the poem without the music and not feel, somehow, robbed.

This is not a musical approach likely to endear com-poser to poet, and there's a long history of writers resent-ing their creations being kidnapped by other art forms (think of Yeats's attitude to musical settings of his poetry; the music associated with the songs from Shakespeare's plays has none of the complexity or magic of the play-wright's composing contemporary John Dowland). It seems to have made Goethe—despite his relative musi-cal sophistication and his valiant attempts to find in a reformed *Singspiel* (the German word for opera with spo-ken text, like Mozart's *Magic Flute*) a way of fusing word and music—edgy. His favoured composers for setting his lyrics—and we have to remember that the founding con-ceit of *lyric* poetry is that these are songs which have lost, and perhaps cry out for, music—were those like his friend Johann Friedrich Reichardt. Reichardt's settings are very different from Schubert's. His ambitions were modest, the means he brought to bear simple, and he saw his first duty as one of accompanying the verse, not body-snatching it without due deference or decency. Schubert clearly spotted the sexual undertow of "Gretchen," the Oedipal confusions of "Erlkönig," and amplified them in the direction of what Goethe, ever the classicist in essence, might have thought of as Romantic hysteria, the sickness which he dreaded. For Schubert himself, the Gretchen poem remained a crucial marker in his life, a text with which he identified despite—or, some would have it, because of—its female protagonist. In the depths of despair after his diagnosis of syphilis in 1823, he repeated her opening words in a letter to a friend—"Meine Ruh' ist hin, mein Herz ist schwer" (My peace is gone, my heart is heavy). This is often read in the light of debates about Schubert's sexuality, as if his ability to inhabit Gretchen in the song, and then to use her words in real life, were a measure of his distance from conventional masculine identity. I like to think it is just as much a measure of Schubert's realisation that "Gretchen" marked a revolution in songwriting which stood right at the beginning of his career. Not every song after "Gretchen" would follow its model, and Schubert was capable of working a much less sophisticated magic. But the Gretchen song stands as a sort of talisman in Schubert's creative life, and the genius Schubert brought to bear upon it is identifiably the same as that at work in his transformation of Müller's poetic cycle *Die Winterreise* into his own *Winterreise*.

. . .

NOTE, FIRST OF ALL, that radical abbreviation of the title. Schubert was quite used to altering literary material to suit his purposes—the repetition of Gretchen's opening words "Meine Ruh ist hin, mein Herz ist schwer" to close "Gretchen am Spinnrade" was an early example. By removing the definite article from Müller's poetic cycle, he did two things. First, he made the work his own, something distinct from its originating material and owing no loyalty to it beyond the use he could make of it in moulding it to his own purposes. Secondly, he made it more abstract, less definite, more open—without its definite article—and, from our perspective, more modern. *Winterreise* has a starkness which is utterly true to its material in a way that *Die Winterreise* would not be. Anyone can own this journey.

Müller's poems appealed to Schubert for all sorts of reasons, some very personal and specific (the cycle ends, for example, with a poem about a musician), some more general (the theme of the outcast cursed by a failed love appealed to a man such as Schubert, who was suffering from the early stages of syphilis). Exploring these is part of what this book is about. But the overarching aesthetic, formal appeal has to be the way in which the *Winterreise* poems seem to beg for music, as Müller himself recognised. Goethe's being resistant to the musical appropriation of his verse didn't stop Schubert setting a great number of his poems, more than by any other poet.

And Goethe's resistance didn't impede Schubert's success in setting them; interestingly, his poems are far more amenable to such treatment than those of his friend and contemporary Schiller, whom Schubert set on almost as many occasions, but often with less startling success. The mysterious subjectivity of Müller's *Die Winterreise*, by contrast, actually cries out to be inhabited and filled in by Schubert's music; the psychology of our wanderer becomes more present to us through music. So too does his physical environment, so dense with metaphor, as the composer brings to bear that complex method of using a motif to suggest a physical analogy (the steady tread of "Gute Nacht," for example; and the cycle yields many, many more) and then subjecting it to the musical invocation of shifting emotion. That inner emotional intensity is externalised, characterised, even dramatised; because the song is written to be sung, it is given voice. Never must we, in the midst of analysis, forget that these songs were made to be sung—whether at the keyboard in private, among friends, or to a larger audience.

Some years before his discovery of the *Winterreise* poems, Schubert made his only attempt at an extended piece of literary prose (a few poems are ascribed to him and, of course, quite a few letters). It's headed "Mein Traum" (My Dream), and it's not clear from the text itself whether it's a record of a dream or an invention, a fable.

What is clear is that in it Schubert imagines himself as exactly the sort of hero—though "hero" is hardly the word—Müller has in mind for his winter's journey:

> With a heart filled with endless love for those who scorned me, I . . . wandered far away. For many and many a year I sang songs. Whenever I tried to sing of love, it turned to pain. And again, when I tried to sing of pain, it turned to love.

It's not surprising that when Schubert came upon twelve of the poems in the almanac *Urania*, some time in the mid-1820s, he was immediately seized by them and almost compelled to set them to music. His friends later wrote of him promising them new songs and then failing to turn up as agreed to sing them, the implication being that he was still immersed in finishing them. Could this have been *Winterreise*? When he did perform the cycle to them, singing to his own accompaniment, they didn't really like it. As Spaun recalled: "Schober said that only one, 'The Linden Tree,' had appealed to him. To this Schubert replied, 'I like these songs more than all the rest, and you will come to like them as well.'" He was engaged in something he himself recognised as revolutionary in the field of song.

In choosing and composing the cycle, Schubert recognised the opportunity that Müller offered him; their musical and poetic methods were quite in tune. Müller's use of Byron's method of absence was even enhanced by the composer, serendipitously as it were, because of the way in which he seems to have discovered the poems. First of all he found the twelve in *Urania*, and composed them straight through as a twelve-song cycle, beginning and ending, as an artistic whole, in the same key, D minor. (I've often performed this ur-*Winterreise* as a cycle in its own right, in concert.) When Müller finally published his complete twenty-four-poem version, in the second volume of his *Gedichte aus den hinterlassenen Papieren eines reisenden Waldhornisten* (Poems from the Surviving Papers of a Travelling Horn Player), subtitled "Songs of Love and Life," he reordered the sequence so that effectively, the new poems were interpolated among the old. Yet Schubert didn't follow Müller in this when he came upon the new version. Instead, he left the first twelve songs as they were, and made them the first half of his cycle; he then took the extra poems and set them in the order that they occurred in Müller's book, one might say higgledy-piggledy.

The composer did make aesthetic choices to craft his own cycle, moulding the poetic source to his own ends as he had so often done before in song after song. He changed the key of the twelfth song, "Einsamkeit" (Loneliness), which had originally ended his set, but which now

fell halfway through; it no longer had the same key as
the first song in the cycle, "Gute Nacht" (Good Night), a
choice which had effected a sort of aesthetic closure for the
twelve-song ur-*Winterreise*. And he did swap around two
of the songs in his second half so that they didn't follow
Müller's order, presumably to effect a particular change
of pace towards the end of the work, avoiding three slow
or slowish songs in a row—"Der Wegweiser" (The
Signpost), "Das Wirtshaus" (The Inn), "Die Nebensonnen" (The Mock Suns)—and avoiding the sense in
Müller that courage is the wanderer's prevailing emotion
directly before he encounters the hurdy-gurdy man of the
last song. But any narrative order that Müller had given
vestigial existence to in the poetic cycle (hints of a story,
a time sequence, a logic of place that have mistakenly led
some commentators to prefer Müller's order for Schubert's
cycle) is utterly expunged by Schubert's compositional
gambit in the second half of the song cycle. The effect is to
redouble the sense of fragmentation from the twelfth song
on. Like all great artists, he makes the most of the acci-
dental, with a serendipitous intensification of the Byronic
method of displacement, a turn of the screw. *Winterreise* is
at one and the same time homely and insistently mysterious, one of the secrets of its enormous power.

Here are Müller's twenty-four songs in their final order:

Gute Nacht—Good Night
Die Wetterfahne—The Weathervane
Gefrorne Tränen—Frozen Tears
Erstarrung—Frozen Stiff
Der Lindenbaum—The Linden Tree
Die Post—The Post
Wasserflut—Flood
Auf dem Flusse—On the Stream
Rückblick—Backwards Glance
Der greise Kopf—The Old Man's Head
Die Krähe—The Crow
Letzte Hoffnung—Last Hope
Im Dorfe—In the Village
Der stürmische Morgen—The Stormy Morning
Täuschung—Delusion
Der Wegweiser—The Signpost
Das Wirtshaus—The Inn
Irrlicht—Will-o'-the-Wisp
Rast—Rest
Die Nebensonnen—The Mock Suns
Frühlingstraum—Dream of Spring
Einsamkeit—Loneliness
Mut—Courage
Der Leiermann—The Hurdy-Gurdy Man

And here is Schubert's order—the first twelve being Müller's original set:

There is, of course, also something immensely contemporary—modern, or is it postmodern?—about the displacement of narrative in Schubert's *Winterreise*. In his book *Reality Hunger,* a montage of unattributed quotations (and self-quotations) dealing with the inadequacy of traditional literary form in confronting a modern, fragmented reality, the American author David Shields tells us that "the absence of plot leaves the reader room to think about other things." "Momentum," he declares, "derives not from narrative but from the subtle buildup of thematic resonances." Many of the patchwork of literary fragments he assembles would do just as good a job as epigraphs to *Winterreise* or a book about or around *Winterreise:*

I have a narrative, but you will be put to it to find it.

I'm not interested in collage as the refuge of the compositionally disabled. I'm interested in collage as (to be honest) an evolution beyond narrative.

Plot, like erected scaffolding, is torn down, and what stands in its place is the thing itself.

How much can one remove and still have the composition be intelligible? This understanding, or its lack, divides those who can write from those who can *really* write. Chekhov removed the plot. Pinter, elaborating, removed the history, the narration; Beckett, the characterisation. We hear it anyway. Omission is a form of creation.

Beckett was a great admirer of Schubert, and of *Winterreise* in particular. And there is something deeply Beckettian about the piece. The fact that Shields's snippets come from such varied twentieth- and twenty-first-century sources (the modernist novelist Djuna Barnes, the playwright David Mamet, David Shields himself) is a measure of the modern persistence of the call to be fragmentary. Looking, in turn, at *Winterreise,* what we need to remember is that none of these urges are modern; they are as old as Müller and Byron and Schubert and, again, much, much older—reality has, after all, always been fragmented, is no more so now than it was then, any then; and we should remember, consequently, that *Winterreise* is by no means old hat.

LET US NOW RETURN to the elements of the poem, the crucial details which set the drama. "*Fremd* bin ich eingezogen," we are told, that word *Fremd* most often translated as a noun rather than the adjective it actually is—"A stranger I came, a stranger I departed." But that commonplace German adjective carries with it a whole penumbra of meaning, a history, and a cloud of connotation. In a modern German dictionary we find the following attempts to capture in English its many meanings:

SOMEONE ELSE'S

DIFFERENT

FOREIGN

ALIEN

STRANGE

OTHER

OUTSIDE.

It is, unexpectedly, an English word too, if a much less
familiar one. We find it in Chaucer, meaning "foreign"
("A faukoun peregryn thanne semed she Of fremde land,"
from "The Squire's Tale"); "strange" ("That nevere yit
was so fremde a cas," from the Dido section in *The Legend
of Good Women*); and "unfriendly" ("Lat be to me your
fremde maner speche," in *Troilus and Criseyde*). Its etymology, shared with the German and also with similar words
in, among many other languages, Swedish (*främmande*),
Dutch (*vreemd*), and West Frisian (*frjemd*), finds its earliest trace, according to some etymologies, in the Proto-
Indo-European *perəm-*, *prom-* ("forth," "forward"),
from *por-* ("forward," "through"): a nice thought given
that trudging sense of going forth that Schubert's music
gives us. "Hostile" is another English meaning; as well as
"not related," or "of another house," akin to the Proto-
Germanic *framaþiz*, or "not one's own," meanings of
singular relevance to this fractured narrative of a marriage
forbidden or foregone. This trawl through the dictionar-
ies is more than idle fact-grubbing; it surely gives us a
poetic handle on our hero's predicament. The word stands
at the head of the poetic cycle, of the song cycle, and it is
repeated. It is crucial.

Fremd can also send us back to a song of Schubert's
which was, in the nineteenth century, as popular as
"Erlkönig" or "Gretchen am Spinnrade," a song whose

central musical theme became the motivic motor of Schubert's titanic piece for solo piano, the so-called "Wanderer" Fantasy. This song, "Der Wanderer," was written in 1816 and published in 1821, setting a poem by Georg Philipp Schmidt von Lübeck (1766–1849). That main middle section, pulsating with melancholia and homesickness, paints a picture of a world emptied of meaning and affect:

> *Die Sonne dünkt mich hier so kalt,*
> *Die Blüte welk, das Leben alt,*
> *Und was sie reden, leerer Schall,*
> *Ich bin ein Fremdling überall.*

> The sun seems so cold here,
> Flowers faded, life old,
> And what people say, empty sound,
> I am everywhere a . . .

Everywhere a what? A *Fremdling*, the poet says. An outcast? A stranger? A foreigner?

The notion of the outcast wanderer was a commonplace of Romantic culture Europe-wide; and wandering is, notoriously, a feature of Schubert's songs. Schubert's other song cycle to poems of Müller, *Die schöne Müllerin*, starts with a song called "Das Wandern"—wandering—

and tells us, with apparent nonchalance and good cheer, that wandering is a miller's delight. Journeymen have to wander, of course, to find work; that's why they're called journeymen. There's nothing darkly existential in play here, not on the surface, at least. Schmidt's wanderer, on the other hand, wanders because he is in some way hollowed out or literally displaced. The song ends with the words "dort wo du nicht bist, dort ist das Glück"—there, where you are not, there is happiness. This reads like depression; but there is also something more historically specific to unpack.

The *Fremdling* is a foreigner in his own land. This was a notion with a particular resonance for people like Georg Schmidt, Wilhelm Müller, or Franz Schubert, living in the territories of what had been the Holy Roman Empire of the German Nation, dissolved by Napoleon in 1806, and only semi-resurrected in the Restoration settlement of 1815, which, while aiming to preserve the territorial integrity of the Hapsburg imperium—a multi-ethnic assemblage of lands half-masquerading as a modern state, its capital city Vienna—put a tight lid on expressions of German nationalism. Germany as a nation did not exist. Outside the Hapsburg domains, German states included small principalities (such as Anhalt-Dessau, where Müller lived and worked as ducal librarian), free cities (like Schmidt's Hanseatic Lübeck), and major powers such as Prussia.

Sovereignty was confused and overlapping. For Germans
in these lands, and in Austria, this was the period known
as Biedermeier, between the nationalistic uprising against
Napoleon of 1814–15 (in which Müller participated as a
soldier, and which Schubert celebrated in song) and the
bourgeois, nationalist revolutions of 1848. Those revolutions failed, but twenty-three years later a new, Prussian-
led German empire was proclaimed at Versailles, forged
by blood and iron; the great Prussian statesman Otto von
Bismarck had managed to exclude the Hapsburgs from
any role in the creation of a German national state. It is
crucial for our purposes, however, to remember that none
of this was preordained, and that a settlement of the German national question could have included Austria, and
that many German speakers hoped that it would.

To live as a German in Dessau, or in Vienna, or in
Lübeck in the 1820s was, then, to live as a *Fremdling,* with
a sense that national borders did not coincide with linguis-
tic realities or cultural yearnings, a sense that to be a German nationalist was to be in opposition to the established
order, to be at odds with authority. It was an experience of
alienation (*Ent*fremd*ung*). Liberalism and nationalism went
hand in hand, both of them suppressed in the clampdown
imposed by the Hapsburg government of Metternich and
its allies in the German Confederation. The Biedermeier
era was one in which the excitement of the revolutionary

and Napoleonic years was to be repressed. The metaphors have been the same in our own time. If there had been a political springtime within living memory—the Josephine reforms of the 1780s in the Hapsburg realms, the nationalist surge of 1814–15 in Germany at large—this was now wintertime. Schubert (born 1797) and Müller (born 1794) give us a *Winter Journey* that became a metaphor for an era. When Heinrich Heine, an admirer of Wilhelm Müller, published his satirical verse-epic on the German political scene in 1844, he called it *Deutschland, ein Wintermärchen* (Germany, a Winter's Tale), making explicit the political undercurrents which swirl beneath *Winterreise*'s Biedermeier surface. In the work of Heine's admirer and correspondent Karl Marx, that Central European, political alienation was to be universalised into a picture of the predicament of humanity in an age of economic transformation, an age in which we still live. We'll return to that picture with a later song, "Im Dorfe" (In the Village).

ALIENATION IS WOVEN all the way through *Winterreise*. There is the very simple, personal sense of the word—the estrangement which follows a love affair is, after all, the way the cycle starts. But there is also the sort of alienation which makes *Winterreise* a pre-echo of so much twentieth-century philosophy and literature. Laid out in its very first

word, *Fremd,* is a connection with absurdism, existential-
ism, and a whole slew of other twentieth-century isms;
with characters out of Beckett, Camus, or Paul Auster.
Schubert's was an age in which, and perhaps for the first
time, to be a human being could seem very lonely in a
metaphysical sense. An empty universe, without meaning; the first hints from a nascent geology (James Hutton

had published his *Theory of the Earth* in 1795) that Earth's
history was built out of a deep time at odds with the work-
ings of the everyday human imagination. Nature was not
friendly, not even hostile; one faced the possibility that
it was simply indifferent. "Schöne Welt, wo bist du?"—
Beautiful world, where are you?—wrote Friedrich Schiller in a poem set, heartbreakingly, by Schubert in 1819, a
poem which was a lament for a world emptied of meaning
and significance, for that lost wholeness which ancient
Greek civilisation mythically embodied. Schubert's
Winterreise is one vessel by which this newborn, fractured,
halfhearted modernity has been transmitted to its even
bleaker successors. Words and music in a dynamic union,
it renders this vision, right at the outset, at its historical
beginning, somehow beautiful.

In late summer 2012, I performed *Winterreise* as part
of the opening season of the Enniskillen International
Beckett Festival. As I stood in a small church, pews and
all, delivering the piece to an English-speaking audience

without translations of the text, an audience which was surely a mixture both of those who knew the piece, and of more who were utterly unfamiliar with the whole genre of song recital, it seemed to become a *Theaterstück,* as the Germans call it, a bit of theatre, a Beckettian drama in the spirit of *Happy Days* or *Not I* or *Krapp's Last Tape.* "A stranger I came; a stranger I departed"; birth and death; "astride of a grave and a difficult birth." The performance was preceded by a reading of Beckett's prose piece *Texts for Nothing* No. 12, by the actor Len Fenton. It begins:

| *33*

> It's a winter night, where I was, where I'm going, remembered, imagined, no matter, believing in me, believing it's me, no, no need . . .

WHAT IS OUR HERO DOING, creeping out of this house at night? Rather negligently, it wasn't something I had given much thought to before I sat down to write this book, and I'm not sure that many of us worry at it before we sing, play, or listen to *Winterreise.* The Byronic mystery is part of it, no doubt; but I think we also have to grapple with the practical realities of how people led their lives in 1820s Europe. Why would a young man, of lower economic status, be living in a house with a young woman and her family? Why did he come to stay?

The most influential writer of the mid-eighteenth century in Europe, beyond all measure, was Jean-Jacques Rousseau; his political writings, notably *The Social Contract* (1762), inspired a revolution; his social and educational theories defined the agenda for generations after him; his *Confessions*, published posthumously in 1782, scandalised and seduced in equal measure. He defined the spirit of the age; and more often than not, the thinkers who came after him were, consciously or unconsciously, agreeing or disagreeing with the Genevan sage.

One of Rousseau's most influential followers in education was Johann Bernhard Basedow, who, drawing on the ideas on education laid out in *Emile* (1762), published his own *Vorstellung an Menschenfreunde für Schulen, nebst dem Plan eines Elementarbuches der menschlichen Erkenntnisse* (Idea to Philanthropists for Schools, along with the Plan of an Elementary Book of Human Knowledge) in 1766. This was followed by a practical system of primary education, the *Elementarwerk*, in 1774, the same year in which, supported by the Prince of Anhalt-Dessau, he set up a new school, the Philanthropinum, in Dessau.

Wilhelm Müller was a Dessau boy—though not a pupil at the Philanthropinum, which had closed in 1793—and he married Basedow's granddaughter; but it's not Rousseau's educational treatise per se that is hinted at in the scenario of *Winterreise*, but rather Basedow's original profession, as a private tutor in a noble family (1749–53), and, beyond that, the plot line of Rousseau's hit novel, published the year before *Emile* and *The Social Contract*: *Julie*, better known by its subtitle as *La Nouvelle Héloïse*. The idea of tutoring in a noble or wealthy family was a familiar one to the intelligentsia of late-eighteenth- and early-nineteenth-century Germany. August Wilhelm Schlegel, Fichte, Hegel, Schelling, and Hölderlin—all of them, and many more, worked as "house tutors," and very often emotional complications ensued. *La Nouvelle Héloïse* was the handbook for tutors and pupils in an emotional tangle: little read today (an epistolary novel in three volumes), but at the time and for long afterwards, a publishing sensation. Robert Darnton, the preeminent scholar of the Enlightenment and historian of the book, has called it "perhaps the biggest bestseller of the century," with at least seventy editions in print before 1800, "probably more than for any other novel in the previous history of publishing." Demand outran supply to such an extent that publishers rented the book out by the day and even the hour. It made Rousseau into the very first celebrity author. Hordes of readers wrote to him, overwhelmed by the emotional intensity of this literary experience:

> I dare not tell you the effect it made on me. No, I was past weeping. A sharp pain convulsed me. My heart was crushed. Julie dying was no longer an unknown person. I believed I was her sister, her friend, her

Claire. My seizure became so strong that if I had
not put the book away I would have been as ill as all
those who attended that virtuous woman in her last
moments.

The story is complex but, for our purposes, simple in
the extreme. Saint-Preux, of humble origins, is tutor to
Julie, a young Swiss woman of noble family. He tries
to resist their growing attachment but, in the end, yields;
social mores compel them to keep their relationship a
secret. He runs away from the dilemma, to Paris and to
London, generating the correspondence which forms such
a large part of the book. Her family discover the liaison
and compel her to marry another, more socially appropriate, but elderly, candidate. "You are the ornament and
oracle of an entire family," writes Saint-Preux to Julie:

> the boast and admiration of a whole town—these, all
> these, divide your sensibility, and what remains for
> love is but a small part in comparison of that which
> is ravished from you by duty, nature, and friendship.
> But I, alas! a wanderer without a family, and almost
> without country, have no-one but you upon earth, and
> am possessed of nothing but my love.

A wanderer without a family, almost without
country . . . If we want to imagine a little more back-

ground for our *Winterreise*, an actor preparing for a complex role, if we want to set the stage more fully, and fill in some of the absent dramatis personae, how about this scene from *La Nouvelle Héloïse*, helping us to paint a picture of the girl's father:

> He began, by exclaiming, but in general terms, against such mothers as indiscreetly invite to their houses young fellows without family or fortune, whose acquaintance only brings shame and scandal on those who cultivated it.

La Nouvelle Héloïse: *the first kiss*

He accuses his wife of introducing into the household "a pretended wit, an empty babbler, more fit to debauch the mind of a modest young woman than to instruct her in anything that is good."

Of course we can't go about endlessly pillaging other works of literature to construct a more detailed narrative for *Winterreise;* and it would be self-defeating given all that we've said about the way that the mystery created by narrative loose ends enhances the cycle's power. But if we want to place the presence of this man in a household in a plausible social and historical context, there's no better place to start than *La Nouvelle Héloïse*. And the next chapter reveals something about Schubert's own career which will make this plot detail seem particularly telling.

DIE WETTERFAHNE

THE WEATHERVANE

Der Wind spielt mit der Wetterfahne
Auf meines schönen Liebchens Haus.
Da dacht' ich schon in meinem Wahne,
Sie pfiff' den armen Flüchtling aus.

Er hätt' es eher bemerken sollen,
Des Hauses aufgestecktes Schild,
So hätt' er nimmer suchen wollen
Im Haus ein treues Frauenbild.

Der Wind spielt drinnen mit den Herzen,
Wie auf dem Dach, nur nicht so laut.
Was fragen sie nach meinen Schmerzen?
Ihr Kind ist eine reiche Braut.

Die Wetterfahne · The Weathervane

The wind plays with the weathervane
On my beautiful sweetheart's house.
I thought already in my madness
It's piping out the poor fugitive.

He ought to have noticed before
The sign of the house, stuck up there,
Then he'd never have wanted to look
In that house for the faithful image of a woman.

The wind plays inside with hearts
Just as it does on the roof, only not so loud.
Why do they ask about my sorrows?
Their child is a rich bride.

*M*OST OF SCHUBERT'S MATURE, published songs start with some sort of a piano introduction. There's a good aesthetic reason for this, one which takes us back to the discussion of "Gretchen am Spinnrade" (Gretchen at the Spinning Wheel) in the last chapter. The introduction gives us the musical idea, puts it out there to be absorbed as music, just music; the voice comes in, and tells us how we should read that musical idea, focusing our attention on a physical or emotional scenario. So here, in "Die Wetterfahne," we have an arpeggio swoosh in the piano (the word arpeggio comes from the harp, and means a chord played in sequence rather than all at once); this rises and falls but also insists, as it travels, with repeated notes and a trill. It seems to start with an eddy of energy and subsides with a nervy, shivering ebbing of impulse. These bars start the song; the musical idea is repeated through the song; and they end it, after the singing has finished.

The description I've given, of course, isn't a purely
musical account, and it isn't an innocent one either,
inflected as it is with my own, informed sense of what's
coming next in the song. But something of that emotional
trajectory is summoned up for the first-time listener, especially after the excursions of the first song. And, of course,
we do know the physical analogue for the musical phrase,
because the song has a title, "The Weathervane." Can we
hear clanking, squeaking, the wind coming and going? In
his orchestral realisation of *Winterreise* (1993), the German
composer Hans Zender gives us something much more
literal in addition: high-pitched whistling from a piccolo;
blowing through the brass instruments, unpitched; hanging cymbals; and a wind machine.

The verse that follows tells us very clearly that this has
been, this piano prelude, a typically Schubertian device,
one which represents something not just in the outside
world but also in the protagonist's—and potentially in
the listener's—heart and head. A sort of prolepsis—the
words have been anticipated by the music. The wind plays
with the weathervane on the beloved's house, and the
protagonist is already thinking in his madness that they're
derisively piping him out, whatever that might be. Three
ideas going on then, jostling for position: the clattering
of the metal weathercock, the madness of the wanderer,
and the crazy picture of the family whistling at him, tell-

ing him to get out—after all, HE DOESN'T BELONG HERE.

First and foremost the weathervane is a symbol for the pretensions of the family, stuck up there on the roof as a *Schild*, a shield, a sort of armorial bearing, blazoning the status of those who dwell within. This is a family that is too good for our fugitive poet; despite the discomfort he feels, though, remember that what exactly happened remains just as unclear as it was in the first song. Did they throw him out, or did he leave? We have no idea.

The squeaking metal device—hardly dignified in itself—becomes the family piping him out. What are we to make of this piping? There's something folkloric about it, perhaps—is it the "rough music," the *Katzenmusik*, or charivari, visited upon social outcasts, or the transgressive, in European villages time out of mind? Is he hearing badly played fifes and banging saucepans? Or is he—a thought that occurs all the more easily to the singer performing the piece before a paying public—being whistled offstage? The self-exposure of a cycle like *Winterreise* often seems indecent, embarrassing; here is a moment where the emotions of the performer and the performed may effectively coalesce.

But then, what does such a device really point us towards? A *Wetterfahne*—literally a "weather flag"—is more often than not a weathercock, a cock that crows, a reminder, often placed on church towers, of the incon-

stancy of the disciple Simon Peter, he who denied Christ
three times before the cock crew. But the very unpredictability of the weathervane as it catches the wind is in
itself enough of a sign that nothing constant, no faithful *Frauenbild,* would be found within those walls. The
use of that rather archaic term—literally "image of a
woman"—to mean a woman, does its own job of distancing and ironising, as if he had been imagining that a dam-
sel dwelt within. That unpredictability is something that
Schubert captures in the music and that, over the years
of performing the cycle, I've wrestled with. Very often
I've suggested to my pianist partner that the best way to
point the meaning of the song is to play the introduction
in a rhythmically unsettled way. But—as we will see with
the ultimate song of unpredictability in the cycle, "Letzte
Hoffnung" (Last Hope)—the composer has done the job
already, and too much fiddling with the pulse unsettles the
representation of inconstancy, which is achieved by the
pattern of short and long notes allied to the sequence of
high and low notes, and a pattern of dynamic swelling and
subsiding: no more, no less.

The last four lines of the poem are the crux of the matter for Schubert, and he repeats them, both to underline
their sense—this is something we mustn't miss—and
to allow for a musical intensification which captures the
wanderer's conviction of his separation from the cosy life
inside the house. Poet Müller unknowingly encapsulates

for us the Schubertian method, the method of "Erlkönig" and of "Gretchen am Spinnrade," in a single couplet— the wind plays inside with hearts just as it plays on the roof, only not so loud—telling us explicitly that the music can represent at one and the same time objective reality and subjective experience. No wonder Schubert wants to repeat it, the second time a little more intensely, in terms of musical contour, but just as quietly (marked "leise," or gently, in the score), to contrast with the violence of the last two lines, which are marked, starkly, "laut," or loud. These two lines are crucial to our understanding of the wanderer's state of mind, and to our understanding of the journey he has been on: "Why do they ask about my sorrows? Their child is a rich bride." "Why do they ask about my sorrows?" has an insistent quality, "Their child is a rich bride" a sort of ironically triumphant upwards flourish. As the first sentence recurs, it is presented with an assertive brutality, repeated twice, rising in pitch, and with jabbing insistence; the second is made more jagged, more hysterical, and to cap it all, in a brilliant musical flourish, we then hear money spilling out from the piano, twelve brilliant, sparkling, rising semiquavers leading us back to the opening piano sequence, the song ending in a final, dying shudder—the weathervane subsiding into silence, the family peaceful within, the outcast trembling in the cold.

The idea of marriage is, of course, encountered in the first song: the girl spoke of love, the mother talked about marriage; the implication being, of course, that the father has been the dissident voice in all this. We hear the echo of possible, idealised companionship in the first song in those interweaving piano voices in alto and baritone registers which accompany those very words, sweetly answering to each other. By the end of this second song, by contrast, the violence of the spurned or spurning lover's feelings is clear, rupturing the peaceful tread of the first song.

MARRIAGE IN VIENNA in the 1820s was a vexed matter. Here is Schubert himself, in a diary entry of September 8, 1816:

Man resembles a ball, to be played with by chance and passion.

This sentence seems extraordinarily true to me . . .

Happy is he who finds a true man-friend. Happier still he who finds a true friend in his wife.

To a free man matrimony is a terrifying thought in these days: he exchanges it either for melancholy or for crude sensuality. Monarchs of today, you see this and are silent. Or do you not see it?

On the January 12 the year before, the repressive post-Napoleonic era regime of Prince Metternich had enacted a new law on marriage, published on March 16: the Ehe-Consens Gesetz, or Marriage Consent Statute. Schubert, at the time a teaching assistant in his father's Vienna high school, fell into the category of those citizens who, according to the new law, needed a permit in order to marry. A permit would only be granted "if the person wishing to marry could prove that he had sufficient means to support a family." When Schubert's older brother Ferdinand married in January 1816, he was exempt from the law because he was a fully fledged teacher in an imperial teaching establishment. When his younger brother, the painter Karl, married in November 1823, he sought permission from the authorities and was required to supply evidence of his profession and of his income, or *Erwerbsfähigkeit* (literally, "capacity for gainful employment").

In April 1816 Schubert had applied for a job, the post of music master in Laibach, supported by a testimonial in Italian from his teacher Salieri (Mozart's legendary rival). It may have been an attempt either to improve his material circumstances or to gain a post (Kapellmeister in a teacher training college) which would make him exempt from the irksome Hapsburg marriage statutes. Whatever the case, on September 7, the day before this despondent diary entry, he received news of his rejection.

It seems clear that Schubert was concerned that he would be unable to marry, condemned then to a life of either "melancholy or . . . crude sensuality." That, remaining unmarried as he did, he subsequently contracted syphilis—probably in November 1822—is sadly unsurprising. Bachelordom was a recognised feature of Biedermeier life in Austria. Taking Schubert's own circle, five never married (Schubert, Jenger, Bauernfeld, Castelli, and Grillparzer); and most waited until they were over thirty to do so, including the painter Kupelwieser, the singer Vogl, and the poet-dilettante Schober (at thirty, fifty-eight, and sixty respectively). Schubert's oldest brother, Ignaz, didn't marry until the age of fifty-one, in 1836, by which time he had inherited his father's position as school director and had become himself exempt from the restrictive Hapsburg marriage laws.

| 49

Did Schubert have anyone particular in mind, anyone he might have wanted to marry in 1816? In the course of that year he wrote out seventeen of his songs in fair copy as a gift for a neighbour with a beautiful voice, one Therese Grob, the daughter of a modestly prosperous, bourgeois couple who owned a silk factory in the Lichtental parish of Vienna. (Recent research suggests the album was actually given to her brother, Heinrich, though presumably with the expectation that he would pass it on to her; it ended up in the possession of his heirs.) Of the seventeen, he probably wrote three with Therese specifically in mind. The last was probably written out in November or December 1816. Therese had sung the soprano solo in Schubert's Mass in F major when it was performed at the Lichtental parish church in September 1814. Here is Schubert's friend Anselm Hüttenbrenner reminiscing to Franz Liszt in 1854:

> During a walk which I took with Schubert into the country, I asked him if he had never been in love. As he was so cold and unforthcoming towards the fair sex at parties, I was almost inclined to think he had a complete aversion for them. "Oh no!" he said, "I loved someone very dearly. She was a schoolmaster's daughter, somewhat younger than myself and in a Mass, which I composed, she sang the soprano solos most beautifully and with deep feeling. She was not exactly pretty and her face had pock-marks; but she had a heart, a heart of gold. For three years she hoped I would marry her; but I could not find a position which would have provided for us both. She then bowed to her parents' wishes and married someone else, which hurt me very much. I still love her and

there has been no one else since who has appealed to
me as much or more than she. She was just not meant
for me."

It may, of course, not have been so clearcut at the time
for the budding bohemian composer, Franz Schubert,
whose own father (a schoolmaster, unlike Therese's—an
easy slip for Hüttenbrenner) was running a successful school which, had the son's priority been bourgeois
security and domestic comfort, he could surely have made
a long-term commitment to. He could have waited for
Therese; he could have made another plan.

    Yet Schubert's self-conception was, in this part of his
life as in his music, that of the outsider, the rejected one.
The disappointments of life could be made into art. In *Die
schöne Müllerin* (The Beautiful Miller Girl), Schubert's
earlier cycle to words of Wilhelm Müller, it is the miller
boy—apprentice, unhappy in love—with whom the composer identifies. There was a family story that when he
arrived for the first time at his boarding choir school, the
Stadtkonvikt, to audition in September 1808, he was wearing a pale whitish-blue coat, provoking teasing from the
other boys—"He must be a miller's son. He'll get in for
sure." And the journeyman miller in *Die schöne Müllerin*
is rejected by a girl who is way above him in social status,
a rich bride, daughter of the master miller. Therese Grob,

continuing the farinaceous theme, went on to marry a
master baker. The Ehe-Consens Gesetz was no obstacle
in this case, and a bill of proclamation, signed and sealed,
sits in the local parish church archive to prove it. Whether
Therese rejected Schubert for a more established figure, or
whether Schubert refused to conform to bourgeois norms
in order to win her, is unclear, as unclear as the opening
scenario of *Winterreise;* it was perhaps, as is so often the
case, unclear to Schubert and Therese themselves. It's
striking that the songs in Therese's album don't include
the peerless "Gretchen am Spinnrade," which was written in this period—was it just too dangerously sexual
for Therese? Did its unbridled sensuality frighten her?
Did Schubert not even show it to her? She was, we may
imagine, part of its inspiration, vocally and perhaps more
deeply.

There is another Schubertian love story, again unrequited, which may help us to understand *Winterreise*. In
1868 Schubert's friend Moritz von Schwind made a sepia
drawing, *A Schubert Evening at Josef von Spaun's.* "Among
other projects," he wrote to Ferdinand von Mayerhofer,
another member of the Schubert circle (not to be confused
with the poet and Schubert intimate Johann Mayrhofer),

I have undertaken the representation of a Schubert-
iad, in which our whole group is portrayed. It is not

quite as beautiful as it was, but rather in the nature of
an old gentleman chattering about events at which he
was present in his youth and to which he still remains
attached in his heart.

Presiding over this imaginary and idealised scene is a
portrait of a lady, a framed oval prominently and centrally
displayed on the back wall of Spaun's drawing room,
directly above the piano at which Schubert is playing,
accompanying the singer Johann Michael Vogl. This is
Countess Karoline von Esterházy von Galánta (1805–
1851), based on a lost watercolour by another Schubert
associate, Josef Teltscher. Karoline's father, Count Johann
Karl Esterházy von Galánta, engaged Schubert in 1818 to
come to the family's summer residence in Zseliz (Hun-
gary) to give music lessons to Karoline and her sister,
Marie, who were both excellent pianists. He continued to
give them lessons on their return to Vienna, and he dedicated his op. 8 songs to the count.

It seems clear that Schubert developed strong feelings
for the young Countess Karoline, feelings which also
fed into his music. He returned to Zseliz in 1824 and
spent four and a half months there. That summer he
wrote to Schwind from Zseliz: "I often feel a wretched
longing for Vienna, despite a certain attractive star."
In February 1828 Schubert's friend the playwright

Eduard von Bauernfeld noted in his diary, "Schubert really seems to be in love with the Countess E. I like him for that. He gives her lessons." In a memoir he wrote in 1863 Bauernfeld gives us more detail, and some sensitive analysis:

> He was, in fact, head over heels in love with one of his pupils, the young Countess Esterházy, to whom he also dedicated one of his most beautiful piano pieces, the Fantasy in F minor for pianoforte duet. In addition to his lessons there, he also visited the Count's home from time to time, under the aegis of his patron, the singer Vogl . . . On such occasions Schubert was quite content to take a back seat, to remain quietly by the side of his adored pupil, and to thrust love's arrow ever deeper into his heart. For the lyric poet, as well as for the composer, an unhappy love affair may have its advantages, provided it is not altogether too unhappy, as it enhances his subjective feelings and stamps the poems and songs, which spring from it, with the colour and tone of purest reality.

Another account by a friend, that of the amateur singer and dedicatee of *Die schöne Müllerin,* Baron Karl Schönstein, tells us how a love affair with a maidservant at Zseliz in 1818 had "subsequently given way to a more poetic flame which sprang up in his heart for . . . the Countess Karoline":

> This flame continued to burn until his death. Karoline
> had the greatest regard for him and for his talent, but
> she did not return his love; perhaps she had no idea of
> the degree to which it existed. I say the *degree*, for *that*
> he loved her must surely have been clear to her from a
> remark of Schubert's—his only declaration in words.
> Once, namely when she reproached Schubert in fun
> for having dedicated no composition to her, he replied
> "What is the point? Everything is dedicated to you
> anyway."

| *55*

The presumably subsequent dedication of the F-minor Fantasy is surely telling—it's more than likely, surely, that the composer would have played the piece, written for two pianists sitting at one instrument, "by the side of his adored pupil," their hands sometimes overlapping. A fantasy indeed, full of longing and yearning, of "subjective feelings."

Karoline had as many as fourteen Schubert autograph manuscripts in her possession—an echo of Therese here, and a hint of Schubert's worshipful wooing—among them copies of songs nine to eleven of *Die schöne Müllerin*, dating from 1824, in a downward transposition which would have suited Karoline's contralto voice. A declaration of love—Impatience ("Ungeduld"), Morning Greeting ("Morgengruß"), and The Miller's Flowers ("Des Müllers Blumen")—who knows? But the notion of an impossible love for a woman far above him in social status, a woman in whose house he has stayed as a teacher, cannot but have made Müller's *Winterreise* poems seem very apt to Schubert, who had himself followed in the tradition of Fichte and Schlegel, of Rousseau's Saint-Preux and, perhaps, Müller's wanderer, as a family tutor.

In many ways this is a return to a way of looking at Schubert that some scholars have seen as discredited. Early on in twentieth-century Schubert studies the nonpareil of Schubert scholarship, Otto Erich Deutsch (who compiled the comprehensive catalogue of Schubert's works, hence the Deutsch or D number that each is given—*Winterreise* is D. 911), wrote of *Die schöne Müllerin* that the composer "of course was not inspired by any maid or any mill, but simply by Müller's poems." There has been an understandable reaction against the sentimental Schubert mythologised in the early twentieth century by Rudolf Bartsch, in his *Schwammerl* ("Little Mushroom," one of Schubert's nicknames) of 1912 (200,000 copies), which in turn inspired the hit operetta based on Schubert melodies, *Das Dreimäderlhaus* (translated into twenty-two languages) and its film version, *Blossom Time* (1934), starring Richard Tauber: the apotheosis, or perhaps the apocalypse of wine, women, and song. But refusing to sugar-coat Schubert doesn't mean that we have to dismiss obvious stages on his inspirational journey. The actual textures of Schubert's relationships with Therese Grob or with Karoline von Esterházy are not part of his art, and we have no record of them; but we can be pretty sure that self-dramatisation in those relationships, as is so often the case in the endless back-and-forth between art and life, steered Schubert in certain directions, narrowed his choices, fuelled his intensity.

The admirable urge to reinvent Schubert, to remove the taint of sentimentality, of cosiness, of Biedermeier in its worst sense, has led in various directions, some of them blind alleys. Schubert's bachelordom has aroused speculation that he may have been homosexual, and twenty years ago this stirred up one of the great controversies in music history, a controversy which has thankfully subsided but which has left its mark, one reason I'd like to flush it out here, at the risk of appearing to have a bee in my bonnet.

In 1989 the former record producer (co-founder of the label Vanguard) and Beethoven biographer Maynard Solomon published an article intriguingly entitled "Franz Schubert and the Peacocks of Benvenuto Cellini" in the scholarly journal *19th-Century Music*. It would take a whole book, perhaps, to enter into the intricacies of the arguments back and forth between Solomon and his primary opponent in the debate, Rita Steblin; and part of the

problem at the time, and subsequently, has been the politi-
cisation of the issue in an era of contested homosexual
liberation. If it had been published today, the fuss would
surely have been much less. Steblin's detailed and convincing work (it is Steblin, for example, who has drawn attention to, and engaged in extensive and admirable research
on, the Ehe-Consens Gesetz) has often been dismissed in
the understandable excitement of finding a new, and previously almost forbidden, way of looking at the composer.

First and foremost, though, it has turned out that there
is nothing new under the sun; Schumann was already
describing Schubert's music—metaphorically, it has to
be said—as feminine, Beethoven's as masculine, in the
period immediately after his death; when the composers' bodies were exhumed for reburial in the new Vienna
cemetery in the 1880s, one commentator remarked upon
the masculine thickness of Beethoven's skull, the feminine delicacy of Schubert's. There are elements of what
has become known as "queer theory" which may help us
better to understand Schubert's music: settings of poems
with a homoerotic theme, such as Goethe's "Ganymed";
settings of poems about homosexual love, such as August
von Platen's "Die Liebe hat gelogen" (Love has lied) and
"Du liebst mich nicht" (You love me not); or even the
analysis of the sexual dynamics of a cycle like *Die schöne
Müllerin*. This was a culture, Greek-obsessed, in which
even artists whose work was primarily heterosexually ori-

entated played with the idea of the homoerotic—Goethe being the best example, with Ganymed and that notorious Venetian epigram I remember from schooldays where he declares that he prefers sex with a woman because having had her as a girl he can then take her as a boy. Figure that one out. But Solomon's attempt to remake Schubert scholarship by reconfiguring our sense of his "primary sexual orientation" seems, on the whole, unhelpful and anachronistic. Schubert may have had some homosexual feelings, he may have had some homosexual experiences. We do not know. He wasn't, and could not have been, in our modern sense, gay. The notion of a gay identity was yet to be invented. And there's plenty of evidence for Schubert's love of women, and for his sexual interest in them, far more than any evidence of homosexual leanings.

Solomon's argument centres on a cryptic, laconic entry in Bauernfeld's diary, August 1826: "Schubert ailing (he needs 'young peacocks' like Benvenuto Cellini)." Until Solomon's intervention, the accepted view was that this was a reference to Schubert's syphilis. Cellini, whose memoirs Goethe had translated in 1806, was a notorious carouser and syphilitic, and peacock flesh was, presumably, a cure for this disease. Solomon quite rightly points out that while peacocks are mentioned in the memoirs, it is never as a cure for syphilis; and he makes an argument that Cellini, also a notorious homosexual, uses bird hunting as a metaphor for pursuing young men, his remedy for low spirits. Hence, Bauernfeld is remarking, in code, on Schubert's need for liaisons with young men. Solomon makes of this an emblem for a new approach to an under-standing of Schubert's life.

The problem is that Solomon makes so many clunking and partisan errors elsewhere in trying to establish his case. Mistranslation, mistranscription, and partial quota-tion are rife, reaching their comical climax with an 1827 party invitation to Schubert and Schober, from a certain Nina, doubtless a good-time girl (or perhaps, probably, a boy en travesti—since the gender of the "nightingales" who will be at this party is suspiciously unspecified). The "snowed-in nightingales will, notwithstanding all the cold rinds, flute with all their might," the invitation reads. Since the cold rinds are "surely" primitive Biedermeier condoms—"How readily would I shed all this cold bark," wrote Schwind to Schober on May 6, 1824—the nature of their flute playing is, as Solomon soberly puts it, "fairly straightforward."

The solution to this particular muddle starts with *Winterreise,* and would stare anyone in the face who had ever heard or sung the seventh song of the cycle, "Auf dem Flusse" (On the River), where that selfsame river has put on a hard, unyielding crust, a "harter, starrer Rinde." Not a condom, nota bene, not one to be seen, even floating down said river. Fluting is singing, of course, and nightingales are singers. Schwind was talking about "breaking the ice" in social contexts. And Nina is not the proprietress of some earlier incarnation of Kander and Ebb's Kit Kat Klub, in drag or out of it, but Mina with an M, a nickname for Wilhelmine, "probably," as Rita Steblin concludes in her dry demolition of Solomon, "Wilhelmine Witteczek, who often invited Schubert to her soirées." Solomon's tin ear for the jokey tone of the invitation doesn't invite confidence in his stylistic antennae (as when he finds irony at work in contemporary accounts of Schubert's relationships with Therese Grob or Countess Esterházy).

| 61

To return to the peacocks, they may mean what Solomon says, or they may not. Having read through the extensive discussions of this little phrase, overfreighted with significance, by Solomon himself, by Rita Steblin, Kristina Muxfeldt, and Marie-Elisabeth Tellenbach, among others, I am none the wiser. If we're not even absolutely sure what it meant for Cellini himself, we are even less so for Bauernfeld or the wider Schubert circle, who would have been reading Cellini's memoirs, let it be said, in Goethe's tame 1806 translation. Bauernfeld may have meant the peacocks to be mythical medicine or actual boys or, indeed, both; the evidence we are presented with is consistent with any of these readings, and nothing Solomon or his supporter Muxfeldt adduces in evidence is in any way conclusive.

In the end, though, the biggest misconception is in

thinking that we have to define Schubert's sexuality, that we can know it or can pin it down. There are figures in the period of whom it might be said such-and-such was homosexual (although that term is as downright anachronistic as calling Michelangelo gay). August von Platen (an inspirational figure for Thomas Mann's novella *Death in Venice*) is one such; and it's telling, but again inconclusive, that Schubert set two of his poems (though it's also worth pointing out that he composed seventy-four songs to poems by Goethe and forty-four by Schiller, and that Brahms set several by Platen). To take the most famous poetic figure of the age, a mega-celebrity whose fame dazzled Europe, Byron, attempts to confine or define his sexuality fail, spectacularly. He had sex with boys, he had sex with women, with his own sister; and his verse reflects both his heterosexual and his homosexual interests. Something similar might be said of Benvenuto Cellini himself; and it's striking that in the only clear instance of "peacock" meaning "pretty boy" in Cellini's memoirs, the artist takes a boy all too convincingly dressed up as a woman to a party in order not to upset his mistress by taking another woman.

There's no denying the strength of highly emotional male relationships within the Schubert circle; the historian Ilija Dürhammer is their most recent and assiduous chronicler. We shall never know if the charged language they used betrayed sexual feelings; that they were touched by them seems plausible or even likely. But these men were, simultaneously, and demonstrably, involved in complicated relationships with women; and it's more than likely that Schubert had some sexual relationships with women too, probably fleeting, and that he contracted syphilis while, say, visiting a run-of-the-mill bordello with his promiscuous, womanising, ne'er-do-well friend Franz von Schober. And it's the two well-attested, idealised relationships, at one and the same time non-relationships, one with a local daughter of the bourgeoisie, the other with a high-born musical devotee, which have very obvious things to tell us about *Winterreise*, and about the force that lies behind this song.

POSTSCRIPT

Friedrich Hölderlin (born 1770) was one of the great German poets of the generation between Goethe (born 1749) and Wilhelm Müller (born 1794). From the late 1790s into the early years of the new century he worked as a tutor in Frankfurt, in Bordeaux, and in Switzerland. In Frankfurt he fell in love with Susette Gontard, the wife of his banker employer, and was dismissed. He went on to immortalise Susette as Diotima in his epistolary novel *Hyperion, or*

the Hermit in Greece, published in 1797 and 1799, a tale
set in the 1770s in which the central character, Hyperion
himself, is dedicated to the liberation of Greece. Hölderlin's philhellenism would surely have drawn Müller to his
work, may even, with Byron, have inspired him. And the
circumstances of Hölderlin's life are another reminder
of the sort of domestic situation which may be at the
origin of *Winterreise*'s mise en scène. In 1806, he began
his inexorable descent into madness and, after a period in
a mental asylum in Tübingen (whose director invented a
mask to inhibit the screaming of the mentally ill), he spent
the years until his death in 1843 living in the home of an
admirer, a carpenter, Ernst Zimmer, in a tower in the
old city wall. He produced, in this period, fragmentary
verse of visionary intensity. Mostly misunderstood in his
own lifetime, he has become perhaps the iconic poet of
German Romanticism, a seer, a dreamer of dreams, his
derangement offering him a key to the unconscious and
the irrational. A year before his descent into insanity, this
poem was published, and it offers us a suggestive poetic
link between Hölderlin and Müller's wanderer, in the form
of a weathervane:

> *Mit gelben Birnen hänget*
> *Und voll mit wilden Rosen*
> *Das Land in den See,*
> *Ihr holden Schwäne,*

Und trunken von Küssen
Tunkt ihr das Haupt
Ins heilignüchterne Wasser.

Weh mir, wo nehm' ich, wenn
Es Winter ist, die Blumen, und wo
Den Sonnenschein,
Und Schatten der Erde?
Die Mauern stehn
Sprachlos und kalt, im Winde
Klirren die Fahnen.

With yellow pears hangs
And full with wild roses
The land in the lake,
You gracious swans
And drunk from kisses
Dip your heads
In the holy, sober water.

Woe is me, from where shall I gather, when
It is winter, flowers, and from where
Sunshine,
And shadows of the earth?
The walls stand
Speechless and cold, in the wind
The weathervanes rattle.

Benjamin Britten set this dark, strange poem—so
much a companion piece to *Winterreise*, if far beyond
Müller in sheer poetic power—as the fifth of his *Hölderlin
Fragments;* and not long after, Hans Werner Henze took
the later, long prose poem *In lieblicher Bläue* (1808) as the
text for his *Kammermusik 1958*, written for Peter Pears.
The weathervane still crows, now silently:

> *In lieblicher Bläue blühet*
> *mit dem metallenen Dache der Kirchthurm.*
>   *Den umschwebet*
> *Geschrey der Schwalben, den umgiebt die*
>   *rührendste Bläue.*
> *Die Sonne gehet hoch darüber und färbet das Blech,*
> *im Winde aber oben stille krähet die Fahne.*

> In the lovely blueness blossoms
> the metal roof of the church tower. Around it glides
> the cry of the swallows, the most touching blue
>   surrounds it.
> The sun rises high above it and gives colour to the
>   metal,
> In the wind however, up there, the weathervane
>   crows silently.

| 3 |

GEFRORNE TRÄNEN

FROZEN TEARS

Gefrorne Tropfen fallen
Von meinen Wangen ab;
Ob es mir denn entgangen
Daß ich geweinet hab'?

Ei Tränen, meine Tränen,
Und seid ihr gar so lau
Daß ihr erstarrt zu Eise,
Wie kühler Morgentau.

Und dringt doch aus der Quelle
Der Brust so glühend heiß,
Als wolltet ihr zerschmelzen
Des ganzen Winters Eis.

Frozen drops fall
From my cheeks.
Has it escaped me, then,
That I have cried?

Oh tears, my tears,
And are you so lukewarm
That you turn to ice
Like the cool morning dew?

And yet you burst out of the source,
Your breast, so glowing hot,
As if you would melt
All of winter's ice.

"You're right: I ought not to have come today," he said, lowering his voice so that the coachman should not hear. She bent forward, and seemed about to speak; but he had already called out the order to drive on, and the carriage rolled away while he stood on the corner. The snow was over, and a tingling wind had sprung up, that lashed his face as he stood gazing. Suddenly he felt something stiff and cold on his lashes, and perceived that he had been crying, and that the wind had frozen his tears.

—EDITH WHARTON, *The Age of Innocence* (1920)

S OME PERFORMANCES of this *Winter Journey*—and I must have sung it around a hundred times—stick in the memory. In the winter of 2010 it was Moscow: with Julius Drake, at the Pushkin Museum of Fine Arts, as part of its December Nights festival. The performance was memorable for all sorts of reasons. December Nights is a series created by the late Sviatoslav Richter, one of the pianistic titans of the twentieth century, whose monumental but vivid live recording of *Winterreise* with the German tenor Peter Schreier was one of my paths to the cycle as a teenager. The Pushkin is a wonderful museum, and beforehand we were able to wander its galleries and meet its formidable director, Irina Antonova, who had been in her post since 1961. A fierce defender of Soviet appropriation of German museum collections at the end of the Second World War, she was already working at the Pushkin in 1945 when almost the entire collection of the Dresden Gallery arrived in Moscow. (Richter and Schreier's *Win-*

terreise, quite coincidentally, was a Dresden performance from the early 1980s.) Antonova was instrumental in establishing the December Nights series. The Pushkin Museum itself was founded by the father of the Russian poet Marina Tsvetaeva, who wrote a poem based on one of the *Winterreise* lyrics, "Die Nebensonnen" (The Mock Suns)." Alexander Pushkin was, like Wilhelm Müller, a participant in the pan-European Byron cult; his Onegin, and Lermontov's Pechorin—the antihero at the centre of the short-story collection *A Hero of Our Time*—are second cousins to Müller's wanderer.

All these historical cross-currents may seem tenuous and beside the point; but they remind us that *Winterreise* is a historical artefact, made in history and transmitted through and by it. When Müller wrote his poems, for example, it was in the wake of a winter journey to end all winter journeys, Napoleon's retreat from Moscow. Müller was a German patriot who fought against Napoleon in 1814; but in the period immediately before, loyalties had been more confused. Napoleon's Grande Armée which invaded Russia in September 1812, six hundred thousand strong, was a multinational entity with a whole corps of Austrian soldiers. The hundred and twenty thousand men who made up the army which left Russia in December 1812 included fifty thousand Austrians, Prussians, and other Germans, more ethnic Germans than Frenchmen.

Franz Krüger's painting *Prussian Cavalry Outpost in the Snow* dates somewhat later, from 1821, but with its chilling snow-covered corpse, barely visible to the viewer's eye, it gives us a wholly other visual context, inspiration for an alternative take on *Winterreise* and what a snowy landscape might mean in the aftermath of those confused and terrible war years.

Schubert himself was, apparently, politically alert, if not hugely politically active, though the evidence from this politically repressed period in Austrian history is not abundant. He seems to have been a bolshie young man in the 1820s, arrested for suspected disaffection (his great friend Johann Senn was with him at the time, probably the ringleader, and ended up in exile, his career in tatters). Earlier on, as a teenager, conversely, he was the patriotic composer of a song which celebrated the allied triumph over Napoleon, "Die Befreier Europas in Paris" (The Liberators of Europe in Paris), written in May 1814, only a few weeks after the Austrian and Russian entry into the French capital. The French bombardment and occupation of the city a few years earlier, in 1809, would have been etched into the young Schubert's memory (he was born in 1797). Joseph von Spaun described the scene at the seminary where both he (a twenty-year-old law student) and Schubert (a choirboy) were living in May 1809:

> It was a magnificent sight to see the glowing cannon-balls curving across the night sky, while the many con-flagrations reddened the sky . . . All of a sudden there was a crash in the house itself, a howitzer shell having fallen on the Seminary building. It penetrated every floor down to the first and burst on the first floor.

The peace conference which ushered in the European settlement after Napoleon's final defeat took place in Schubert's home city, filling it with foreign dignitaries and

social activity. After the inevitable flurry and excitement
the result—especially after the enactment of the repressive Karlsbad Decrees in 1819—was a German-speaking
world under a spell a little like that which the White Witch
casts in *The Lion, the Witch and the Wardrobe:* always
winter and never Christmas. Censorship was at work;
suspicion bred disaffection. Schubert and his friends were
denizens of this Biedermeier world, in which domestic
pursuits were at the forefront, art foreswore the heroism of
yesteryear, and any opposition to the way things were was
coded and discreet. The Austrian system was, according
to Schubert's playwright friend Bauernfeld, "rein nega-
tives: die Furcht vor dem Geiste, die Negation des Geistes,
der absolute Stillstand, die Versumpfung, die Verdum-
mung" (purely negative: the fear of spiritual things, the
negation of spirit, absolute stasis, waterlogged, stultified).
Winterreise might remind us of wars gone by; but also of a
frozen peace.

IN *WAR AND PEACE,* Tolstoy reflects on the historical
meaning of the campaign of 1812 and its aftermath: "The
fundamental and essential significance of the European
events of the beginning of the nineteenth century lies in
the movement of the mass of the European peoples from
west to east and afterwards from east to west." The Ger-

man invasion of Russia in 1941 echoed this at full volume and more—more grandiose, more foolish, infinitely more savage. Around the time Antonova was starting work as a curator in Moscow, a month or so before the Battle for Berlin, the German tenor Peter Anders was completing a recording of *Winterreise* in a studio in the heavily bombarded city as a token of German civilisation, part of a complete account of German song on record planned by Goebbels's client and Hitler's favourite, the accompanist Michael Raucheisen (reportedly the first pianist to play Lieder with the piano lid fully open in concert).

The relationship between the Nazi regime and classical music is a more than vexed one. The maverick Marxist philosopher Slavoj Žižek is typically provocative in his dealings with *Winterreise*, making explicit and specific the problematic of German high culture which has been worried at by George Steiner and others—"the paradox that modern barbarism sprang in some intuitive, perhaps necessary way, from the very core and locale of humanistic civilisation"—and represented with crude filmic brilliance in Steven Spielberg's *Schindler's List* (in which, as the Lodz ghetto is exterminated, a German soldier plays graceful fugal music at the piano in the Jewish apartment they are breaking up: "Bach or Mozart?" his two, less "civilised," comrades wonder aloud to each other). Here is Žižek on the cultural role of *Winterreise* c. 1942, around

the time the bass-baritone Hans Hotter made a very
famous recording of the cycle with the same Raucheisen
we noted above:

> It is easy to imagine German officers and soldiers
> listening to this recording in the Stalingrad trenches
> in the cold Winter of 42/43. Does the topic of *Winter-
> reise* not evoke a unique consonance with the historical
> moment? Was not the whole campaign to Stalingrad a
> gigantic *Winterreise*, where each German soldier can
> say for himself the very first lines of the cycle: "I came
> here a stranger, / As a stranger I depart"? Do the fol-
> lowing lines not render their basic experience: "Now
> the world is so gloomy, / The Road shrouded in snow.
> I cannot choose the time / To begin my journey, /
> Must find my own way / In this darkness."

Žižek goes on to make the same point for a number of
the *Winterreise* songs, further illustrating that "unique
consonance with the historical moment." Here is the
"endless meaningless march," the resonant retreat, in
"Rückblick" (Looking Back): "Es brennt mir unter
beiden Sohlen, / tret ich auch schon auf Eis und Schnee.
/ Ich möcht' nicht wieder Atem holen, / Bis ich nicht
mehr die Türme seh'." (The soles of my feet burn, / even
though I'm walking on ice and snow. / I don't want to

draw breath again / until I no longer see the towers.) The soldier can only dream of returning home in spring, his *Frühlingstraum;* he waits nervously for the arrival of the post (song thirteen); while the stormy morning of number eighteen is very like the "shock of the morning artillery attack":

> The cloud tatters flutter
> Around in weary strife.
> And fiery red flames
> Dart around among them.

Utterly exhausted, the soldiers are not allowed to embrace the peace of death (the theme of the twenty-first song, "Das Wirtshaus," The Inn), and the only way is onwards—"closing one's ears to the complaint of the heart" ("Mut," Courage):

> If the snow flies in my face,
> I shake it off again . . .
> Complaining is for fools.

Žižek's analysis might seem forced, but it makes a deep historical sense; the Lied has a longstanding, if unexpected, connection with world historical events, seemingly at odds with its domestic origins, its aesthetic of interiority. For Žižek, on the contrary, it's precisely that "displacement" that could have made *Winterreise* a consoling companion on that other winter journey in 1942, abstract emotions allowing "an escape from the concrete." Is this what art is for, to hide the terrible truth?

EARLIER ON in the trajectory of German nationalism, in 1894, Anton von Werner painted his sumptuous *Billet outside Paris, 24th October 1870*. Werner was an establishment figure, director of the Royal Academy of the Arts in Berlin, most celebrated for his much-reproduced painting of the declaration of the new German Empire at Versailles in 1871. Werner was attached to the chief of the Prussian General Staff, Helmuth von Moltke, during the preceding Franco-Prussian War; the anecdotal detail of this famous painting suggests that he was recalling, if perhaps also improving on, a real incident. Dishevelled Prussian soldiers are discovered by the viewer in a luxurious rococo French salon (in the Château de Brunoy). We're struck by the muddy boots, the scattered wood by the fire which is being stoked. There is an immediate visual contrast between the roughness which the soldiers have brought into this somewhat effeminate environment, a juxtaposition between French civilisation and German culture, between sturdy male values and the degeneracy of a

Anton von Werner, *Billet Outside Paris, 24th October 1870*, 1894

defeated people. But we notice, too, that these rough men have not demolished the elegance of their surroundings: they are essentially decent. The luxury furnishings have not been looted; a helmeted veteran is in restrained conversation with an elderly servant of the house. In front of them a young girl is transfixed by what is going on at the centre of the picture space. There's a grand piano, open-lidded; and to the accompaniment of one of his comrades an officer is singing, with casual elegance, one hand in his waistband, the other delicately resting on the piano desk, for all the world as if he were at the Wigmore Hall. The music being played, legible on the piano, and mentioned in Werner's own notes on the picture, is a Schubert song, from the 1828 Heine set, "Am Meer": "Das Meer erglänzte weit hinaus . . ." ("The sea shimmered far out . . ."). This song, again according to Werner's notes was, rather unexpectedly (given its dark psychological colouring), a favourite with military bands.

So we see how Schubert song may have mediated German triumphs and German disasters over that whole troubling period from 1813—the birth of modern German nationalism—to 1945, its ultimate shame and catastrophe. Schubert invented his new way of writing songs in a period of political retrenchment in Mitteleuropa, and within a circle which valued and exalted the concept of *Bildung*—the cultivation of the self and its powers. This involved both *Anbildung* (the widening of cultural horizons through a programme of cultural immersion, reading and the like) and *Ausbildung* (the blossoming of natural gifts). Schubert song drew deeply on this culture. A conflict is embedded in Werner's picture, over and above the message which it overtly conveys of German strength and French weakness. On the one hand the image of war: muddy boots and uniforms, the notion of Prussian militarism placed at the heart of the German national mission, as means in the first place but also, ultimately, as value system; on the other hand, the notion of *Bildung*, of cultivation, of personal expression through quiet music, which is the apotheosis of sensitivity: this is the conflict which nervously inhabits the centre of the picture. Can they co-exist?

Lieder singers today are the inheritors of this history, in both its positive and its negative aspects; we cannot escape it, nor should we wish to; we can, instead, seek to understand it. The period immediately after 1945 saw the reinvention of the Lied, with an alliance between new technical means—high fidelity and the long-playing record—and a new generation of Lieder singers dominated by the extraordinary sensitivity and quicksilver imagination of the Prussian schoolmaster's son Dietrich Fischer-Dieskau. Out of the red-hot furnace of Fischer-Dieskau's interpretative gift—on recordings and on the concert platform, over a period of nearly half a century—the full panoply of Schubert's lyrical genius could be revealed to the world, with a missionary zeal which privileged *Bildung* over power. In a sense the new Lieder singing was forged out of war, but suited for peace. Fischer-Dieskau's first *Winterreise*:

> My school was preparing a concert in which I was to sing the *Winterreise*, in response to my fervent desire (and my mother's) to perform the song cycle before a larger audience; Professor Walter was in the audience.

In my zeal I miscalculated: Two songs (I don't remember which ones) were not properly memorised—so I simply left them out. When the concert was roughly at the halfway mark, the air raid sirens began to sound. It was January 30th, 1943, the tenth anniversary of the Nazi seizure of power, and the British were commemorating it with heavy bombardment. My audience of two hundred or so in the Zehlendorf town hall joined me in fleeing to the basement. After about two hours, during which all hell broke loose outside though fortunately not in Zehlendorf itself, we all went upstairs again for the second installment of the song cycle. It was a debut out of the ordinary, but it showed me that I could confront difficult circumstances and work through them to the end.

The legend is that after his first performance of *Winterreise* in London in the early 1950s, the young Fischer-Dieskau was so disorientated that he walked off the wrong side of the stage.

And so we come full circle, *Bildung* to *Bildung*. The new Lieder singing which took the world by storm in the 1950s and 1960s—and in the face of which we contemporaries all stand in awe—was an ambassador for the new Germany and an inheritance from its liberal beginnings, all the way back in the 1820s.

. . .

SO MUCH FOR the tangled historical and cultural complexities, or just the sheer irony, of two English musicians performing Schubert's *Winterreise* in the Pushkin Museum in Moscow in 2010. This particular song, "Frozen Tears," brought our Moscow performance to mind for two, related reasons. We arrived and left the city to the accompaniment of an unparalleled demonstration of winter's physical and aesthetic power, an ice storm which turned the trees into glassy sculptures, overfreighted with crystals, a weird landscape frozen heavy, fit for *Winterreise*. Frozen tears indeed: with icicle droplets decorating the branches, the very trees were weeping. How often we have performed this cycle in the summer, we thought, and how odd that sometimes seems, how inappropriate. Odd too, perhaps, that we always give the cycle in a warm hall, that we never feel the cold or live in the silence of the snowy landscape. How often do the audience really imagine it? Should it be part of the recipe?

Before the performance, a very courteous Russian journalist interviewed me, in English, for the radio. In song recitals, as opposed to opera—where a wall of light can separate the actor from the auditorium—the audience are usually visible, part of the performing equation, to play with and against. Towards the end of the concert, look-

ing into the hall, some way back, I saw my interviewer in
tears, something I'd never noticed before in a performance
of *Winterreise*. It may have meant something very particular for him, he may have had an upsetting day, week
or month; but I couldn't help ascribing it to the mythical
Russian soul, that literary trope in which for these people,
the emotions lie very close to the surface.

WINTERREISE WAS WRITTEN in a period in which
overmuch crying was becoming suspect. The mid to late
eighteenth century, the so-called age of sentiment, had
been awash with tears. Copious crying had moved from
the realm of pietistic religion (codified in the Bach of can-
tatas such as "Weinen, Klagen, Sorgen, Zagen," Weeping, Wailing, Fretting, Fearing) to stand at the centre of
a barely concealed sensual economy. Tears meant sympathy; but they also stood in, imaginatively at least, for a
more carnally imagined exchange of body fluids. The hit
book of the 1770s, with a currency which went right down
to the wire and the storming of the Bastille, was Goethe's
The Sorrows of Young Werther. A must-read for hip young
Germans on its publication, it stimulated a craze which
soon spread the length and breadth of Europe. Werther
had his copycats sartorially—a vogue for blue coats and
buff breeches—and more existentially: older and wiser

heads worried that the book was encouraging not only Romantic moping (Werther loves Charlotte; she is married; he pines) but even suicide (Werther's fate). What became known as sentimentalism was the order of the day in much English and French writing of the time, but Goethe pushed weeping to its ecstatic, erotic limit. Reading Klopstock, Charlotte and Werther touch and weep. As Roland Barthes describes it:

> By releasing his tears without constraint, [Werther] follows the order of the amorous body, which is in liquid expansion, a bathed body: to weep together, to flow together: delicious tears finish off the reading of Klopstock which Charlotte and Werther perform together.

By the 1820s, the cult of sensibility and its crying were becoming old hat. Dickens's Sam Weller, created in 1836 but channeling the manners of the previous decade, declares that as for feelings, it's better that a man "keep 'em in his own buzzum, than let 'em ewaporate in hot water, 'specially as they do no good. Tears never yet wound up a clock, or worked a steam ingin'." It's partly a question of the whirligig of fashion, but sensibility was also one of the dangerous doctrines associated with the era of revolution.

So, influenced by the hipsterish irony of Byron, anticipating the Romantic deflatus of Heine, Müller's wanderer
is almost amused by, and certainly affects surprise at,
his own tears; and at first sight, they are not the flow-
ing, lubricating, intoxicating tears of sentiment, but tears
which fall frozen from his cheeks. A contradiction is built
into the poem, though, for while the wanderer derides
his tears as being so lukewarm that they turn to ice like
the morning dew, at the same time they are glowing hot
as they emerge from their source, the breast. They come
from within, and within is a raging furnace of emotion.
It's a song about repression, about the objectification of
feeling, and Schubert reflects every turn of the poem in
his musical setting, from the frozen, almost mocking call-
and-answer motif of the opening bars in the piano part to
the repeated cry of the words "des ganzen Winters Eis,"
all winter's ice.

Crying, of course, is twofold—vocalisation and the
production of tears. It comes in many varieties, different
combinations, a kaleidoscope of grieving: silent tears;
dry-eyed keening; sobbing, muffled or less restrained;
and the all-devouring weeping which seems to rack the
body, monstrous but cleansing. Infants cry all the time,
adults much less so; and while crying is a physiological
process—the tears shed in emotion contain twenty to
twenty-five percent more protein than those produced

when chopping onions, and particular stress-related hormones seem to be secreted in emotional tears—it remains culturally and historically mediated. The idea that crying provides some sort of possibly healthy release has a long history. For Seneca, "tears ease the soul"; Ovid wrote that "by weeping we disperse our wrath . . . It is a relief to weep; grief is satisfied and carried off by tears."

At the same time, we live in a society suspicious of tears, or embarrassed by them. Men cry much less often than women in our society, and this has not always been the case. Music is one of the most powerful ways of calling up the emotions that lead to crying; but whenever I find myself crying at a piece of music, I experience two conflicting, overlapping feelings—my satisfaction (I hesitate to call it such) at the authenticity and intensity of my response is, in its very self-consciousness, somehow shameful. One should not give way to the tears which music elicits—they come and are staunched. People in concert halls do not, unlike people at funerals, cry openly and demonstratively, despite the huge emotional impact of what they are listening to. Only that once did I catch someone, just one person, crying in the audience.

| 4 |

ERSTARRUNG

FROZEN STIFF

Ich such' im Schnee vergebens
Nach ihrer Tritte Spur,
Wo sie an meinem Arme
Durchstrich die grüne Flur.

Ich will den Boden küssen
Durchdringen Eis und Schnee
Mit meinen heißen Tränen,
Bis ich die Erde seh'.

Wo find' ich eine Blüte,
Wo find' ich grünes Gras?
Die Blumen sind erstorben,
Der Rasen sieht so blaß.

Soll denn kein Angedenken
Ich nehmen mit von hier?
Wenn meine Schmerzen schweigen,
Wer sagt mir dann von ihr?

Mein Herz ist wie erfroren,
Kalt starrt ihr Bild darin:
Schmilzt je das Herz mir wieder,
Fließt auch ihr Bild dahin.

In vain I search for traces of her footprints in the
    snow, where she walked through the green
    fields on my arm.

I will kiss the ground, piercing through the ice
    and snow with my hot tears, until I see earth.

Where can I find one flower, where can I find
    green grass, the flowers are dead, the grass
    looks so washed-out.

Shall I then take no keepsake from this place?
When my griefs are silent, who else will say
    anything about her to me?

My heart is as if frozen, the picture of her is
    frozen stiff inside me.
If my heart ever melts again her image will flow
    away as well.

ERSTARRUNG IS A TRICKY WORD to translate. The standard translation—"numbness"—doesn't seem altogether adequate, summoning up notions of anaesthesia and insensibility which have very little to do with this song, as listening to the first few bars will confirm. There's urgency and obsessiveness and intensity at work, even before we are given the poet's words to tell us more. The noun *Erstarrung*, not an everyday one, derives from the verb *erstarren*—to stiffen, to grow rigid, to solidify. That verb in turn derives from the adjective *starr*, or stiff. "Frozen rigidity"; "frozen solid"; "turned to ice"? Then again, *erstarren* can simply mean to freeze. "Frozen," then, or "frozenness" literally, the idea of the poem surely being that the ground is frozen and that our hero wants to cut through it somehow and recover what is lying underneath—memories, the past, lost love?

In vain I search for traces of her footprints in the snow,
where she walked through the green fields on my arm.

There is a despairing sense of loss—that telling *verge-bens*, "in vain," with its moaning appoggiatura, a leaning note. Spring is only a memory, as is companionable love, and the green fields are covered with snow. It is winter. Those traces in the snow, the quest for them is driven—this is the first fast, busy song we have encountered on our journey—and they remind us of those other footprints in the first song, the animal tracks that were to help the wanderer find his way in the darkness. Somehow the girl is assimilated to prey, and I am reminded of Sir Thomas Wyatt.

> Whoso list to hunt, I know where is an hind,
> But as for me, hélas, I may no more.
> The vain travail hath wearied me so sore,
> I am of them that farthest cometh behind.
> Yet may I by no means my wearied mind
> Draw from the deer, but as she fleeth afore
> Fainting I follow. I leave off therefore,
> Sithens in a net I seek to hold a wind.
> Who list her hunt, I put him out of doubt,
> As well as I may spend his time in vain.

"Fainting I follow . . ." Our protagonist is that oh-so-modern man, a stalker; but isn't the notion of stalking built into our very concept of romantic love, our founding myth, our sentimental solace, one which might all too easily keel over into pathology and abuse?

Schubert had already set a substantial set of poems by a real-life Romantic stalker, Ernst Schulze, whose *Poetisches Tagebuch* (Poetical Diary) charted his obsession with the seventeen-year-old Cäcilie Tychsen: famous songs among them, like "Im Frühling" (In Spring) and "Auf der Bruck" (On the Bruck, also known as "Auf der Brücke," On the Bridge).

AND NOW the mania is at full pelt, in the words and in the music:

> I will kiss the ground, piercing through the ice and
> snow with my hot tears, until I see earth.

The vocal line reaches right up to a high A-flat, keening, shrieking; but despite the drama of that, it's a passing note, that A-flat, within a phrase which must surely emphasise either the tears themselves—"mit meinen heissen *Tränen*"—or their hotness—"mit meinen *heiss*en Tränen." These are the sort of minuscule decisions the singer must make, usually in the heat of the moment. Their scorching quality is certainly something of a change from the last song, in which the poet's tears were so lukewarm that they froze like morning dew.

This is one of the craziest moments in the cycle, the most hysterical. It moves from a quiet scurrying to those piercing cries and it seems, above all, to have a sexual quality, a priapic tempest of repressed urgency and desire for release, which sets it apart from the rest of the *Winterreise* songs. It is also, surely, of all those songs, the most psychoanalytical in flavour.

Psychoanalytical because it is, figuratively, about feelings which are buried, repressed and seek to escape, to vent themselves. We feel that very strongly in this song, as great waves of emotion stemming from the piano (the unconscious? the id?) are ridden and struggled with by the voice (the conscious mind, the ego?). This is a theme we shall return to.

Heterosexual sex is not something we readily or easily associate with Schubert's music; those who want to present Schubert's primary sexual orientation as homosexual (see my second chapter) have this as a point in their favour. The homoerotic is indeed well or at least prominently represented in Schubert songs—most famously by the initially languorous but increasingly heated setting of Goethe's "Ganymed," the allegorised tale of the boy seized into the heavens by Zeus to become cupbearer of the gods. "Gretchen am Spinnrade" (Gretchen at the Spinning Wheel) is, of course, one of the most erotic songs ever written, but it is sung from a female perspective, a voice which Schubert, as composer, was very good at adopting. There's not a single song in *Die schöne Müllerin* (The Beautiful Miller Girl), the quintessential cycle about unrequited love, which could properly be described as either sexy or sensual. The whole work is seemingly predicated on the avoidance of adult male sexuality, threateningly embodied in the hairy male hunter who gets the girl. There is a palpable lack of erotic charge in the miller boy's utterances. A plainly and energetically erotic poem like Goethe's "Versunken" (another tricky translation; perhaps "Immersed" is best—it's all about the pleasures of the poet or his persona sinking his fingers into his girlfriend's hair, tousling, kissing, caressing) is not obviously sexy music. The Schubert scholar John Reed complained that "the on-running semiquavers, the shifting tonalities and even the chromaticisms suggest impatience, emotional disturbance, excitement, but not erotic pleasure." Here we hit on one nub of the problem. Languorous, panting eroticism is well catered for in music; active desire, less so. If Wagner's *Tristan und Isolde* is the touchstone of the musical erotic with its waves of desire and endless deferred climaxes, Schubert can certainly evoke the same passions on what is, perhaps, a more human, less frustrating—and exhausting—level. His song "Sei mir gegrüsst" (I greet you) is one which I have sung a lot in recital. Performed slowly as Schubert indicates, self-consciously slowly, it brilliantly suggests this sort of emotional and physical state, a song in suspended animation, touching on but also oversensitively withdrawing from overmuch ecstasy.

It may be that the Wagnerian eros is too dominant, that we underplay the tangled and energetic pleasure of a song like "Versunken," and that if we open our minds and hearts and bodies a little more, we may find unexpected things in Wagner's predecessor and preemptor Franz Schubert. Perhaps not quite in the way J. M. Coetzee comically suggests in a scene in his novel-cum-memoir, *Summertime*. It's a collection of recollections about the half-fictionalised John Coetzee, and this is an old girl-friend talking to the interviewer (collecting memories in order to compile some sort of biography) about her relationship with this strange man:

> One night John arrived in an unusually excited state. He had with him a little cassette player, and put on a tape, the Schubert string quintet. It was not what I would call sexy music, nor was I particularly in the mood, but he wanted to make love, and specifically— excuse the explicitness—wanted us to co-ordinate our activities to the music, to the slow movement.

The sheer eccentricity of using the slow movement of the quintet, the nonpareil of serious, deep, transcendent classicism (frequently one of the pieces chosen on BBC

Radio 4's *Desert Island Discs* as a sublime marker of final
things), as an aid to seduction or soundtrack for sex is a
measure of Coetzee's view of John Coetzee, his alter ego,
his doppelgänger, as an emotional oddball.

"The slow movement in question may be very beautiful
but I found it far from arousing. Added to which I could
not shake off the image on the box containing the tape:
Franz Schubert looking not like a god of music but like
a harried Viennese clerk with a head-cold. I don't know
if you remember the slow movement, but there is a long
violin aria with the viola throbbing below, and I could
feel John trying to keep time with it. The whole business
struck me as forced, ridiculous."

John Coetzee's reasons for this "erotic experiment"
are further evidence of his strange detachment: the artist
is an outsider (rather like the protagonist of *Winterreise*),
and more than a little creepy. They also offer something
between a fascinated engagement with and a sly satirical
dig at the whole apparatus of both the new cultural history and historical reenactment in performance. It starts
out reasonable and intriguing, beautifully nuanced and
convincing:

> He wanted to prove something to me about the history
> of feeling. Feelings had natural histories of their own.
> They came into being within time, flourished for a

while or failed to flourish, then died or died out. The kinds of feeling that had flourished in Schubert's day were by now, most of them, dead. The sole way left to us to re-experience them was via the music of the times. Because music was the trace, the inscription, of feeling.

This does eloquently summarise a strong sense we have about music, about its special ability to summon up, to encapsulate the moods and subjectivities of past times, whether in our own histories as individuals or those of other cultures. The feelings aroused may be illusory; then again, if most of the feelings of Schubert's day were dead and buried, surely we wouldn't be so interested in a work like *Winterreise*. There may be other ways to investigate the history of feeling, but surely none that offer the promise of such interiority, such power. Coetzee the author swoops down to his comical endgame:

Okay, I said, but why do we have to fuck while we listen to the music?

Because the slow movement of the quintet happens to be about fucking, he replied. If, instead of resisting, I had let the music flow into me and animate me, I would have experienced glimmerings of something quite

unusual: what it had felt like to make love in post-
Bonaparte Austria.

"Music isn't about fucking" is the reasoned response to all
this nerdy role play. "Music is about foreplay. It's about
courtship. You sing to the maiden *before* you go to bed
with her, not while you are in bed with her."

Of course, Coetzee's quondam lover is simply opposing
robust common sense to her partner's eccentric experi-
mentalising. There is, however, at least one example in
Schubert's song output of music which does experiment
with the idea of fucking, or at least with a more active
and thrusting male sexual persona. This is the song "Der
zürnenden Diana" (To the Angry Diana), not especially
well-known, a setting of a poem by Schubert's friend
and flatmate, Johann Mayrhofer. It is, poetically, the
clearest example in Schubert's oeuvre of a heterosexual
poem to set against the homoeroticism of a poem like
"Ganymed"—both, let it be noted, on classical subjects. The voice in the poem is that of the young hunter
Actaeon, who has seen Diana bathing with her companions. As she flushes with anger, the language is sensual,
the breathless excitement in the vocal setting and in
the surging of the piano line palpable as the composer
responds to the words: "am buschigen Gestade / Die
Nymphen überragen in dem Bade" (on the bushy bank, /

Towering over the nymphs in the bath); "der Schönheit
Funken in die Wildnis streuen" (showering sparks of
beauty on the wilderness). Actaeon must die, of course,
but he shall never regret, "nie bereuen," that he has seen
what he has seen; and he shall die at Diana's hand, by her
own arrow. The final stanza is intensely erotic, with all
that age-old association between death and orgasm:

> *Dein Pfeil, er traf, doch linde rinnen*
> *Die warmen Wellen aus der Wunde;*
> *Noch zittert vor den matten Sinnen*
> *Des Schauens-süsse letzte Stunde.*

(Your arrow, it hits its mark—yet gently warm waves
run from the wound; still tremble my failing senses in
contemplation of this sweet last hour.)

Gender relations in the poem are not straightforward
or traditional, of course. Death by an arrow shot from
a female bow may remind us of the reverse symbolism
of Shakespeare's *Venus and Adonis,* in which the nonpareil of male beauty is slain by a boar in a scene drenched
in sexual frisson as, "nuzzling in his flank, the loving
swine / Sheathed unaware the tusk in his soft groin."
Mayrhofer's Diana is like Shakespeare's Venus, who,
in a reversal of the norms of antique gender relations,

seems to have the power: "Backward she push'd him, as she would be thrust, / And govern'd him in strength, though not in lust." But if there is something phallic about Diana's arrow, and if her anger and Actaeon's desire seem to merge in the insistent thrusting of the opening piano part (fiery and resolute), it remains the case that the poem and, even more, the song present the picture of a very masculine desire, starting with those thrusts and ending in waves of exhausted shuddering, a musical ejaculation a long way from the slow movement of Schubert's quintet.

Without getting bogged down all over again in the muddy issue of Schubert's sexuality, or his sex life, "Der zürnenden Diana" reminds us not to dismiss the hetero-sexual side of the Schubertian equation, or to assume (as Maynard Solomon and his followers do) that adopting this sort of perspective means returning to the kitsch view of Schubert as a devotee of wine, women, and song. "To the Angry Diana" is a disturbing song, and in performance (for this performer at least, and his audience) quite a shocking one. On a biographical note, it is interesting that the song was dedicated to one of the most extraordi-nary women in Schubert's circle, the singer and courtesan (Graham Johnson calls her the "Dame aux Camélias" of Biedermeier Vienna) Katharina von Laczny. "What a woman!" Moritz von Schwind declared. She was in "ill repute" all over the city, according to an overexcited

Schwind, and Schubert and his friends clearly adored
and admired her combination of raciness, intelligence and
conversational flair. Her powerful sexuality haunts this
song.

REPRESSED SEXUALITY—very different from the efflo-
rescence of "To the Angry Diana," but closely related—is
the motor of "Erstarrung," driving right through to the
exhausted throbs of its last couple of bars. Constrained
sexual rigidity and prowling sexual hunger fuel the song.
The erotic impulse is to penetrate through to the earth—
Mother Earth—and the verb Müller uses, *durchdringen* (to
pierce), has *imprägnieren* (to impregnate) as one of its syn-
onyms. When, in its central section, the song's obsessive
movement lulls slightly, it is to notice how the fecundity of
nature is denied to the protagonist:

> Where can I find one flower,
> Where can I find green grass—
> The flowers are dead,
> The grass looks so washed-out.

The tone, and the repetitions made by the composer,
remain expressive of obsession.

The middle section closes by introducing the idea of

memory, which will connect this song with the next, "Der Lindenbaum" (The Linden Tree):

> Shall I then take no keepsake from this place?
> When my griefs are silent, who else will say
>   anything about her to me?

As the main musical tactus is resumed, the notion of memory is joined to that of winter:

> My heart is as if frozen,
> The picture of her is frozen stiff inside me.
> If my heart ever melts again
> Her image will flow away as well.

It's an extraordinarily complex image, difficult to unpack, retaining an ambiguity which connects with the way that, as the cycle commences, we are not really told why the wanderer left the house—who was rejector, who rejected? His heart is frozen, which implies a certain inability to respond emotionally, a state all of a piece with what we would call clinical depression. At the same time it is her image, "ihr Bild," which is cold, with that wonderful equivocation of meaning in the word *starrt*—the image is frozen and it stares (*starren* also means to stare, to look fixedly). Who is the cold one in this story?

There is something about the frozenness of our wanderer's heart in which he finds both comfort and terror. It has the immobility, the impermeability, that the bereaved seek: the bereaved who do not want to forget the departed, the dead, but must hence, paradoxically, cling to the pain of bereavement. Returning to the inevitable sexual thrust of the song, he wants to be cold because only coldness preserves him from the disappointment of fulfilled desire, the desire which ebbs in the last measures. At the same time, that image of the cold lover staring at him from within is a compelling and scary one. What one takes away from "Erstarrung," in the end, is the overwhelming sense of runaway emotions held down, repressed but unprocessed.

| 5 |

DER LINDENBAUM

THE LINDEN TREE

Am Brunnen vor dem Tore,
Da steht ein Lindenbaum:
Ich träumt' in seinem Schatten
So manchen süßen Traum.

Ich schnitt in seine Rinde
So manches liebe Wort;
Es zog in Freud' und Leide
Zu ihm mich immer fort.

Ich mußt' auch heute wandern
Vorbei in tiefer Nacht,
Da hab' ich noch im Dunkel
Die Augen zugemacht.

Und seine Zweige rauschten,
Als riefen sie mir zu:
Komm' her zu mir, Geselle,
Hier findst du deine Ruh'!

Die kalten Winde bliesen
Mir grad' ins Angesicht,
Der Hut flog mir vom Kopfe,
Ich wendete mich nicht.

At the well before the gate
There stands a linden tree;
I dreamt in its shade
So many a sweet dream.

I cut into its bark
So many a word of love;
In happiness and sadness it drew
Me back to it again and again

Today I had to wander too
Past it in the depths of night,
Even in the dark
I had to close my eyes.

And its branches rustled
As if it was calling out to me:
Come here to me, old chap,
Here you find your rest.

The cold winds blew
Straight in my face;
My hat flew from my head,
I didn't turn back.

Nun bin ich manche Stunde
Entfernt von jenem Ort,
Und immer hör' ich's rauschen:
Du fändest Ruhe dort!

Now I am many hours
Distant from that spot,
And always I hear that rustling:
You would find rest there.

Well, gate (out of shot), *lime tree: Bad Sooden-Allendorf, spurious original for Müller's* Lindenbaum. *The old tree fell in 1912.*

The unification of Germany would not have been possible without German art, without German science, and without German music—the German Lied in particular.

—BISMARCK (1892)

Let no one underestimate the power of German song as an ally in wartime.

—BISMARCK (1893)

If we are to take it as a truth that knows no exception that everything living dies for internal reasons—becomes inorganic once again—then we shall be compelled to say that "the aim of all life is death."

—FREUD, *Beyond the Pleasure Principle* (1920)

THE URGENT PULSE of "Erstarrung" turns into the rustling of Schubert's most famous song, "Der Lindenbaum," a transfiguration of the driven triplet figure the pianist can reflect in performance by allowing one song to melt seamlessly into the other. In another act of motivic binding, the simple tune which is dislocated by the triplets at the beginning of "Der Lindenbaum" is a major-key version of the driven melody which propels "Erstarrung." The openings of each song are closely related.

The present tense melts into the past—"I seek in vain" becomes "I dreamed so many sweet dreams." C minor becomes E major, the first time in the cycle that a song starts in a major key; the fact that it is a semitone above the relative major (which would have been E-flat) lifts the song, taking us to another place, another time, a transla-

tion best effected not by pausing between the songs in
performance but by juxtaposing them as intimately as
possible. Key relations between songs in *Winterreise* often
have a powerful dramatic or emotional effect, one which
can be lost when the original sequence is disrupted by
transposition to, say, baritone or bass keys. This issue will
recur in the next chapter.

That gentle rustling—of the leaves of last summer | *115*
rather than the winter branches of the present, specified
later in the poem—is then itself gently interrupted by
horn calls, the Romantic sound par excellence, the call of
the past, of memory, sensuality at a distance, "distance,
absence and regret," as Charles Rosen puts it in his book
The Romantic Generation. Remember those horns, for they
will return, later in this song; and horns will play a significant role later in the cycle—a posthorn at midpoint and a
funereal brass ensemble towards the end.

The *Lindenbaum*—the lime or linden tree in English—is a magical, mythical tree, freighted with alle-
gorical significance; something the art historian Michael
Baxandall alerts us to in his classic study *The Limewood
Sculptors of Renaissance Germany:*

> There are reports of holy limetrees hung with votive
> tablets against the plague; of many limegroves visited
> as places of pilgrimage; of lime seeds eaten by the

women of upper Bavaria; of the leaves, blossom and bark of the tree applied to the body as a means to strength and beauty . . . The lime did have, broadly speaking, festal associations: as Hieronymus Bock said, it was a tree to dance under.

Here is the lime tree in Bock's *Kreuter Buch* (1546), his herbarium:

As far back as Homer, the linden had been a magical
tree. In Ovid's *Metamorphoses* the transformation of the
old couple Baucis and Philemon into a lime tree and an
oak, respectively, made it a symbol of female conjugal
fidelity. The *Lindenbaum* is deeply embedded in European,
and more specifically in German, culture. Walther von der
Vogelweide, one of the greatest German poets of the high
Middle Ages, wrote a song some time in the late twelfth
or early thirteenth century which crystallises the wider
association between love and the linden:

> *Under der linden*
> *an der heide,*
> *dâ unser zweier bette was,*
> *dâ mugt ir vinden*
> *schône beide*
> *gebrochen bluomen unde gras.*
> *vor dem wald in einem tal,*
> *tandaradei,*
> *schône sanc diu nahtegal.*

> Under the linden tree
> on the open field,
> where we two had our bed,
> you still can see
> lovely both

> broken flowers and grass.
> On the edge of the woods in a vale,
> tandaradei,
> sweetly sang the nightingale.

Walther's is a courtly song about love and a relationship between a low-born girl and a man of substance: *Winterreise*'s tale told topsy turvy.

We have met Goethe's *Werther* already—as famous a book in German literary culture as was Rousseau's *La Nouvelle Héloïse* in French—and seen him crying his eyes out with his beloved but unattainable Charlotte. Linden trees figure in his story at iconic moments. Here he is just having parted from Charlotte and her fiancé, Albert—he has made friends with them both—perhaps forever. The pain of seeing her with Albert has been too much:

> I stood gazing after them in the moonlight. I threw myself upon the ground, and wept: I then sprang up, and ran out upon the terrace, and saw, under the shade of the linden-trees, her white dress disappearing near the garden-gate. I stretched out my arms, and she vanished.

When Werther has shot himself in the head, dispirited in impossible love, it takes him twelve hours to die (I was

one of the children in Massenet's opera *Werther* in 1977
at the English National Opera, and remember laughing,
with the cruelty of childhood, at the meal the operatic
hero manages to make of his end, singing clarion-voiced
to the last). He tells Charlotte where he wishes to be buried: "At the corner of the churchyard, looking toward the
fields, there are two lime-trees . . ."

If the associations between the linden and Romantic
love are of striking and obvious relevance to Schubert's
song, the political resonances too should not be forgotten, given all that can be said about *Winterreise*'s role as a
secret, coded lament for the reactionary climate at large
in Germany and Austria in the 1820s. Linden trees can
live to an enormous age. The oldest in Germany today
is said to be in the marketplace of the village of Schenk-
lengsfeld in eastern Hessen, reputedly planted in the ninth
century. Trees like this were planted in many settlements
in German-speaking lands in a custom dating back to
pre-Christian times. Sacred to Freya, and known as the
Tanzlinde (the dance linden, back to the festal significance
identified by Baxandall), they were often rededicated
to the Virgin Mary or the Apostles. Village meeting
places, these *Dorflinden* (village lindens) were a symbol
of community and, indeed, of Germanness, an aura only
intensified by the holding of assemblies and judicial courts
under their branches. The terms *Thing Linde* and *Gerichts-
linde* refer, respectively, to the immemorial institution

of German folk government (the Thing or *Ding*) and
to the execution of community justice (*Gericht*), held in
the shadow of the tree. In the political wintertime of the
1820s, the dreams the dreamer dreams in this song might
well be of an idealised past in which Germans of all sorts
governed themselves under the linden tree, free from
foreign interference or bureaucratic oppression alike.

It is surely that folkloric, national symbolism that has
helped make "Der Lindenbaum" into the most popular of
Schubert songs. Not popular in the way his "An die Musik"
and "Die Forelle" are, as songs of the concert hall or, once
upon a time, the drawing room—though "Lindenbaum"
used to be taken out of context in recital more than any
other song from Schubert's cycles—but as an outdoorsy,
jovial, community-singing or Boy Scouting sort of a song.

The main tune itself is folklike in its simplicity: firmly
rooted in one, major key; constructed from simple triads
and scales. Müller's poem is at one with this. What the
great German poet Heinrich Heine wrote in a letter of
1826 to Müller—"Wie rein, wie klar sind Ihre Lieder, und
sämmtlich sind es Volkslieder" (How pure, how transparent are your songs, they're just like folk songs)—is
especially true of "Der Lindenbaum," a real *Kunstlied im
Volkston* (art song in the popular style).

I remember going to Berlin around 2005 and telling my
taxi driver that I was to be singing Schubert's *Winterreise*

the following night at the Philharmonie (home of the Berlin Philharmonic). "Ah"—or rather "Ach"—he said, and started to sing a little, *im Volkston*. It sounded very much like "Der Lindenbaum," and in essence it was; the very mention of *Winterreise* had, after all, elicited the taxicab rendition. But it wasn't Schubert's "Der Lindenbaum," not really, and a single variant note—rising at the end of the first sung phrase, rather than falling—identified it as the folk song fashioned from Schubert's original by the composer Friedrich Silcher (1789–1860).

In order to work his questionable magic, launching "Der Lindenbaum," transformed, into the anonymous stream of folk music—not all singers of the song have known, like my taxi driver, what they are singing, its history or its pedigree—Silcher had to eviscerate what Schubert had made. The minor key that characterises the wanderer's journey in the darkness, eyes closed, cannot be allowed; nor can the turbulent musical episode which evokes the wind blowing in his face and his hat being blown from his head. It all has to be much simpler. In Silcher's solo version, for voice and piano or guitar, it's a strophic song with a basic chordal accompaniment. That fabulous rustling in the piano had to go; the melodic line was altered in the direction of greater psychological uplift. You can hear the great Lieder, Mozart, and operetta tenor Richard Tauber sing Silcher's version, lederhosen and all, in a 1930 movie, *Das lockende Ziel* (The End of the Rainbow—it's on YouTube). "Am Brunnen vor dem Tore" (as it became known, in true folk style) went on to become one of the most anthologised of German folk songs, to be sung a capella, with unison voices or a mixed choir, or perhaps accompanied by guitar around a campfire. A songbook for "secondary school and years 7 and 8 in primary school" included an adaptation of Silcher's version; the book was compulsory teaching material for the *Volksschulen* of the Zurich canton (3rd edition, 1931). More often than not, however, the song would have been orally transmitted, with little variations in the melody according to the mood of the singer, and radical departures, no doubt, from Müller's *völkisch* (popular or folksy) but still artful text. Here's the beginning of a version recorded in Silesia in the early 1900s:

> *Am Brunnen vor dem Tore*
> *Da steht mein Liebchens Haus.*
> *Sie hat mir Treu geschworen,*
> *Ging mit ihr ein und aus.*

> By the well in front of the gate
> There stands my beloved's house.
> She swore to be true to me,
> I went in and out with her.

The oddest thing about this version is that it contains never a mention of the fabled linden tree.

This sort of shared musical culture had largely disappeared by the end of the twentieth century, to be replaced by the commodified commonality of rock and pop music. Even in this sort of popular culture, however, "Der Lindenbaum" and its derivatives could make a mark. The Greek chanteuse Nana Mouskouri, a Eurovision fixture from the 1960s to the 1980s, had an unlikely version, derived from Silcher's, which can be seen on YouTube: ancient Greek ruins; white quasi-priestly gown; birdsong; catchy beat; and, of course, like Schubert himself, a musician with trademark glasses (somewhat larger). There's even a German-language episode of the hit American satirical cartoon *The Simpsons* in which a version of the song is rapped by Bart on the school bus outside the local nuclear power station, where his father works:

> *Am Brunnen vor dem großen Tor, uff,*
> *da steht so ein affengeiler Lindenbaum oh yea,*
> *ich träumte in seinem Schatten, so manchen süßen*
>   *Traum,*
> *so manchen süßen Traum*
> *unter diesem affengeilen Lindenbaum,*
> *oh yea, oh yea.*

> At the well in front of the great gate, uff,
> There stands such an ape-horny linden tree oh
>   yeah,
> I dreamt in its shade so many sweet dreams,
> So many sweet dreams
> Under this ape-horny linden tree,
> Oh yeah, oh yeah.

Here "Der Lindenbaum" replaces a folk song about the all-American mythical hero the former slave John Henry, who dies pitting his solitary strength against a newfangled steam-driven hammer, trying to save his own job and those of his men. Two very different cultures . . .

WHEN, AT THE VERY OUTSET of the 1990s, I was researching a television programme about nineteenth-century German song and the new, post–Cold War Germany—hoping to sell a documentary about Fischer-Dieskau to *The South Bank Show* on the back of the cultural roots and references of impending German reunification—my reading included a stimulating study by the preeminent American historian of Germany, Gordon A. Craig, *The Germans*, first published in 1982. I was delighted to find some grist to my Lieder mill in his chapter on Romanticism. Craig's quest, in a long and

distinguished career as a historian, had been to explain
how a culture as crucial and illuminating to Western
civilisation as German culture had become entangled in
the corrupting darkness that was Nazism. What were
the cultural conditions which led to what historians have
called Germany's *Sonderweg*, that other path which led it
away from the mainstream political evolution of the West?
Romanticism was one part of his answer, and in particular
he cited "the fascination with death that was so prominent
among the first Romantic generation."

| *125*

The evidence he brings to bear is wide-ranging, from
Ludwig Tieck's notes on Novalis's plans for the conclusion of his novel *Heinrich von Offerdingen*—"Human
beings must learn to kill each other . . . they seek
death"—to Wagner in 1854, five years before the deathly
consummation of *Tristan und Isolde:* "We must learn to
die, and indeed to die in the most complete sense of the
word." Craig goes on to connect this fascination with
extinction to the German embrace of war in the first half
of the twentieth century. Already in 1815, Joseph von
Eichendorff could write how "out of the magic incense of
our making a ghost of war will materialise, armoured with
the blanched face of Death." This is the same Eichendorff whom Schumann set to music in his sublime op. 39
Liederkreis of 1840. "Wolken ziehn wie schwere Träume"
(Clouds gather like oppressive dreams), Eichendorff

wrote and Schumann's singer sings; Craig saw something
sinister in all this gloom. When, in 1914, the German
chancellor Theobald von Bethmann-Hollweg called his
own policy on the eve of war "a leap into the dark and
the heaviest duty," Craig read it less as a commonplace
metaphor comparable to Edward Grey's lights going out
all over Europe, and more as the culmination of a century

of dubious German philosophising.

Romanticism's death obsession was to bear a terrible fruit; it was "omnipresent in Romantic prose and
verse," and it is not surprising that Craig detected its
baleful shadow in some of the most treasured passages
of Schubert song—in the whisper of the Erl King, in
the murmuring of the brook in *Die schöne Müllerin*, in
the seductive tread of Death himself in "Death and the
Maiden." Standing at the head of all these, though, is the
rustle of the linden tree:

> *Komm her zu mir, Geselle,*
> *Hier findst du deine Ruh.*

> Come here to me, good fellow
> Here you will find rest.

This analysis was shocking to me when I first read it. I'm
not sure I had ever before made the connection between

the songs I loved and the Nazi catastrophe, however much
I was aware of the moral degradation of the Wagner cult.
And, of course, the analysis is tendentious: enthusiasm for
war and fear of peacetime degeneration were just as alive
in England in August 1914 as in Germany; English poetry
had its own, longstanding love affair with death; much of
what deathly spirit there is to be found in Schubert song
is old-fashioned Christianity, whether Catholic or Pietist,
rather than newfangled Romanticism.

Craig's argument about Romanticism has its own roots
in two German literary titans, one pre-Romantic and one
post-Romantic. Johann Wolfgang von Goethe himself,
disturbed by the cultural trends for which he himself was
partly responsible, made his famous declaration in 1829,
towards the end of his long life: "I call the classical what
is healthy, and the Romantic what is sick." It is Craig's
adducing of "Der Lindenbaum," however, that reveals
his debt to another disciple of Goethe, Thomas Mann.
The song features crucially at the climax of Mann's novel
The Magic Mountain (1924), though what precisely it has
to say is, in a way typical of the whole book, unclear—
much less so than the black-and-white certainties of either
Craig or Goethe. This is partly a question of Mann's
expansive method, his ability to see and capture (often
at great length) every side of every question. It is also a
function of how the book came to be. Conceived in 1913

as a comical and novella-length pendant to the tragical *Death in Venice* (1912)—one treating of cholera on the lagoons, the other of tuberculosis in a Swiss mountain sanatorium—it took more than a decade to reach its final form, years dominated by the Great War, its prelude, its course, and its aftermath. Mann had started writing it just as his commitment to German nationalism was intensifying in response to the threat and outbreak of hostilities. War was, as for many others, a solution to Mann's political fears of decadence at large in German society, but also a distraction from his personal crisis, his writer's block. Since his first, breakthrough success, *Buddenbrooks*, a family chronicle published in 1902, no further fat novel had appeared, but only a succession of smaller works. In *Death in Venice*, which has at its heart a psychopathology of exhausted creative genius, he quite deliberately assigned to his protagonist, Gustav von Aschenbach, all the big books with which he, Mann himself, had struggled and which he had failed to finish. In Aschenbach's fictional world, the books were completed masterpieces, and therefore no longer available as projects for the flesh-and-blood Thomas Mann. This act of artistic semi-suicide was quickly followed by the huge and energising excitement of war. If Mann himself did not fight, he was a propagandist for what he saw as German cultural values against the vapid French and the commercial Englanders, deep *Kultur* against superficial *Zivilisation*.

By the end of the conflict he was not much further
on with *The Magic Mountain*, but he had penned the
monumental and reactionary *Reflections of an Unpolitical
Man*, and engaged in the famous spat with his liberal-
minded brother Heinrich. The novel grew and grew, but
its achievement of a final form coincided with Mann's
conversion to a republican politics and his commitment
to the Weimar settlement. This involved his increasing
disavowal of the opinions he had propounded during and
immediately after the war, opinions which he now saw as
dangerously Romantic—the fascination with death, the
aversion to democracy. Yet he never entirely discarded
his Romantic disposition, and while his political trajectory was clear—from nationalism to republicanism to a
quasi-socialist anti-Nazism—his creative vision remained
multifaceted. We see this in his attitude towards Wagner,
the arch-Romantic—his love and admiration of the composer, even his technical debt to his leitmotivic method,
combined with a need to grapple with and escape from his
influence. Writing about Nietzsche, Mann was describing himself: Nietzsche, whose love for Wagner "knew
no end," a love "which his commanding spirit had to
overcome." And what was at issue here was "the paradoxical and eternally interesting phenomenon of the world-
conquering intoxication with death."

The Magic Mountain, by turns meditative and comical, is never narratively driven: exasperating and intrigu-

ing by turn, it is half allegory, half bildungsroman. The hero, young Hans Castorp, goes to visit his sick soldier cousin, Joachim, in a sanatorium outside Davos, and ends up staying there for almost all of the novel. He falls for a fellow patient, Clavdia Chauchat, an echo of a same-sex schoolboy crush on a fellow pupil, and a relationship one of whose erotic climaxes is the acquisition of an X-ray plate of the sick beloved. He philosophises, more than half in love with Keats's easeful death (it wasn't only the German Romantics who were at it, after all), much of the time with his odd-couple mentors, the warm-hearted rationalist Settembrini (based partly on Thomas's brother Heinrich) and the mystical, fascistic Jesuit Naphtha (echoes of Wagner, with all that silk, incense, blood, and sacrifice). In the end, and paradoxically, only the outbreak of war in 1914 forces him to leave. Hans's relationship with sickness and death is constantly in play, and never quite resolved in the way Gordon Craig would like to suggest ("The dominion of Death over the Romantic temperament is perhaps the major theme . . . and the climax of his hero's *Bildung* comes when he frees himself from it"). By the middle of the book, we know that Hans doesn't really have tuberculosis, but he insists, like a true Romantic, on dwelling among the sick and dying; he does make a bid for escape midway, on skis, gets lost amidst the snow, but resists the temptation, the strong temptation, to give up and die buried under "hexagonal symmetry"; when he leaves the

sanatorium, it is to join a war which seems to embody
the love of death; and he is discovered at the end in a
muddy, martial landscape singing to himself those rustling
words from "Der Lindenbaum," as he advances to what
must surely be extinction. What *The Magic Mountain*
seems to do is to play with the notion that to grapple
with death is the business of life and art; but that, at the
same time, a "sympathy with death" can all too easily
become pathological. Castorp understands that he must
"keep faith with death in his heart, but always be aware
that allegiance to death and what is past is only evil and
misanthropy and revelling in darkness if it controls our
thinking."

131

That extraordinary popular dissemination of "Der
Lindenbaum" discussed earlier must have been one of the
things that led Mann to choose it to play such a crucial,
if mysterious, symbolic role in *The Magic Mountain*. It
meant that most readers would recognise the song; it also
meant that it could at the same time summon up visions
of profound art and intimations of the folkloric. Mann
himself dwells on the subject at length in the chapter
entitled "Fullness of Harmony." The sanatorium, "in its
never-resting concern for its guests," makes an acquisition, rescuing Castorp from "his mania for solitaire," a
mysterious object whose "secret charms" intrigue even the
narrator. It is a gramophone. The sanatorium's director
waxes lyrical about it:

> This is no apparatus, no machine . . . this is an instrument, this is a Stradivarius, a Guarneri . . . Music, most faithful, in its modern, mechanical form. The German soul, up-to-date . . .

The music supplied on the brittle black discs is varied—Italian arias, a French horn playing folk-song variations, the latest dance music. Lieder too, of which Hans's favourite is "Der Lindenbaum," "which he had known since childhood, and for which he now developed a mysterious, multifaceted love." The narrator describes the song as "exemplarily German" and as being one of those special Lieder which is at one and the same time a masterpiece and a folk song—"and that simultaneity was what stamped it with its particular intellectual and spiritual view of the world."

THAT VIEW OF THE WORLD is handled subtly in *The Magic Mountain*—"the greatest care must be given to nuance," as Mann writes—but it comes down to the Romantic worldview, that deathly obsession:

> The song meant a great deal to him, a whole world . . . [H]is fate might have been different if his disposition had not been so highly susceptible to the charms of the

emotional sphere, to the universal state of mind that this song epitomized so intensely, so mysteriously . . . [W]hat were Hans Castorp's scruples, what questions did he ask himself . . . about the ultimate legitimacy of his love for this enchanting song and its world? What was this world that stood behind it, which his intuitive scruples told him was a world of forbidden love?

It was death.

Hans's rational-minded friend and adviser, Settembrini, has earlier warned him of the dangers of music; and the association between death and music is signalled throughout the novel. As he looks at an X-ray of his hand, for the first time connecting with his own mortality, "there came upon his face the expression it usually wore when he listened to music: a little dull, sleepy, and pious, his mouth half open, his head inclined toward the shoulder."

Introduced in the chapter on the gramophone—a nice juxtaposition between the ultimately Romantic and the utterly mechanical—Hans's favourite song returns at the very end of the book.

"Where are we? What is that? Where has our dream brought us?" the narrator asks. It is a landscape straight out of *Winterreise*, be it the "murky sky that bellows incessantly with dull thunder" ("The Stormy Morning")

or the jagged, tattered signpost which points nowhere
("The Signpost"). Mud instead of snow, and three
thousand "feverish lads" who "shout courage in brash,
young voices." One of them, the hero of the book, who
has spent most of its thousand or so pages holed up in
that sanatorium in the snowy mountains—"There is our
friend, there is Hans Castorp"—is singing. His feet are
weighed down by mud, he's soaked through, his face is
flushed, he clutches a bayoneted rifle in his hand, it hangs
by his side, he treads on a fallen comrade—but he sings,
sings to himself—"the way a man sings to himself in
moments of dazed, thoughtless excitement, without even
knowing—and he uses what tatters of breath he has left to
sing to himself." What he sings is "Der Lindenbaum"—
"Ich schnitt in seine Rinde / so manche liebe Wort . . .
Und seine Zweige rauschten, / als riefen sie mich zu"
(I cut into its bark / so many a word of love . . . And its
branches rustled / as if it was calling out to me):

> And so in the tumult, in the rain, in the dusk, he disap-
> pears from sight.

Half a book earlier, Hans has already made that one,
unsuccessful attempt to escape from the Magic Mountain.
The landscape was a snowy one. Knowing that "Der Lindenbaum" features at, and indeed as, the climax, it is easy
to read *Winterreise* into Hans's abortive expedition.

The chapter itself is called "Snow," and it creates, suggests, hints at a parallel between the predicament of the wanderer in *Winterreise,* compelled by his own nature to wander through a winter landscape, and that of Castorp, Mann's protagonist, tubercular sufferer, who has sunk into the comfortable but deathly embrace of the snowbound sanatorium where most of the story plays out. In "Snow," Castorp escapes from his confinement, venturing outside, and gets lost; in so doing he confronts ultimate questions. Reading "Snow" is, if nothing more, a good imaginative and mental workout for singing, or experiencing, *Winterreise.*

| *135*

There are many more detailed parallels. The relationship between this winter landscape and the confronting of existential questions, to start with: snowy blankness, "white whirling nothing," "white darkness" as a blank screen upon which the ultimate can be projected and grappled with in a sort of ironic, almost jocular, tone which the two works share. "He realised," Mann tells us, "that he was talking to himself"—just like our other wanderer—"and saying rather strange things at that." Like Schubert and Müller's protagonist, Castorp seems to want to lose his way. "He had secretly," Mann writes, "and more or less on purpose been trying to lose his bearings," as the wanderer seems to suggest elsewhere in the song cycle. And, like our wanderer, Hans is tempted to give in: "the desire, the temptation, to lie down and rest crept into his mind"; but in the end, he doesn't succumb, refusing to surrender to snowflakes, to that "hexagonal symmetry": "My stormily pounding heart does not intend to lie down and be covered by stupid, precise crystallometry."

THAT NOTION of the stupidity of brute nature is moot. Nature is the Romantic topos par excellence, of course, at the heart of the Romantic literary tradition from which both Müller and Schubert emerged; and many, many of Schubert's songs conform to the classical Romantic pattern which is to be found, for example, in Coleridge's great linden-tree poem, "This Lime Tree Bower, My Prison." The bower may be a prison—the poet is confined, having stayed behind when his friends went for a country walk—but nature is a source of delight and healing, both when he considers, in his imagination, his companions "wander[ing] on," but also when he returns to his own situation:

> A delight
> Comes sudden on my heart, and I am glad
> As I myself were there! Nor in this bower,
> This little lime-tree bower, have I not mark'd
> Much that has sooth'd me. Pale beneath the blaze
> Hung the transparent foliage; and I watch'd

Some broad and sunny leaf, and lov'd to see
The shadow of the leaf and stem above
Dappling its sunshine!

How different is this tree, however, from Müller and
Schubert's whispering tempter, and Coleridge's conclusion
is resolutely positive: "no sound is dissonant which tells of
Life."

Nature in *Winterreise* is very differently conceived.
Only at the outset do we hear the authentically early
Romantic strain—"Der Mai war mir gewogen / mit
manchem Blumenstrauß" (May was good to me, / with
many a garland of flowers)—though even here the image
is formal enough to verge on the sarcastic. We are presented in subsequent songs with a succession of images
of a hostile Nature: sometimes that brute, stupid Nature
which Castorp confronts; sometimes Nature personified
as something sinister or malicious. The branches tempt the
wanderer in this song, "Der Lindenbaum," to lie down
and freeze to death; will-o'-the-wisps will lure him into
dangerous places ("Irrlicht"); the ice will mock him by
painting illusory leaves on the windowpanes ("Frühlingstraum"). That very personification, though, is pushed to
the limit and, hence, essentially satirical—look at how the
reality of birds dislodging snow from roofs onto the wanderer's head is poetically transformed into the ludicrous

image of crows throwing snowballs at his hat from every house ("Rückblick"). We end up, then, with much the same vision of winter as Castorp's—"a fairy-tale world, childlike and funny," with something "roguish and fantastic" about it, but in the final analysis "simply indifferent and deadly," "monstrously indifferent." This, surely, is one of the lessons the wanderer learns in the course of

Winterreise. In an earlier song, written in 1819, setting lines of Schiller, "Die Götter Griechenlands" (The Gods of Greece), Schubert had mourned the loss of that "beautiful world" in which nature was infused with godhead, the world of Greek mythology. By the end of *Winterreise* and its twenty-second song, "Mut" (Courage), he seems instead to be recommending defiance in the face of a *deus absconditus,* with music that is very obviously, if again ironically, celebratory—"Will kein Gott auf Erden sein, / sind wir selber Götter" (If there's no God on earth, / we're gods ourselves).

The thematic connection between the two journeys in the snow, Mann's and Schubert's, is clinched by the refuge both men find in or about an isolated hut in the frozen landscape ("Rast"—Rest). They both dream dreams ("Frühlingstraum"—Dream of Spring). Schubert's is a spring dream of love and happiness which is shattered by crowing birds and bitter cold; Mann's is one of the most commented-upon dreams in German literature, in which a vision of a sunny and civilised people conceals horror in the sanctuary at its heart:

> Two half-naked old women were busy at a ghastly chore . . . dismembering a child held above a basin . . . They devoured it piece by piece.

The web of associations is extensive—Aschenbach's orgiastic dream in *Death in Venice*, Goethe's witches in *Faust*, even H. G. Wells's Eloi and Morlocks from *The Time Machine* (1895; Wells and Mann dined together on more than one occasion) and Conrad's *Heart of Darkness* (1899). The moral conundrum is explicit: the deathly horror which lies at the heart of civilisation.

Castorp marches forward to what seems certain death singing "Der Lindenbaum," a participant in what Mann calls this "worldwide festival of death," the Great War. It is in this festival, this orgy of killing, this "ugly rutting fever," that Germany has found the dangerous solution to the pre-war creative slough of despond which is represented in the book by the endless, semi-comical disputes between Settembrini and Naphtha, and by the healthy Hans's refusal to leave his asylum of sickness. Germany is Mann writ large. Self-mythologising, he had found the solution to his own personal crisis—so brilliantly exposed in *Death in Venice*—in the outbreak of war. For that failure to resist sympathy with death, he blamed Romanticism, while at the same time he remained unable utterly to reject its aesthetic and human potential. For Mann the novelist, "Der Lindenbaum" may be an anthem for doomed youth, but the possibility of love remains. And so the novel ends:

> . . . you saw the intimation of a dream of love rising up out of death and this carnal body. And out of this worldwide festival of death, this ugly rutting fever that inflames the evening sky all round—will love rise up out of this, too?

As Mann put it in 1930: "The war forced us out of the metaphysical and individual stage into the social." For Mann the republican citizen, Schubert's song became a much simpler symbol of reaction, and his nation's unhealthy sympathy with death and immersion in the past. Not long after the publication of *The Magic Mountain*, in April 1925, he wrote in a letter to the dramatist and critic Julius Bab commenting on the proposed candidacy of Paul von Hindenburg, the reactionary general, for the presidency of the German Republic, the so-called Weimar Republic. The attempted embrace of Goethe's healthy classicism over the sickness of the Romantic is contained in that very sobriquet. Hindenburg's election would be, Mann declared, "merest 'Lindenbaum.'"

.   .   .

WHEN I FIRST GOT TO KNOW *Winterreise* in my teens,
I was a little confused about "Der Lindenbaum." I had
the idea that the leaves were whispering to the traveller
to lie down under their branches not because he might
then freeze to death, but because they would rain down
some sort of poisonous narcotic blossom on him. I was,
probably, confusing the genus *Tilia* with the suburban
Laburnum familiar to me from my South London childhood, poisonous in every part (the plant, not the childhood) and, hence, an object of nervous fascination.
Even if wrongheaded in any literal sense, the idea of
some sort of active ingredient lurking in the tree is a
fruitful one, because it points us away from death, and
Mann's use of the song, to its other significance, which
is memory.

> No sooner had the warm liquid mixed with the
> crumbs touched my palate than a shudder ran through
> me and I stopped, intent upon the extraordinary thing
> that was happening to me. An exquisite pleasure had
> invaded my senses, something isolated, detached,
> with no suggestion of its origin. And at once the
> vicissitudes of life had become indifferent to me, its
> disasters innocuous, its brevity illusory—this new
> sensation having had on me the effect which love has

of filling me with a precious essence; or rather this
essence was not in me, it was me. . . . Whence did
it come? What did it mean? How could I seize and
apprehend it? . . .

In this celebrated madeleine-eating moment from
Marcel Proust's *A la recherche du temps perdu* (In Search
of Lost Time), the recovery of memory, that cascade of
reminiscence which is initiated by the madeleine, has its
own occult connection with the linden tree, for the warm
liquid in which the madeleine is dipped is the French infu-
sion of lime flowers, tilleul. Proust was not the only writer
of the Belle Epoque to express a connection between the
lime flower and the process of involuntary memory. In his
1904 study *La Fonction de la mémoire et le souvenir affectif*
(The Function of Memory and Affective Recollection)
the French psychological researcher Frédéric Paulhan
recounted his own epiphany, a less poetic transcription of
what Proust was to describe:

We thus rediscover here and there, in our memory,
distant recollections of impressions which seem to
have nothing to do with the present, but which struck
our mind at a favourable moment . . . I thus recall the
impression which the bland odor of falling linden blossoms [*fleurs de tilleul*] made upon me in the courtyard

of the little school where as a young child I learned to read.

LIKE MOST GREAT poems or songs, "Der Lindenbaum" has about it a complexity which forestalls any attempt to be too prescriptive. It is very easy to take Mann's line, and see the subject as death, its subtle temptations, whispering in the traveller's ear—you will find peace if only you lie down and go to sleep in the snow under that tree, the sleep of death. And of course, the subject is death, just as many have interpreted the hurdy-gurdy player at the end of the cycle as a figure straight out of the mediaeval and early Renaissance *danse macabre* or *Totentanz*. "Komm her zu mir, Geselle" (Come here to me, old chap), the tree whispers, and that word *Geselle* is telling. Originally deriving from the Old High German *gisello*, or housemate, the person you share a room with, the word came to mean a journeyman or apprentice. Here it means companion, travelling companion, and the mode of address is familiar, even chummy. In the earlier set of poems which Schubert set to music, *Die schöne Müllerin*, Müller uses the same word, as the miller boy stares at the mill race and feels drawn to plunge into its waters, the waters he will kill himself in at the end of the cycle. The draw is hypnotic, friendly, perhaps sinister:

Und in den Bach versunken
Der ganze Himmel schien
Und wollte mich mit hinunter
In seine Tiefe ziehn.

Und über den Wolken und Sternen,
Da rieselte munter der Bach
Und rief mit Singen und Klingen:
Geselle, Geselle, mir nach!

And sunk into the stream
The whole of heaven appeared
And it wanted to pull me down
With it into its depths.

And over the clouds and stars
The stream murmured, lively,
And called to me with singing
And tinkling: Geselle, Geselle.

At the same time, the lime tree is, as its liquor had been for Proust, a spur to memory. Under a very different aspect, it is love, and the remembrance of love, that we find in "Der Lindenbaum." The tree reminds the wanderer of the happiness he once had, and it tempts him to try again; the openness of the first song—did he leave or was he cast out?—makes that a possibility. The key to this is in the music. The song mixes memory and desire in its very opening bars, which so subtly remind us of the passionate torment of the preceding song "Erstarrung." And it is to those sounds that we return in the piano postlude.

Anyway, be it love or death that tries to call him back, our wanderer walks on.

POSTSCRIPT

Mahler's *Lieder eines fahrenden Gesellen* (Songs of a Travelling Wayfarer; first completed in 1885) is a piece I have sung many times—if not as often as *Winterreise*. The best-known version is for orchestra, with baritone or mezzo-soprano (Dietrich Fischer-Dieskau and Janet Baker were legendary exponents); but, in the original version for piano and transposed up for the tenor voice, stripped of its late Romantic orchestral colouring, it has its own potency and, what is more, a relationship to Schubert's two cycles which becomes all the more clear. It is more than the *Gesell'* of the title—the travelling wayfarer, the apprentice, first cousin to the miller boy of *Die schöne Müllerin* and the wanderer of *Winterreise*. The first song sets out with a figure in the piano whose broken conclusion is an echo of the clumsy numbfingeredness of the hurdy-gurdy in the last song of *Winterreise:*

Mahler's is a *Sommerreise* to match Schubert's winter

journey; and while much of the verse, put together by
Mahler himself, is inspired by or even derived from the
famous folk collection *Des Knaben Wunderhorn* (The
Boy's Magic Horn; 1805 and 1808), it is just as artful and
carefully contrived as Müller's. "The idea of the songs as
a whole," as Mahler wrote to a friend in 1885, "is that a
wayfaring man, who has been stricken by fate, now sets
forth into the world, travelling wherever his road may
lead him." Many of the elements of Schubert's journey
are there: the solitary farewell, the departure at night, the
girl who will marry another man, and, at the very end,
the linden tree. Mahler's traveller is the emanation of a
Romanticism much closer to Mann's notion of sickness
and sympathy with death, or Freud's of the death instinct.
The linden tree comes at the end of the cycle, and, unlike
Schubert and Müller's wanderer, Mahler's surrenders
to it:

> *Auf der Straße steht ein Lindenbaum,*
> *Da hab' ich zum ersten Mal*
> *im Schlaf geruht!*
> *Unter dem Lindenbaum,*
> *Der hat seine Blüten*
> *über mich geschneit,*
> *Da wußt' ich nicht, wie das Leben tut,*
> *War alles, alles wieder gut!*

Alles! Alles, Lieb und Leid
Und Welt und Traum!

On the street stands a linden tree,
there for the first time
I found rest in sleep!
Under the linden tree,
Whose blossoms
snowed down on me.
There I didn't know what life did,
Everything was good again,
Everything—love and suffering
And world and dream!

| 6 |

WASSERFLUT

FLOOD

Manche Trän' aus meinen Augen
Ist gefallen in den Schnee;
Seine kalten Flocken saugen
Durstig ein das heiße Weh.

Wenn die Gräser sprossen wollen,
Weht daher ein lauer Wind,
Und das Eis zerspringt in Schollen,
Und der weiche Schnee zerrinnt.

Schnee, du weißt von meinem Sehnen:
Sag', wohin doch geht dein Lauf?
Folge nach nur meinen Tränen,
Nimmt dich bald das Bächlein auf.

Wirst mit ihm die Stadt durchziehen,
Muntre Straßen ein und aus:
Fühlst du meine Tränen glühen,
Da ist meiner Liebsten Haus.

Many a tear from my eyes
Has fallen in the snow;
Its cold flakes suck in
Thirstily the hot grief.

When the grass wants to sprout,
A mild wind blows around,
And the ice breaks into pieces
And the soft snow melts away.

Snow, you know my longing:
Say, where does your path lead?
Only follow my tears
And the stream will soon swallow you up.

You'll go through the town with it,
In and out of the lively streets;
When you feel my tears are glowing hot,
There's where my beloved's house is.

"W ASSERFLUT" picks up where "Der Lindenbaum" left off:

That insistent phrase in the piano in the last verse (which originated in the second, minor-key, nighttime verse), repeated twelve times, and in the end perhaps a little irritating, a little trite, a little too chirpy—the sentimental appeal of the linden tree mocked by the traveller—is transformed, stretched out, into the keening opening figure of the next song. That figure itself, though, is a matter of intense debate.

. . .

GOING TO A LIEDER RECITAL can be a little dangerous
for your average audience member. Mostly, you're part of
a compact group, well lit (so texts can be read or referred
to in translation), easy to pick on if the singer wants to
direct his or her emotional effusions directly to or at you.
It's sometimes said that the measure of a great singer
is that it feels as if he or she is singing to you alone; in
somewhere like London's Wigmore Hall this can often be
quite literally true, and this resource—the address to the
individual as well as to the mass—is a crucial part of the
aesthetic transaction.

It's odd for us singers that other instrumentalists—
especially solo pianists, who look away from the audience
and don't know singers well—don't realise this. How
often have I been asked: "So, you recognise people in the
audience?" Of course I do; and the psychological state
one enters to process that recognition—"Why, there's
mother!"—while staying in "character," is tricky to
plumb. It must be a matter of layered (re)cognition.

It's particularly important to remember that if you're a
well-known musician, or a colleague, and come to a recital
in the Wigmore Hall, you have to come back afterwards
and enthuse or at the very least engage, and perhaps lie.
That is part of the etiquette, for if you don't come back

(or at least send a note), every half-human singer will be convinced that you hated the performance.

Some time around the beginning of the millennium, I was performing all three Schubert cycles twice through, with Julius Drake, at the Wigmore Hall (not some strange endurance test, but spread over a couple of weeks). In one of the *Winterreise*s I noticed that an exceptionally distinguished pianist, and great Schubertian to boot, was sitting at the end of row H on the right. I had recognised him fairly quickly as I scanned the hall in the moments before the cycle kicked off, making that initial visual connection with the audience that has become almost a ritual. Only a little later did I see that he was following the music with his score (always a little off-putting if you're singing something by heart) and that he was sitting next to another, younger, but also distinguished instrumentalist. As Julius launched into the first bars of "Wasserflut," the pianist in the audience—let us call him A—started to look with incredulity at the music. Shaking his head, he turned to his companion—let us call him B—and jabbed a finger at the notes. I don't remember B's reaction, but the coup de grâce came when A swung his body right round to communicate his artistic dissent, revealing that the person in the row directly behind him was another famous pianist, C, who seemed rather taken aback at the disturbance.

What was going on? Why was our harmless performance of this harmless little song causing such a fluster?

It's all about what is known as triplet assimilation. In
the very first bar of this song, Schubert writes a triplet—
three even notes—in the treble, upper clef, to be played
by the right hand; in the same bar, in the bass, lower clef,
to be played by the left hand, he writes a syncopated
rhythm, a dotted quaver and a semiquaver, thus:

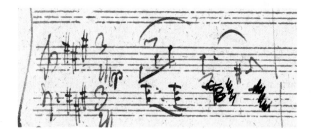

To be clear: the time signature of the song is in three,
3/4, three crotchet beats to a bar, but the first beat of that
bar is divided up into three in the right hand—three
even quavers—and into four in the left hand—a dotted
quaver and a semiquaver. How should that smooth triplet
be played against the so-called "duplet" dotted rhythm?
Assimilating it means "tripletising" the dotted figure
in the lower stave and allowing its semiquaver to sound
together with the last triplet in the upper. The alternative,
strictly logical treatment, is for that semiquaver to sound

after the triplet, producing a more complex, jagged texture
in which the two voices in either hand have more of an
independent life. In our Wigmore performance, Julius and
I had plumped for the latter, hence the visible dissent from
row H. The pattern runs all through the song; in the first
two bars where the voice joins the piano, the singer has
triplets against the piano's dotted rhythm ("Manche Trän'
aus meinen Augen"), then falling into the piano's dotted
scheme in the third bar ("Ist gefallen in den Schnee").

Triplet assimilation has been a matter for the sort of
musicological debate which can seem inward-looking and
trivial but does, in fact, have an impact on the way we play
and hear music. Musicologists (mostly) believe in rules, in
the notion that the symbols on the page require an accu-
rate rendering, first and foremost, before any performer's
intuition can be allowed to engage, and in order to make
possible the flowering, from what is mere ink and paper,
of what the composer had in mind. The ideal is realised.
Hence, working out what the rules of notation required
in 1827 when Schubert wrote "Wasserflut" is crucial to
presenting a proper performance of the song.

In 1972 Josef Dichler published an article in an Austrian musicological journal concerning interpretative
issues in Schubert's piano music, describing a failure to
assimilate dotted rhythms to triplets in Schubert as "poly-
rhythmic madness," a position taken up by one of the

greatest of Schubertians, Alfred Brendel, in a programme
note written in the same year, a note he has reprinted in
his widely read collection of essays *On Music*. As a pianist
whose performances of Schubert piano sonatas have such
an exceptional way with Schubert's aesthetic—the cosy,
the brutal, and the uncanny in luminous coexistence—
Brendel's opinion carries a lot of weight. There can be
not the "slightest doubt," he wrote, "that the Brahmsian
polyrhythm usually produced is wrong: the dotted rhythm
has to be adjusted to the triplets where they occur together
and, I should like to add, most probably where it stands
alone as well."

Brendel's first argument is technical and negative: if
Schubert wanted to hear the smooth, Brendelian version of those notes, he had no other way to write it down:
"Some of Schubert's notation habits are surprisingly old-
fashioned." A tripletised dotted quaver/semiquaver (the
figure Brendel wants to hear in the left hand) was not part
of Schubert's notational armoury. "Whenever," Brendel
writes, "Schubert wants to use triplets in a quadruplet
time scheme he writes not ♩ ³ ♪ but ♩. ♩ ."

In 1969 another distinguished pianist, Paul Badura-
Skoda, wrote that he had never seen ♩ ³ ♪ or what is called
a "broken triplet" in Schubert's music. However, more
thorough research on Schubert's notation by the musicologist David Montgomery has uncovered at least three

hundred and sixty examples of such triplets in Schubert's oeuvre in twenty-three different works written over a period of fourteen years. Including other forms of broken triplet, the count reaches into the thousands. So, if Schubert had wanted what Brendel characterises as the "soft" sound of a tripletised dotted quaver/semiquaver against a triplet in the other hand, he could have made that clear in his notation and written ♩ ³ ♪ . We do not need to give a preference to "soft" rhythms in Schubert's piano writing, as Brendel suggests; the danger is of falling into the old, nineteenth-century opposition (popularised by Robert Schumann) between the "masculine" Beethoven and the "feminine" Schubert.

Assimilation of triplet to dotted rhythm could and did occur but, even in the eighteenth century, was no more than a practical solution, depending on the tempo of the piece (it was easier to achieve distinct non-assimilation if the piece was slow) or the capacity of the player to play three against two; it wasn't what the composer "meant." Here's the great flute player and pedagogue (Frederick the Great's teacher, no less) Johann Joachim Quantz, in 1752: "If one tried to assimilate the dotted figure to the value of the triplet figure, the expression created thereby would not be brilliant and splendid, but lame and monotonous instead." This, according to the theorist and keyboard player Johann Friedrich Agricola, "is what J. S.

Bach taught all his pupils." Here is D. G. Türk in 1789, advising caution: "The dividing of dotted notes against triplets presents difficulties, and is therefore also not to be expected of beginners with any exactitude."

It is true, as Brendel says, that in both the manuscript and the printed score, that of the first and of many subsequent editions, the relevant passage in "Wasserflut" is printed so that the first and third of the triplets in the right hand are directly above the two chords in the left hand. Montgomery, the musicologist, contends that this is mere printer's convention (and Schubert wrote his manuscript for the printer), a matter of reading convenience. To support this, he points to Beethoven's annotations on a copy of Cramer's Piano Etudes, which insist upon the rhythmic independence of triplet and dotted rhythms in a passage which has these "mixed" rhythms precisely aligned on the printed page.

By this point I want to shout—and so does my gentle reader, I guess—"Enough with the musicology already!" But whatever the ins and outs of the arguments, the question of triplet assimilation seems to be open enough to allow for a variety of approaches. Julius, my pianist, and I grew up listening to LPs, and our pianistic idol in *Winterreise*, as in much of the Lieder repertoire, was (and probably remains) Gerald Moore, who started playing the piece in the 1930s and made at least four classic recordings, three with Dietrich Fischer-Dieskau and one with Hans Hotter. Moore, of an older generation, before this hoohah blew up, plays our favoured, jagged version, and describes its affect like this: "The semiquaver comes after the triplet . . . not merely because it is slow moving, but because it has a dragging effect giving verisimilitude to the picture of the tired wanderer half blinded by tears."

Arnold Feil, the distinguished musicologist, argued, if less colourfully, for just the same weariness in the song, but concluded that this required the very triplet assimilation which Moore eschewed. Rather than weariness, and Moore's very specific (and limiting) pictorialism, I would want to stress dissociation and complexity as the virtues of the unassimilated version—weirdness, if you like. For pianists a generation after Moore, this seemed just a little too modern, perhaps; yet thinking that they were being true to some sort of Viennese classical practice, they were then overtaken by the authenticity generation, who studied the sources exhaustively and left us better informed, but still having to make a choice. And how do we musicians make those choices?

If I were to question, honestly, my motives for choosing which version of Schubert's rhythmic configuration in "Wasserflut" to go with, I would have to suspect that it was familiarity and the pull of Gerald Moore's extraordinary piano playing. Beyond that, I didn't think about it much; and, after all, it is a notational complexity that we're talking about, and I am not a trained musician, and indeed started my life as a singer learning music by ear. After a few years of singing the piece professionally, hearing about all the experts who favoured that strategy of assimilation, I, slightly cussedly no doubt, thought we should stick to our guns, and that we had freedom, as performers, to do so. I wasn't, after all, so displeased to see the ruffled feathers in row H of the Wigmore. Now, of course, I am more than delighted to have found justification for our reading. (It was Leif Ove Andsnes who, years ago, when we were touring the piece, told me that a violinist friend of his, steeped in baroque music, had said that the issue of assimilation wasn't as clear as some seemed to think.) These three positions represent some sort of sequence, I suppose: following an old performance tradition; asserting one's freedom; refinement in the archive.

The freedom of performance is crucial. The status of the score in classical music is the subject of enormous philosophical nitpicking and logic chopping, but even if it is the score that distinguishes ours from other, even most, probably all other musical traditions (jazz or Indian classical music, for example), it is still the performance that is the reality, especially in a contemporary culture in which playing through a score oneself is, for most music lovers, an ideal lost in the distant past. The score is of course

more than a mere recipe, and it provides a necessary and
containing discipline for performers, something to kick
against (a discipline which gives meaning and force to the
eccentricities of such performers as Glenn Gould). At the
same time, so much of what we have to do as "realisers" of
the score is not in the score, either in words or in notation;
that gap is what makes "interpretation" necessary. And
interpretation is really a misnomer, because what goes on
in the gap is so much more than interpretation—crucial
matters like colour and timbre and timing and pauses
between pieces and absolute (rather than relative) dynamics and so on and so on. The performance is a meeting
between the composer and the performer and the listener,
and it is only together that they can create the piece.

The issue of how to realise rhythmic notation in actual
sound stretches way beyond the issue of triplet assimilation, even if one confines oneself to the rhythmic relation
between voices in piano writing. The musicologist Julian
Hook has compiled and analysed a whole host of conun-
dra in his brilliant work on what he calls "impossible
rhythms." Singers, in particular, grapple with notational
inexactitude all the time, because they do not sing notes
but words, and phrases, and sentences, the relationship
between consonant and vowel and syntactic emphasis in
continual counterpoint with the bald quavers, crotchets,
minims, and semibreves written on the page. This, and

the importance of breath, is something that every song accompanist has to learn. If the pianist in a performance of *Winterreise* is playing music, and not just notes, and given the apparent ambiguity of notation we have highlighted, then different solutions to the opening of "Wasserflut" will be possible, and indeed necessary.

I want to end this rather technical excursus—which does, nonetheless, tell us a lot about how musicians grapple microscopically with the stuff of music in preparation and in performance—by remembering that, in fact, the first recording of *Winterreise* I owned was not one of Fischer-Dieskau and Gerald Moore's but Fischer-Dieskau and Daniel Barenboim's. It was as I was writing this that it came to me and, wonders of the information age, I could immediately call up Barenboim's handling of those first few bars online. In the opening bar he assimilates; in the second bar the same phrase is repeated and he doesn't: an intuitive solution. By contrast, listening to Brendel's version (with the same singer)—and I yield to no-one in my admiration for him as a Schubert player—am I imagining a slight inhibiting self-consciousness in the very precisely articulated assimilation of the third bar?

When I sing *Winterreise*, different performances fall out different ways, different groupings of songs emerge from the logic of performance, and different emotional trajectories are pursued. But "Wasserflut" has a very particular

quality in the sequence which I notice every time. It is
created by that extraordinary marriage of musical playfulness and expressive extremity which the song presents,
something which is to recur again and again in the cycle;
it is a crucial step on the journey Schubert makes towards
the hollowed-out, bare music at the end of the work, and
also, coincidentally, an anticipation of the sort of effect
Stravinsky achieves (much more radically, of course) in a
work like *Oedipus Rex,* which I happen to be preparing as
I write this.

164

   If one needed a final argument in favour of playing or
singing the triplets against the dotted rhythm, this would
be it. The first eight sung bars give us a whole host of
rhythmic possibilities, and they feel, at first, like a sort of
game. In bars one and two ("Manche Trän' aus meinen
Augen") piano and voice just miss each other, and it's
crucial that they should do so, pace Brendel; at the beginning of bar three, on the contrary ("ist gefallen"), they
mirror each other exactly in a spiky dotted rhythm. And
then back to the triplet against dotted figure with "in den
Schnee." This is partly a matter of Schubert's exquisite
way with word-setting, trying to ensure that the notes
he writes embody the natural gesture of the language;
and partly a matter, beyond that, of colouring the words
with rhythm, of picturing the falling tears in the jerki-
ness of the notes. But it also produces an objectivity and

emotional distance, a dissociation, that is then rudely interrupted by the passionate outburst of the climactic bar and the word "Weh," or woe. Marked by a forte stab in the piano accompaniment, it swells and lingers on a dotted crotchet F-sharp which conflicts dissonantly with the G which the piano sounds before the voice itself can reach it. The quaver rhythm makes a sort of ululation, drawn out and whining: it is the first proper quaver rhythm the voice has had, and it lacks the lilting sway of the preceding triplets. By the end of the song, the vocal line is at its most extreme. We are left with a phrase, "da ist meiner Liebsten Haus" (there is my beloved's house), which repeats the notes of the first verse, reaching a top A for the first time in the cycle, but on more open vowels ("da ist meiner Liebsten Haus" versus "und der weiche Schnee zerrinnt"), which lend a sense of greater desperation. The game starts up in the piano again, pianissimo now, triplet against dotted rhythm, leaving us with that very bleak, lonely semiquaver which precedes the final resolving chord.

"Wasserflut" is significant in a singerly way because there are those top A's to be negotiated, the first of only a handful in the cycle, and a pitch that lies outside the domestic zone of comfortable *Hausmusik* in which Schubert song originated. As happened on other occasions, and with other songs in this cycle ("Rast," "Einsamkeit," "Mut"), it seems that Schubert was prevailed

upon by his publisher to publish it in a lower and, for those
buying the music to sing and play through at home, more
manageable key, without that tricky high note.

In putting *Winterreise* together, the issue of tessitura
seems not to have been a central concern for Schubert.
Tessitura literally means "texture"; in vocal music, it refers
to the area in which most of the singing line lies. The tessitura of the Evangelist, a tenor, in the Bach Passions is,
for example, high, although high B appears only once, and
high B-flat not at all. Even at baroque pitch (A=415 hz,
about a semitone lower than modern pitch) the role "sits"
high. On the other hand, many operatic roles for a tenor
may have a tessitura which sits lower than the Evangelist's in terms of its vocal centre of gravity, but stretches
up much higher for individual notes—those B's, C's,
and even C-sharps and D's which operatic tenors call the
"money notes." Singing *Winterreise* in public concert,
projecting in a large hall, one notices that the keys—
those published and those higher keys Schubert originally
wrote, as in the case of "Wasserflut"—do not really
cohere around one voice type. Many songs—including
almost all of Schubert's first, manuscript versions—are
too high for a regular baritone (though Fischer-Dieskau's
1948 recording with Klaus Billing starts in the original key). But both the original and the published key
sequences—surely preferred versions, although some of

my favourite *Winterreise* singers are baritones, mezzos, or sopranos—also occasionally present a phrase which is a little low when competing with a seven-foot Steinway in a modern concert hall. It is a reminder that the first performer of these songs was Schubert himself, sitting at a fragile Graf or Broadwood instrument, accompanying himself among friends in a Viennese apartment.

If I seem a little insistent about the original key sequence—in either the manuscript or the published score—it is because *Winterreise* is forever, and to my exasperation, being described as a "dark" cycle, best performed by a low voice. Oversensitive perhaps, I find my right to sing the cycle being questioned. The reasons for this misascription are largely historical. The two best-known Schubert singers within the composer's own circle were the retired opera star Johann Michael Vogl and the accomplished gentleman amateur Baron Karl von Schön-stein, both baritones. The first singer to perform the whole piece in a public concert, in 1860, Julius Stockhausen, was a baritone. The singers on the most famous recordings of the work in the modern era, Dietrich Fischer-Dieskau and Hans Hotter, were baritone and bass-baritone, respectively. The contrast is usually made with *Die schöne Müllerin*, a young man's cycle, best performed by a fresh tenor: the tessitura is consistently higher. But if there is no reason to see *Winterreise* as a special province of the older singer (two famous tenor exponents, Peter Pears and Peter Schreier, refused, bizarrely in my view, to perform the piece until they were over fifty), neither does it belong by any means to the lower voices. The keening sound of those high-lying phrases in the original version of "Wasserflut," tenor territory, are a special reminder of that.

| 7 |

AUF DEM FLUSSE

ON THE RIVER

Der du so lustig rauschtest,
Du heller, wilder Fluß,
Wie still bist du geworden,
Gibst keinen Scheidegruß.

Mit harter, starrer Rinde
Hast du dich überdeckt,
Liegst kalt und unbeweglich
Im Sande ausgestreckt.

In deine Decke grab' ich
Mit einem spitzen Stein
Den Namen meiner Liebsten
Und Stund' und Tag hinein:

Den Tag des ersten Grußes,
Den Tag, an dem ich ging,
Um Nam' und Zahlen windet
Sich ein zerbrochner Ring.

Mein Herz, in diesem Bache
Erkennst du nun dein Bild?
Ob's unter seiner Rinde
Wohl auch so reißend schwillt?

You who rushed along so heartily,
You gleaming, wild river,
How still you've become,
You don't say goodbye.

With a hard, stiff crust
You have covered yourself,
You lie cold and unmoving
Stretched out in the sand.

On your surface I engrave
With a sharp stone
The name of my beloved,
The hour and the day.

The day of our first greeting,
The day I left,
Around name and numbers
Winds a broken ring.

My heart, in this river
Do you now recognise your image?
Under its crust does it
Swell to bursting in the same way?

Franz Josef Glacier, New Zealand

D URING THE EARLY nineteenth century rivers of
ice, in the sublime form of Alpine glaciers, were a
subject of enormous interest to the European intellectual
world. In 1816, the English poet Percy Bysshe Shelley
visited Chamonix in the company of his wife, Mary, and
her stepsister Claire Clairmont. Shelley was awed by the
"stream of solid ice" which he observed, glaciers which

> flow perpetually into the valley, ravaging in their slow
> but irresistible progress the pastures & the forests
> which surround them, & performing a work of desola-

tion in ages, which a river of lava might accomplish in
an hour.

Beautiful in its crystalline forms and undulating
masses, the icy landscape was almost alive, "frozen blood
forever circulating slowly thro' his stony veins."

The era from which *Winterreise* emerged was one in
which the whole notion of time was being reconfigured.
Geological discoveries and geological thinking led to the
inescapable conclusion that the Earth was much older than
had previously been thought; that the processes that had
shaped it had been taking place with extraordinary and
unhuman slowness over unimaginable epochs of deep,
deep time. Ice was a crucial part of this, and glaciers were
the evidence which Schubert and Müller's contemporaries—in England, in the German lands, in Switzerland
and elsewhere—were analysing with a new and systematic vigour. The notion that the Earth had been subject
to ice ages arose from the consideration of glaciers in the
Alpine regions and of the mysterious deposit of massive
boulders (erratics) in unexpected geological locales. Glaciation had once been more extensive. The landscape—its
peaks, its troughs, its scattered debris—had been formed
by the slow might of the ice as much as by the catastrophic
engines of volcano and earthquake. It was glaciers that
had, in previous epochs, carried those massive rocky

giants to their present-day isolation on the north German plain. The theory achieved its first definitive expression in the 1830s and 40s in the work of Jean de Charpentier and Louis Agassiz, but both men paid tribute to the role of Goethe—poet, playwright, novelist, Weimar minister of mines, natural philosopher—in the solving of the puzzle. "Goethe alone," wrote Agassiz in 1837, "unified all the indications into a definitive theory." Charpentier headed his *Essai sur les glaciers* with a quotation from Goethe. It came from a passage which the author had added to his novel *Wilhelm Meisters Wanderjahre* (Wilhelm Meister's Journeyman Years: sequel to *Wilhelm Meisters Lehrjahre*, Wilhelm Meister's Apprenticeship, from which Schubert had set so many poems) in March 1828, ready for publication of a second edition the following year. Chapter nine is an account of a mining festival which our hero attends and at which a debate takes place on the "creation and origin of the Earth." Various theories are canvassed: Neptunism and the gradual recession of an all-encompassing ocean; Vulcanism and its "all-pervading fire"; even, fantastically, the notion that such inexplicable geological forms can only have fallen from the heavens. Finally "two or three quiet guests" espouse the theory with which Goethe had been dabbling throughout the 1820s, that there was once a period of "fierce cold" when glaciers grew and descended "from the highest mountain chains far into the land."

The Shelleys' visit to Chamonix and exposure to the
awesome glacial phenomena had a lasting impact. They
published their *History of a Six Weeks' Tour Through a
Part of France, Switzerland, Germany and Holland*, which
included Percy's poem "Mont Blanc," in 1817. In the
following year Mary Shelley published her novel *Frankenstein; or, the Modern Prometheus*, a text suffused with
images of distressed and alienated wanderings in an icy
landscape, and irresistibly reminiscent of *Winterreise*. It is
to the frozen mountains that Victor Frankenstein retreats
after creating his monster; it is on a massive glacier that
his creation tracks him down. The monster is Frankenstein's doppelgänger as well as his creation, estranged
from those around him, not at home in the world; and just
as Victor disposes of the female creature he has made as
companion for the monster, the monster kills Frankenstein's own bride, Elizabeth. Both are left bereft of female
companionship. The novel's opening, and its dénouement,
play out in the Arctic. Victor pursues his prey across the
boundless ice, and it is into the frozen wastes that the
monster escapes to die after the demise of his creator.

THE FREEZING-OVER of rivers is something that must
have been much more common in Schubert's day than in
our own. In the Netherlands not so long ago for a series of

Winterreisen, I arrived during exceptionally cold weather. The townsfolk of Amsterdam, the Hague, Eindhoven had taken to the canals and lakes and streams on skates, like something out of a painting by David Teniers or the younger Brueghel. It was the first time in about fifteen years, apparently, that such a big freeze had occurred. In the time of Teniers, or of Franz Schubert, it was commonplace. *Winterreise* was created in a period when the rigours of winter bulked larger in the European imagination than it does in ours, cosseted as we are by central heating, and transfixed by the prospect of global warming. Typical winter effects—frozen rivers, ice storms, snow blizzards—were then a Europe-wide phenomenon.

The detailed effects of climate change are complex, of course. Climate isn't weather; and global warming might mean even colder winters for those of us dependent on the Gulf Stream for our moderated weather patterns. My own anecdotal experience, imaginatively powerful if factually unreliable, probably reinvented in memory, is that things aren't as cold as they used to be. At university in Oxford in the 1980s, when I first performed *Winterreise*, winter was a much more powerful presence. Huge dagger-like icicles hung from the guttering outside my second-floor window in January and February; it snowed in May one year; and I can remember repeatedly falling off my bicycle on some fruitless errand (actually looking for a banjo player for a production of *The Threepenny Opera*), not because I was student drunk or nerdily clumsy but because the streets were covered in a thick and slippery crust of ice. We are cut off from Schubert's wintertime; but also from the wintertime of our own imagined past.

THE CONCEPT OF ICE AGE which emerged in the early nineteenth century has been refined and investigated. There have been five true ice ages in Earth's history; outside such periods of glaciation, even the high latitudes on the Earth's surface have been ice-free. Now of course—though they are melting apace courtesy of global warming—we have polar ice caps. Which means that we are in fact, and a little confusingly, living in an ice age, one which started 2.6 million years ago; but in a period of intermittent warmth known as an interglacial (periods of intense cold are known as glacials, popularly and confusingly often also called "ice ages"). The current interglacial began about 11,400 years ago, and it has been, one might argue, the climatic precondition for the birth, and perhaps for the flourishing, of human civilisation.

Within that interglacial itself, wheels within wheels, climate has fluctuated. From around 800 to 1200 northern Europe experienced unusually mild and stable weather, perhaps the warmest four centuries of the last eight thou-

sand years: the so-called Mediaeval Warm Period, an era
of settlement, expansion, exploration, and agricultural
plenty. This era of plenitude was succeeded by what has
been called the Little Ice Age. Around the mid-thirteenth
century, pack ice in the North Atlantic began to advance
southwards, as did glaciers in Greenland. Carbon dating shows plants being killed by the cold from around
1275; from around 1300, warm summers in Europe ceased
to be a matter of course; rivers and seas froze over in
wintertime.

One way of defining the so-called Little Ice Age is in
terms of the advance of glaciers. Looking at the largest
glacier in the Alps, the Great Aletsch Glacier, over this
period, one can see that its maxima during the period of
the Little Ice Age—in 1350, 1650, and 1850—exceeded
those in the previous epoch. The devastating reality of
glacierisation is well evidenced in the historical record.
In 1601 the peasants of Chamonix were panicked by the
drastic encroachment of their local glacier (the "mer de
glace" which Goethe and the Shelleys visited). Two villages had been destroyed and a third was under threat.
They appealed to the Savoyard authorities. Nearly a century later, in 1690, they were asking the bishop of Annecy
to exorcise the glacier. The mid-century depredations
of the Grindelwald Glacier were terrifyingly conveyed
by Martin Zeiler in the *Topographia Helvetia:* a chapel

destroyed by the spreading ice; the earth driven before the encroaching flow, turning pastureland into desolate mountain waste; rough ice floes, rocks, and whole pieces of cliff carried by the glacial ice and destroying houses and trees in their wake.

The other way of looking at the Little Ice Age is in terms of climate. There remain a lot of disagreements about the precise shape of this period of cooler summers and colder winters, and local or regional conditions could make all the difference, but it seems fair to say that from 1350 to 1850 it was cooler in Europe than it had been in the centuries before and the century and a half since. Here is a rough visual guide, a comparison of ten different published reconstructions of mean temperature changes during the last two thousand years:

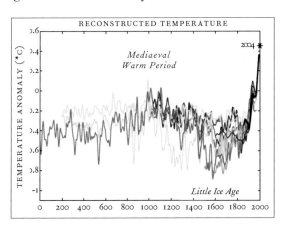

Winterreise was written and composed in a Europe in which winter had a greater imaginative impact than in our own time; at the same time, it was the product of a culture fascinated by the uncanny power and symbolism of ice.

"AUF DEM FLUSSE" starts off with icy nonchalance in the piano, a dissociated tread, an emotionless plodding which conjures up, at one and the same time, a frozen river and a frozen state of mind. With the tempo indication "langsam," slow, it was originally marked as "mässig," moderate: the crucial consideration is that the staccato quavers, bass note answered by triad in the left hand, remain separate and without real contour. There's something amused about the wanderer's calm consideration of the frozen river, an almost cabaret-like quality to the modern ear. The absurd, the comical should never be resisted in *Winterreise*.

Detachment is preserved for the first two stanzas, which repeat their music in a minor key which doesn't engage with melancholy. The little turn on "You don't say goodbye" sends itself up, a graceful farewell, a little wave in the vocal line which contradicts the meaning of the words it sets. The vocal phrases which relate the stillness and motionlessness of the frozen river ("Wie still bist du geworden," How still you've become, and "Liegst kalt und

unbeweglich," You lie cold and unmoving) are marked
"sehr leise" (very soft), and for me they seem to demand
an inwardness and smoothness, as well as a pianissimo,
which contrasts with the hardness of the opening phrases
("Der du so lustig rauschtest," You who rushed along so
heartily, and "Mit harter, starrer Rinde," With a hard, stiff
crust). Inwardness, but still detachment.

The following two stanzas, with their change into
the major key, offer us a sort of cosiness almost, a musical warmth quite at odds with the words, which paint
the image of a gravestone made of ice. The idea of words
written vainly in water is a poetic trope. Keats's epitaph is
perhaps the most familiar in English: "Here lies one whose
name was writ in water." Goethe uses the same image in
his poem "Am Flusse." It's worth quoting in full, because
it seems likely that Müller would have read it and we know
that Schubert certainly did, because he set it to music in
1822:

| 181

> *Verfließet, vielgeliebte Lieder,*
> *Zum Meere der Vergessenheit!*
> *Kein Knabe sing' entzückt euch wieder,*
> *Kein Mädchen in der Blütenzeit.*
>
> *Ihr sanget nur von meiner Lieben;*
> *Nun spricht sie meiner Treue Hohn.*

Ihr wart ins Wasser eingeschrieben;
So fließt denn auch mit ihm davon.

(Flow away, much loved songs, to the sea of forgetting. No boy will sing to you again with delight, no girl in the blossom-time. You sang only of my love; now she speaks with scorn of my fidelity. You were written in water, so flow away with it.)

To write on ice is an image of ambivalence: like writing on water but not quite letting go, wanting to delay the oblivion of forgetting, the inevitable bereavement, by freezing it. Freezing feeling is, though, at the same time, both to preserve and to anaesthetise it. The wanderer doesn't scratch songs or love poems in the ice, but a laconic record of his affair: the name of his love (which we never learn), the day of the first greeting, the day he left, and, winding around the name and the numbers, a broken ring. Again, the music pulls against the words as the sinuous unbroken vocal line tells us about the broken ring.

The final stanza is repeated twice and introduces an unprecedented flood of strong emotion into the hitherto detached emotional landscape of the song. Under all this ice, is feeling still surging? The music gives us the answer, as it rises up to a passionate climax. The final phrase reaches a top A and on this occasion (unlike "Wasserflut"

or, later in the cycle, "Rast") Schubert doesn't alter the
manuscript key to accommodate the less vocally accomplished singer. He wants this key, and he is committed to
the idea of that climactic top note—although (as a sop
to his publisher, no doubt) he offers a patently inadequate
alternative phrase (known as an ossia) which no singer
would dream of singing.

The song ends as nonchalant as ever, diminishing
into pianissimo with broken octaves which are taken up
in the next song, ending with a chord spread over two
beats—a wonderful example of how something totally
commonplace can sound quite extraordinary in the context which Schubert creates for it, a moment of glassy,
wondering stasis after all the disjointed black notes of
the preceding pages.

| *183*

| 8 |

RÜCKBLICK

BACKWARDS GLANCE

Es brennt mir unter beiden Sohlen,
Tret' ich auch schon auf Eis und Schnee.
Ich möcht' nicht wieder Atem holen,
Bis ich nicht mehr die Türme seh'.

Hab' mich an jeden Stein gestoßen,
So eilt' ich zu der Stadt hinaus;
Die Krähen warfen Bäll' und Schloßen
Auf meinen Hut von jedem Haus.

Wie anders hast du mich empfangen,
Du Stadt der Unbeständigkeit!
An deinen blanken Fenstern sangen
Die Lerch' und Nachtigall im Streit.

Die runden Lindenbäume blühten,
Die klaren Rinnen rauschten hell,
Und ach, zwei Mädchenaugen glühten!
Da war's geschehn um dich, Gesell!

Kömmt mir der Tag in die Gedanken,
Möcht' ich noch einmal rückwärts sehn,
Möcht' ich zurücke wieder wanken,
Vor ihrem Hause stille stehn.

It burns under both the soles of my feet,
Even though I walk on ice and snow,
I don't want to draw breath again,
Until I can no longer see the towers.

I have stumbled on every stone
In my hurry to leave town;
The crows threw snowballs and hailstones
At my hat from every house.

How differently you welcomed me,
You town of inconstancy!
At your gleaming windows sang
The lark and nightingale in contest.

The round linden trees blossomed,
The clear fountains splashed sparkling,
And, oh, a girl's two eyes glowed!
Then you were done for, my friend.

If I think of that day,
I want to look back once again,
I want to stagger back again,
Stand still in front of her house.

Orpheus and Eurydice, *1806, by the Danish painter*
Christian Gottlieb Kratzenstein (1783–1816)

*T*HE NOTION OF THE LOVER, a singer, looking back, is inscribed as a frightful mistake in Greek myth. Things did not go well for Orpheus. And our wanderer knows that if he turns round, his former lover will be as fugitive as Eurydice, as evanescent as the will-o'-the-wisp of the next song.

The emotion that was released in the previous song seems to surge afresh in this, great pulses of it, connected motivically by those rocking octaves which mark the end of each rising wave of music in the piano.

In the first bar the bass line drives on, punctured by semiquavers in the right hand, towards the forte piano (a sort of accent) on which the wave breaks. The song is marked "Nicht zu geschwind," but as always "not too fast" still means fast—but with enough weight to allow those crotchet octaves in the bass line in the second bar to achieve their utmost hollow brutality, and enough room for the words, when the voice enters, not to become an incomprehensible gabble. The difficulty of spitting them out, though, the breathlessness of expression, is crucial, as is the sense in the piano of the quavers in the bass line sort of chasing the offbeat semiquavers in the right hand. When the voice enters, the piano imitates it out of synch, a graphic picture of pursuit. It is an extraordinary effect.

The quasi-mythological grandeur of burning feet on ice is succeeded by a poetic image of comical, almost cartoon, absurdity—those hostile crows throwing snow and ice from the rooftops.

"Rückblick" might also carry the sense of "flashback," and that is what the middle of the section of the song is. It is possible to read it as a simple and sweet reminiscence of lost delights, but two things point in the other direction. First, the intrusive jabs of negativity right from the start—the mention of inconstancy, the fact that the lark and the nightingale are at odds with each other rather than in harmony (a little vocal caesura before "im Streit" can underline this). Secondly, the cheapness of the imagery and the jingle-jangle banality of the music Schubert has used to set it, with that insistent D going on and on in the right hand, the voice doubled in the left, reaching an apex of insincere Romantic flummery in the piano as a descent into renewed savagery sets off the last verse, with that chasing motif at work again. But it soon peters out, with an exhaustion which is palpable in the strange dragging accents which mark the vocal line—"Möcht ich zurücke wieder wanken" (I want to stagger back again)—as if some sort of effort to continue is being made, as if something, at the same time, is pulling us backwards.

By the end of the song all energy in the voice is dissipated, and after a final flutter in the piano, with churchy, antique harmonies which will recur later in the cycle, the great first arc of the cycle is done with. The next song will take us into another world.

| 9 |

IRRLICHT

WILL-O'-THE-WISP

In die tiefsten Felsengründe
Lockte mich ein Irrlicht hin:
Wie ich einen Ausgang finde,
Liegt nicht schwer mir in dem Sinn.

Bin gewohnt das Irregehen,
'S führt ja jeder Weg zum Ziel:
Unsre Freuden, Unsre Wehen,
Alles eines Irrlichts Spiel!

Durch des Bergstroms trockne Rinnen
Wind' ich ruhig mich hinab—
Jeder Strom wird's Meer gewinnen,
Jedes Leiden auch sein Grab.

Into the deepest rocky ravines
A will-o'-the-wisp lured me:
How I'll find my way out,
Doesn't lie heavily on my mind.

I'm used to losing my way,
Every path leads to the goal:
Our joys, our woes:
They're all a will-o'-the-wisp game.

Along the mountain stream's dry bed
I wander peacefully down—
Every stream will reach the sea,
So every suffering will find its grave.

. . . a wandering fire,

Compact of unctuous vapour, which the night

Condenses, and the cold environs round,

Kindled through agitation to a flame,

Which oft, they say, some evil spirit attends

Hovering and blazing with delusive light,

Misleads the amazed night-wanderer from his way

To bogs and mires, and oft through pond or pool,

There swallowed up and lost, from succour far.

—JOHN MILTON, *Paradise Lost*, BOOK IX, LINES 633–42

IRRLICHT

Aus Ehrfurcht, hoff ich, soll es mir gelingen,
Mein leichtes Naturell zu zwingen;
Nur zickzak geht gewöhnlich unser Lauf.

(I'll try out of respect for your honour to bend
my natural flightiness; usually we take the
zigzag way.)

MEPHISTOPHELES

Ei! Ei! Er denkt's den Menschen nachzuahmen.

(Aha! He likes to imitate mankind.)

—JOHANN WOLFGANG VON GOETHE, *Faust, Part One*

*W*RITING IN EDINBURGH's *New Philosophical Journal* in 1832, Louis Blesson, major of engineers in far-off Berlin, set out his dogged pursuit of the strange phenomenon of the *Irrlicht,* ignis fatuus, or will-o'-the-wisp. Born in 1790, a near contemporary of both poet and composer of this song, Blesson was doubtless a military man reminiscing about his philosophical investigations while on the manoeuvres of his youth, only a year or so before Wilhelm Müller himself volunteered for service against the French:

In the year 1811, I was at Malapane, in Upper Silesia, and passed several nights in the forest, because ignes fatui were observed there . . . In the year 1812, I spent half a night in the Rubenzahl Garden, on the ridge of the Riesengebirge, close on the Schneekoppe, which constantly exhibits the Will-with-the-Wisp [sic], but having a very pale colour. The flame appeared and disappeared, but was so mobile that I could never

approach sufficiently near . . . In the course of the
same year I visited a place at Walkenried, in the Hartz,
where these lights are said always to occur . . .

Blesson had first seen the ignis fatuus "in a valley in
the Forest of Gorbitz, in the Newmark." This valley was
marshy on its lower part, and during the day bubbles
could be seen rising from the water of the marsh. Carefully marking these places, Blesson had returned at night
and observed "bluish-purple" flames which retreated upon
his approaching them for a closer look:

> I conjectured that the motion of the air, on my
> approaching the spot, forced forward the burning
> gas . . . I concluded that a continuous thin stream of
> inflammable air was formed by these bubbles, which,
> once inflamed, continued to burn—but which, owing
> to the paleness of the light of the flame, could not be
> observed during the day.

He could not be doubtful but that "this ignis fatuus
was caused by the evolution of inflammable gas from the
marsh." He manages to get close to the lights and first
singes paper ("which became covered with a viscous moisture"), then sets it alight. "The gas was evidently inflammable, and not a phosphorescent luminous one, as some
have maintained."

This is, in essence, the modern explanation of a mysterious phenomenon which had been known since time immemorial, and had been given any number of mystical and dark connotations. As a recent authority wrote in 2001, in the journal *Bioresource Technology:* "The curious natural phenomenon known as *Ignis fatuus* or *Will-o'-the-wisp*—flickering lights observed in darkness over burial sites, peat-bogs and swamps—has been ascribed to the spontaneous ignition of phosphine evolved with other gases (methane) originating from the decomposition of organic materials under anaerobic conditions."

That bible of the Enlightenment, the *Encyclopédie,* half a century or so before Blesson's researches, had offered a different account, in which the *feux follets* can actually be caught—they are nothing other than a "luminous material, viscous and slimy, like frogspawn. This material," the contributor insists, "is neither burning nor hot." In a typical imaginative leap towards one of the obsessions of eighteenth-century physical science, the conclusion is that the substance of the *feu follet* is identical to that which constitutes electricity. Other contemporary theories were closer to the apparent truth—both Alessandro Volta and Joseph Priestley (the inventor of the battery and one of the discoverers of oxygen, respectively) diagnosed the ignis fatuus as the result of an interaction between lightning and methane. This is half right, but Blesson was resolute that "they are of a chemical nature, and become inflamed on coming into contact with the atmosphere, owing to the nature of their constitution." They were nothing to do with "luminous meteors," either.

IN 1795, Goethe had published his "Märchen," or tale, known in English as "The Green Snake and the Beautiful Lily," in his friend Friedrich Schiller's magazine *Die Horen*. In its opening scene, a sleepy ferryman is awoken by two noisy, rather bumptious will-o'-the-wisps who "wiffle and hiss together, in an unknown very rapid tongue." To pay the ferryman for their passage across the river, the lights shake themselves and scatter a "heap of glittering gold pieces" into his wet boat, gold which threatens the stability of his craft, but which they will not take back. The ferryman takes the gold and buries it in a rocky chasm. A fair green snake is awoken by the gold "coming clinking down." Swallowing them "with extreme delight, she began to feel the metal melting in her innards, and spreading all over her body; and soon, to her lively joy, she observed that she was grown transparent and luminous." The tale continues for some pages in similar vein, and seems to be in total a parable about human freedom.

There's no clear connection between Goethe's text

and Müller's but, reading it, I can't help thinking of the clinking of gold coins that we heard in "Die Wetterfahne" (The Weather Vane), of the "tiefsten Felsengründe" (deepest rocky ravines) of this song, or of the luminous *Nebensonnen* (mock suns) in part two of the cycle. What's more, the joshing, humorous tone of Goethe's fairy tale makes a good note for how to play the opening of the song, which surely represents the wanderer's approach to the wisp, and its shy retreat. A will-o'-the-wisp game indeed.

These bars do not sound like regular music; they are not "classical," or slightly melancholic, or serious, or high-minded. The first two bars can be something like a shrug of the shoulders—expressive of indifference, feigned indifference, or something else, but with a distinctly casual feel about them. Then the third bar can be playful, a little sticky on the first of those F-sharp triplets and then with an accelerando that is somehow surprising or teasing, as the wisp, or whatever it is we are seeking,

eludes us and pokes out its tongue. The whole shtick is
repeated when the voice comes in: "In die tiefsten Felsengründe," with another sort of shrug and a comically literal
descent to a bottom B; "Lockte mich ein Irrlicht hin"
racing forwards to that nonchalant fourth in the piano:

Then Schubert invents the most wonderful variation
on that initial stuttering, lurching, groping third bar—a
veritable arabesque, a thing of wonder and wonderment,
underpinned by a slower version of the stuttering in the
piano:

The wanderer is dazed, hallucinating, on the edge. The cycle is repeated again for verse two of the poem and then hard reality intrudes in the music, assertive, robust even, in comparison to what has gone before. "Durch des Bergstroms trockne Rinnen . . ."—the dryness of the river bed is also the dryness of his own eyes in the suspension of grief. But the effort is quickly spent as "Wind ich ruhig mich hinab" returns to piano. The notion of winding that the words summon up is reflected in the keening excess which is brought to bear on the last two lines. The wanderer's attitude throughout the cycle so far has been one which seesaws between the expression of true emotion, and a sort of ironic distancing from it, even an embarrassment at it. Here the first expression, with its growly beginnings (look how low it is), seems, if not formulaic, then at least to retain some degree of detachment:

The very last phrase, with the weird extended pause (like an all-seeing eye) over the painful diphthongs "auch sein," turns it into a real wail of anguish:

Lei _ den auch sein Grab.

And so back to the beginning again in the piano, with a
reflective pause at the end.

Those—dying then,
Knew where they went—
They went to God's Right Hand—
That Hand is amputated now
And God cannot be found—

The abdication of Belief
Makes the Behavior small—
Better an ignis fatuus
Than no illume at all—

—EMILY DICKINSON

| 10 |

RAST

REST

Nun merk' ich erst, wie müd' ich bin,
Da ich zur Ruh' mich lege;
Das Wandern hielt mich munter hin
Auf unwirtbarem Wege.

Die Füße frugen nicht nach Rast,
Es war zu kalt zum stehen,
Der Rücken fühlte keine Last,
Der Sturm half fort mich wehen.

In eines Köhlers engem Haus
Hab' Obdach ich gefunden;
Doch meine Glieder ruhn nicht aus:
So brennen ihre Wunden.

Auch du, mein Herz, in Kampf und Sturm
So wild und so verwegen,
Fühlst in der Still' erst deinen Wurm
Mit heißem Stich sich regen!

Only now that I lie down for a rest
Do I notice for the first time how tired I am.
Wandering kept me merry
On the inhospitable path.

My feet didn't ask for a rest,
It was too cold to stand still;
My back felt no burden
The storm helped to blow me on.

In the cramped house of a charcoal burner
I found refuge.
But my limbs won't rest,
Their wounds burn so much

You too, my heart, in battle and storm
So wild and so daring,
You feel in the stillness for the first time your
    worm
Stirring with hot pang.

*R*AST" IS ANOTHER ONE of those songs which underwent a transposition between the manuscript and the first printing: perhaps the publisher asked Schubert to take out that tricky high A-natural which comes at the end of each verse. Avoiding the key of the final song, "Einsamkeit," in the original twelve-song *Winterreise* may also have been a consideration, Schubert not wanting to anticipate that arrival and return to the key of the opening song, "Gute Nacht." So, D minor became C minor and that final phrase of each verse with the high note had its contours slightly changed. In the original version, the octave leap from a low A to a high A is accomplished on one syllable—"fort" (onwards) in verse one and "Stich" (literally sting or fang) in verse two; in the revision, the lower tessitura encourages Schubert to make the high note more aggressive, less bound into the line, and it begins the words "fort" and "Stich," giving them an extra punchiness that matches the marking "stark," or strong, which he has added above the vocal line.

The poem starts off with a paradox, the paradox of the compulsive wanderer: it is only now that I lie down to rest that I feel tired. The inhospitable features of the path he has taken spur him on: it is too cold to stand, the wind blows him on. The tempo marking is "mässig," or moderate, so the idea of tiredness is not evoked by a collapse into slowness or virtual stasis. Instead, Schubert's piano introduction embodies the struggle to continue. There are probably more technically correct and exhaustive ways of describing what happens in those six bars, but what I hear each time is a struggle to rise, a painful struggle through those intervals which sound in the right hand—an augmented fifth (stretch), a fourth (withdraw), another, higher augmented fifth (stretch), major third (withdraw), and then a bare octave which settles into a sort of illusory major key, A major, before the song sets off again in its home key of D minor. Each of the accents in this painful process has a different character and a different weight.

That jagged vocal phrase at the end of each verse— "Der Sturm half fort mich wehen" (The storm helped to blow me on) and "Mit heissem Stich sich regen" (Stirring with hot fang)—shows us a wanderer who, if tired, is still able to mount a bravado display of athletic, loud, thrusting singing. In the second verse it accompanies the notion of the worm stirring in the stillness that rest has brought. I have always taken this worm for granted. The English idiom of the worm turning has been at the back of my

Thirty-ninth plate from William Blake's Songs of Innocence
and of Experience Showing the Two Contrary States of the
Human Soul, *1794, in a hand-coloured print c. 1825–6*

mind, perhaps—not necessarily appropriately—and that of Blake's invisible worm which infests the sick rose.

The *Wurm* is not really a worm, though, in the modern sense, but more the sort of creature we meet in *Beowulf*, a serpent or perhaps even a dragon, the *Lindwurm* of German mythology, which writhes insidiously in the slippery pianissimo phrases which prepare for the vocal climax where it strikes.

And as the opening music plays us out, *piano* and somehow emptied of its force by repetition, the final chord in the piano, with a pause mark above it, might represent the overtired traveller finally falling asleep in the hut in which he has sheltered, waking for the spring dream of the next song.

MÜLLER IS INTRIGUINGLY SPECIFIC about this hut in which the wanderer falls asleep. It is in "eines Köhlers engem Haus," a charcoal burner's narrow dwelling, that he takes refuge, and that lowly figure is the first addition to the ghostly dramatis personae of the poem since we met the girl's family back in the second song. It is deep winter and the house, or rather the hut, is empty, but this non-encounter with an absent artisan only intensifies our sense of the protagonist's isolation. Charcoal burners could be loners, often living and working by themselves, and

this one is a sort of double for the wanderer to match the
hurdy-gurdy man who appears in the last song. One
of Aesop's fables is about such a man:

> There was once a charcoal burner who lived and
> worked by himself. A fuller, however, happened to
> come and settle in the same neighborhood; and the
> charcoal burner, having made his acquaintance and
> finding he was an agreeable sort of fellow, asked him
> if he would come and share his house. "We shall get
> to know one another better that way," he said, "and,
> besides, our household expenses would be dimin-
> ished." The fuller thanked him, but replied, "I couldn't
> think of it, sir. Why, everything I take such pains
> to whiten would be blackened in no time by your
> charcoal."

Aesop's tale reminds us of the visual contrast that the
inkling of a charcoal burner introduces into the blinding
blank hallucinogenic whiteness of the winter's journey,
a premonition of a later companion—the crow—and a
contrast that is there all the time, unremarked, in recital,
black on white: the black and white keys of the piano, the
black of its case, the black and white of the singer's formal
attire.

·   ·   ·

WHY DOES MÜLLER INTRODUCE the ghost of a charcoal burner into his sparsely inhabited poetic sequence? We can look at this absentee quite literally, as the manufacturer of a crucial pre- and proto-industrial material without which the smelting of metals and the production of iron would have been impossible; wood burns at a significantly lower temperature than charcoal (1500 versus 2700 degrees Celsius). Over a period of millennia charcoal burners were familiar denizens of the forest, plying their trade close to the supply of raw material, building great conical piles of wood around a central shaft, covering the whole structure with turf or clay, starting a fire at the bottom of the flue and then tending and repairing the furnace as the fire carbonised the wood, driving out moisture and reducing it in volume by as much as a third. The kilning process would take weeks, and it was a skilled business with its own distinctive expertise. The experienced burner would know from the smell of smoke how his kiln was doing; it was unwise to depend too much on the colour of the vapours. Lonely as it often was, this could also be a family business, nomadic, with one family working several sites and carrying food to the burners. It was seasonal too, which is why the hut in *Winterreise* is empty.

The charcoal burner's hut is the simplest dwelling imaginable: and, widely distributed in both time and space, across both continents and millennia, it is the very archetype of the prehistoric hut, in its most primitive form, which existed in unbroken tradition from the days of the Stone Age. A simple conical structure—echoing the furnace which was the burner's livelihood—it consisted of a circular framework of around twelve wooden poles. These sloped inwards to cross at the apex, teepee-like, this skeleton being then covered with turf, hides, thatch, or cloth. It was, sure enough, a narrow dwelling with a rough bed, made out of logs and straw, and little else. A small charcoal fire would be kept burning near the door, for heat. A small entrance porch would be constructed, furnished with a wooden door or a piece of sacking to keep the wind out.

The conservation of the form of the charcoal burner's hut, and the family nature of the occupation, has suggested to some anthropologists and archaeologists that this was a craft pursued by some sort of in-group who preserved and transmitted their traditions. Be that as it may, during the 1820s, charcoal burning must be seen as a liminal activity: these men were living on a social and on a historical boundary. Many burners were loners, most were at least outsiders; and, from our perspective at least, the craft which they followed was in decline. The replacement of charcoal by coke is one of the markers of the Industrial Revolution which accelerated in England in the mid-eighteenth century and which ultimately led, as the economic historian Tony Wrigley has characterised

it, to human liberation from the drudgery of the organic
economy. The exploitation of the prehistoric stockpile of
the products of photosynthesis in the form of first coal,
then oil and gas, enabled the smashing of traditional
restraints on growth and the creation of the modern world
as we know it. By 1788 two thirds of the blast furnaces in
Britain were using coke, and the shift in the deployment
of power sources over the period 1560 to 1860 in England
and Wales was staggering:

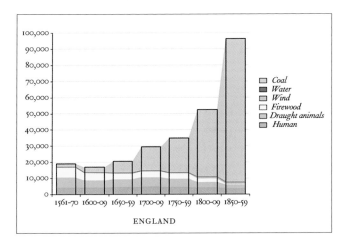

The *y* axis is energy consumption per head in mega-
joules. Orange is coal; red, water; blue, wind; yellow,
firewood; green, draught animals; mauve, human.
German-speaking Central Europe lagged far behind the

front-runner, Great Britain, in this process, of course, but already in 1810 Friedrich Krupp had built a pioneering steel foundry in Essen, producing smelted steel by 1816 and laying the foundations of what was to become, in the course of the nineteenth century, the world's largest industrial company.

All this gives our absent charcoal burner quite a symbolic role in understanding the culture from which *Winterreise* emerged, whether or not Müller and Schubert were fully aware of his activities and fate. The avatar of a traditional way of life that had transformed the European landscape, with a large responsibility for the deforestation which, in its turn, created shortages of charcoal and drove the exploitation of coke, he was also a poignant figure, living deep in the immemorial forest—so crucial to German self-understanding since the time of the Roman Empire—but at the same time poised on the edge of industrial modernity and extinction.

Living a piece as complex and resonant as *Winterreise* means engaging with it in all sorts of ways: understanding what it might mean for us now, as a message in a bottle set afloat in the cultural ocean in 1828. How does it relate to our current concerns? How does it connect with us, however unexpectedly? Müller's charcoal burner is intriguing in this regard. Whatever Müller or Schubert intended him to be or to point to, it is undeniable that his presence in the poem is a mystery calling out for an explanation. Why a charcoal burner's hut? Why not a shepherd's hut or a little non-specific hut? Part of his appeal for us is the way he can summon up a lost way of life and an economy in flux. The other surprise, a much more hidden one, is that he might be giving us a secret political message, intended by Müller and, in all likelihood, adopted by Franz Schubert.

The Denker Club, 1819, a satirical response to the Carlsbad Decrees: the sign on the wall behind the table reads: "Important question to be considered in today's meeting: 'How long will we be allowed to think?'"

In this wintertime of post-Napoleonic, Metternich-sponsored repression in the German lands—in Prussian-dominated Dessau (Müller's hometown) as much as in Hapsburg-ruled Vienna (Schubert's)—political allegiances, personal and national, were shifting, complex, and concealed. The continental powers who had defeated the Napoleonic assault on traditional monarchy—the Prussians, the Austrians, and the Russians—had, in September 1815, forged their notorious Holy Alliance, dedicated to the "perpetuation of mundane institutions" at home and abroad, and the adjustment of their "imperfections" through "justice, love and peace." The Quadruple Alliance of November 1815 and the Quintuple Alliance which took shape at the Congress of Aix-la-Chapelle in autumn 1818 brought Britain and the restored French monarchy on board, although the English refusal at Aix to agree to Tsar Alexander's "universal union of guarantee" was a sign of the fragility of this international effort to resist democracy, revolution, and secularism. Eighteen nineteen, the year of the Peterloo Massacre in England, saw student riots in Germany, the murder of the prolific conservative playwright August von Kotzebue by a deranged member of one of the university *Burschenschaften* (fraternities), and the attempted assassination of the president of Nassau, Karl Friedrich von Ibell. The resulting Carlsbad Decrees applied throughout the German Confederation, including Austria and Prussia. They intensified censorship, banned the *Burschenschaften*, removed reform-minded professors from their posts, and set up an investigative committee to uncover revolutionary

plots. The Karlsbad Decrees, and the Vienna Final Acts,
which followed, limiting constitutional government and
requiring monarchical government for all states within
the federation—these were the keystones of the political regime under which both Wilhelm Müller and Franz
Schubert lived their Biedermeier lives. No compromise
with liberalism was conceivable for the powers-that-be;
the satirist Ludwig Börne (1786–1837) described Kotzebue's murder as "the point at which the modern history of
the Germans crystallizes."

Artists in Schubert's Vienna—poets, musicians, play-
wrights, painters—lived under the shadow of this system
and reached their own accommodations with it. Foreign
travel was restricted to ensure domestic security, but
also to impose a degree of isolation from foreign innovation. One branch of the police system, the *Polizeihofstelle*,
focused its attention on political and moral crimes. As
Alice Hanson, the historian of musical life in Vienna in
this period, puts it: "The Polizeihofstelle directed censorship and the collection of information about foreign or
domestic persons engaged in revolutionary, criminal, or
immoral activities. The secretive nature of the investigations, together with the draconian punishments for con-
victed offenders, helped to create an atmosphere of tension
and mistrust in Viennese public life." Censorship was not
necessarily thoroughgoing or watertight, but it delayed
and harried and undermined. By 1826 the three-year

battle over his play *König Ottakars Glück und Ende* (King Ottakar's Happiness and End)—which even the emperor was longing to see—had reduced Franz von Grillparzer to despair, and he confessed to Beethoven that the censors had destroyed him. The Austro-American journalist and novelist Charles Sealsfield, who had fled Metternich's repressive system, wrote *Austria as It Is, or, Sketches of Continental Courts, by an Eye-witness*, in 1828. He summed up the state-sponsored idiocy under which Austrian writers existed:

> A more fettered being than an Austrian writer surely never existed. A writer in Austria must not offend against any Government, nor against any minister; nor against any hierarchy, if its members be influential; nor against aristocracy. He must not be liberal—nor philosophical—nor humorous—in short, he must be nothing at all. Under the catalogues of offenses are comprehended not only satires, and witticism; nay, he must not explain things at all because they might lead to serious thoughts.

Schubert's own encounters with this world of constraint, pedantry, and doublethink were not inconsiderable. He ran into trouble with a few songs, and with his German Mass, which used an unsanctioned translation.

Each of his Latin masses omits the words "Et unam sanctam catholicam et apostolicam Ecclesiam" (And one holy, catholic and apostolic Church), a significant absence which the censor missed or overlooked. More important were his run-ins with the censors over his operas, and it has to be admitted that his choices of libretto were provocative in the circumstances. While *Fierrabras* passed the censors in 1823 with only a few changes, the dangerously titled *Die Verschworenen* (The Conspirators) was renamed *Der häusliche Krieg* (The Domestic War). *Der Graf von Gleichen*, a tale of aristocratic bigamy, was, not surprisingly, banned outright in 1826. The impression is of a young man twisting the tail of the authorities and flirting with defiance. "Enviable Nero!" wrote Schubert in an excited 2 a.m. diary entry in 1824. "You were strong enough to destroy a corrupt people with the sound of stringed instruments and of song."

| *223*

The central anxiety for the Metternich-sponsored regimes within the German confederation was student unrest and revolutionary activity. One of Schubert's former schoolfellows, whom he counted among his "best and dearest friends" in 1818, was the poet Johann Senn, described by their mutual friend Josef Kenner as "warm-hearted . . . candid with his friends, reserved with others, forthright, vehement, hating all constraint," surely exactly the sort of young man in whom the secret police would have taken an especial interest. Senn had indeed been on a police list from as early as 1813, as a participant in radical student politics. In March 1820, the police raided his lodgings in the early hours of the morning, and filed the following report:

> Concerning the stubborn and insulting behaviour evinced by Johann Senn, native of Pfunds in the Tyrol, on being arrested as one of the Freshmen Students' Association, on the occasion of the examination and confiscation of his papers carried out by regulation in his lodgings, during which he used the expressions, among others, that "he did not care a hang about the police," and further, that "the Government was too stupid to be able to penetrate into his secrets."

Some of Senn's friends—Schubert, Johann von Streinsberg, Johann Zechenter, and Franz von Bruchmann—were present and also "inveighed against the authorised official with insulting and opprobrious language." Senn was arrested and detained for fourteen months before being deported to his Tyrolean homeland, his career in tatters. Schubert was released with a black eye and a severe reprimand. Senn was not forgotten within Schubert's circle of friends, viewed as a hero and a martyr, his health drunk on numerous festive occasions.

Some years after the Senn incident itself, and after a few of his friends had travelled to the Tyrol to meet the poet-in-exile, Schubert set two of his poems to music, full of Biedermeier resignation—"Selige Welt" (Blessed World) and "Schwanengesang" (Swan Song).

Any sort of social gathering was viewed with suspicion in Metternich's Vienna, even the most apparently innocent. Youthful high spirits were suspect in this system later characterised as "ein durch Schlamperei gemilderter Absolutismus" (absolutism mitigated by sloppiness). Vienna had long been home to societies for discussion, literary, artistic, and otherwise, and these too were under scrutiny in the Metternich era. Schubert's name was associated with three. What has come to be known as the Bildung Circle was a like-minded group of young men from Linz (including many of the poets of Schubert songs and some of his dearest friends—Josef von Spaun, Franz von Bruchmann, Josef Kenner, Johann Mayrhofer, Franz von Schober, and Johann Senn himself), who met regularly to pursue the Goethe-inspired goal of self-improvement through education. The circle attracted police attention as early as 1815, and the annual the group started publishing in 1817, *Contributions to the Cultivation of Youth*, was viewed with suspicion. It withered, although the ideal of the like-minded reading group was intermittently part of Schubert's life until his last illness. Vienna also briefly hosted the Unsinngesellschaft (the Nonsense Club), which met between 1817 and 1818 and of which Schubert was the only musician member. It had its own weekly newsletter, the *Archive of Human Nonsense*. Whether the japes and jollity which dominated the activities of this group may have been cover for disaffection, the resort to nonsense itself a coded protest against the new dispensation, we cannot be certain. The more famous Ludlamshöhle (Ludlam's Cave), with its very distinguished list of members (Grillparzer, the great Carl Maria von Weber, composer of *Der Freischütz*, and the actor Heinrich Anschütz among them), was similarly silly on the surface, with a lot of drinking, ribaldry, and dirty jokes, but eventually the authorities came to suspect it of something more sinister. One night in April 1826 thirty-two policemen broke into the premises, confiscating papers and detaining suspects. They failed to penetrate the club's wall of surreal facetiousness, and the papers they took away, full of riddles and hints of conspiracy, may have been no more than Viennese teasing. The agents certainly made fools of themselves, requiring earnest decodings of Ludlam tomfoolery. At the same time, the consequences were serious—Grillparzer was placed under house arrest—and the club was apparently closed down (Schubert's membership application lapsed). Eighteen twenty-six was a nervous year in the Hapsburg dominions, with an increase of activity by the Carbonari;

and Ludlam's password and colours were all too redolent of that much-feared Italian revolutionary front, devoted to the liberation of the peninsula from Austrian rule: "Red is black, black red."

REVERED AS THE SUPREME TRANSLATOR of poetry into song, Schubert was also an occasional poet on his own account. His last surviving poem, written in 1824, tells its own story of the idealistic hopes of youth crushed. The diagnosis of syphilis in 1823 had done its work, and Schubert had written to his brother Ferdinand in July 1824 of "a miserable reality, which I endeavour to beautify as far as possible by my imagination." In September, Schubert wrote to Schober about his "fits of depression, when the sterility and insignificance that characterise the life of today are brought home to me." Thoughts such as these inspired Schubert to write a poem in which the political trajectory of disappointment, and the typically Biedermeier consolatory role of art, are foremost. "Klage an das Volk" (Lament over the Nation) has been beautifully translated by the Australian poet Peter Porter:

> Youth of our Days, gone like the Days of our
>   Youth!
> The People's strength, unnumbered impotence,

The crowd's gross pressure without consequence,
The Insignificant our only glimpse of Truth!

The Power I wield springs always from my Pain,
That remnant of a preternatural striving.
I cannot act, and Time with its conniving
Treats all our deeds with infinite disdain.

The Nation lets its sickness make it old,
Youth's works are dreams which every dawn
    disperses—
So soon forgotten are those sacred Verses
That Faith would once have written out in gold.

To Art alone, that noble calling, falls
The task of leavening a world of Action
And give relief in time of brawling Faction
To all whom Fate has huddled within walls.

THE RELATIONSHIP between art and power has always
been a vexed one. The artist seeks the freedom of self-
expression, and probably always has done, however
much the ideology of Romanticism and the cult of the
artist-rebel may have given the age-old desire for artistic independence a new intensity. Yet "art" and the

"artist"—by which we mean an autonomous realm of art and a specialist practitioner in music, painting, literature, whatever—are the historical creation of the division of labour and the existence of surplus value within the host society. Subsistence economies may have individuals who tell stories, sing songs, draw drawings, but they don't have artists. The marketplace has been an added complication since the late eighteenth century. The genius who bridled against the demands of the aristocratic patron must also suspect too close an alignment with the demands of his or her audience. The true creator creates new needs and travels where no-one has thought to travel before; hence the whole notion of the avant-garde.

What we nowadays call "classical music" has a particular set of anxieties in these days of economic transformation and capitalist crisis. The more market-driven side of our activities, the recording business, is in meltdown. While technology has allowed more people than ever before to listen both to the classical music of the past and to the new music which hopes to reach out to the future, ways of "monetising" this are in decline. People have come to expect much of their electronically reproduced music free or for a vanishingly small sum. There's no such thing as a free market, of course, the markets in every product or service being mediated by government, regulation, custom, law, expectation, what you will. But the classical recording business was always a peculiarly flexible creature, where status and the preferences of those running and owning the companies always allowed for cross-subsidy and the making of records which could be sure of making not a penny. Concert life has, during the twentieth and twenty-first centuries, become even more divorced from the idealised practices of the marketplace.

The classical music we want to listen to in concert and at the opera was produced in a period during which labour costs were relatively much lower than today. The labour-intensive model of music making which classical music requires—a symphony orchestra of a hundred highly trained individuals, for example—means that classical music performances are relatively more expensive now than they were in their heyday in the nineteenth century. Classical music is not susceptible to the efficiency savings which innovation, competition, and mass manufacturing introduced during the nineteenth and twentieth centuries. Most other luxury goods became more affordable. Classical music did not, and surely that is also part of its appeal as an art form free from the tendency to commodification. At the same time, just as previously discretionary goods had become virtual necessities in liberal democracies, access to the arts in all their questioning splendour came to be seen no longer as the prerogative of the wealthy and powerful, or even of the bourgeois, but as a part of demo-

cratic citizenship. This, in the end, is the justification for
the subsidies (in direct form or as tax breaks) which keep
the traditional arts alive in capitalist society. A musical
tradition embroidered for the court and the aristocratic
salon has hence found its way into the modern age.

The paradoxes remain. It is all too easy to paint the
support of classical music less as a civic necessity than as
a middle-class subsidy. Private sponsorship, corporate
sponsorship—in fact just as reliant as government subsidy
upon the diversion of funds to minority interests—are
held up as an ideal. All this may seem two hundred years
and many miles away from Franz Schubert in Biedermeier
Vienna. Schubert struggled to assert his autonomy in a
political system which denied his freedom, offered him
up to indignity, and made it hard for him to earn a decent
living following his own aesthetic imperatives. Artists—
performers as well as composers—still wrestle with how
to assert their independence from money or from government, less urgently than Schubert perhaps, but often with
as much irritation or embarrassment. There is no easy
solution. Just before the great financial crash of 2008
I was asked to give a speech celebrating the City's contribution to the arts. As a regular performer at the Barbican,
and a beneficiary of its imaginative programming and the
opportunities that it gave me, I was delighted. Unaware,
in retrospect embarrassingly unaware, of what was about

to be unleashed, I praised the innovativeness and free-wheeling spirit of the financial sector which allowed it to appreciate parallel innovation and boundary-breaking in the realm of artistic endeavour. Government, concerned to ensure that money was well spent, that outreach was prioritised, could not indulge such blue-skies thinking. Living in the aftermath of the great bubble bursting, it is easy to see that I had been drawn into the frenzy as much as any overexcited day trader or purblind ratings agency. The hangover from which we are suffering, some much more than others, makes us all feel a little disturbed at how much our lives have hung on these activities of which we now mightily disapprove. But no one, not even the most austere of artists, can escape from his or her time, from social, political, economic reality. Real autonomy is a chimera, but we have to keep trying to imagine it into life, a necessary fiction, by balancing interests and encouraging pluralism. Being aware of these pressures now can help us understand a little better what the transcendent artistry of a composer like Schubert cost; the force that underlies much of his music; how we connect with it. His anger, his domesticity, his alienation are ours too.

WHAT OF WILHELM MÜLLER? He is the classic model of the comfortable German intellectual in the line of

Goethe in Weimar. Born in Dessau, the son of a master tailor, after military service against the French and travels to Berlin and Italy, he was installed as ducal librarian at Dessau in 1820, a privy councillor by 1824, an upwardly mobile protégé of the duke of Anhalt-Dessau, himself a client of the Prussian royal house. Yet, at the same time, Müller had definite liberal form in a period when liberalism was anathematised by Prussia and the Holy Alliance; benefiting from the patriarchal benevolence of his prince, he managed to preserve and occasionally assert his intellectual independence in a manner typical of the Biedermeier era.

In 1816, while a student in Berlin, Müller and a group of friends had published an anthology of poetry called *Die Bundesblüthen* (Flowers of Union), which made a provocative nod towards the dangerous territory of secret societies. A reference in one of Müller's poems to the recent fighting in which he had participated during the Wars of Liberation against Napoleon—"Für Gott, die Freyheit, Frauenlieb und Sang" (For God, freedom, love of women, and song)—was cut by the censor. In reply to Müller's faux-naïf comeback that it was the king of Prussia who had asked his subjects to fight for freedom, the censor replied laconically, "Ja, damals" (Yes, once).

In 1817 and 1818 Müller travelled in Italy, first as companion to Baron von Sack and then on his own. The literary outcome was his *Rom, Römer und Römerinnen* (Rome, Roman Men and Roman Women), published in 1820: not a straightforward travel guide but rather a series of glimpses into the life of a people, the hidden sides of Italian life and customs. Müller presented his own immersion in the charms of Italy as a distraction from the troubles of Europe at large. There was something disingenuous in this, however. Italy was alive with anti-Austrian feeling, channelled through the revolutionary Carbonari. Already in 1817 there had been revolts in the Papal States; and in 1820, the very year in which Müller's book on Rome appeared, revolution broke out in Naples, crushed by Hapsburg forces in 1821. Müller's engagement with and promotion of a native Italian culture (his pioneering collection of Italian folk songs, *Egeria*, was published posthumously in 1829) was of a piece with the philohellenism he imbibed from his hero Lord Byron, and which gave him his familiar sobriquet "Greek Müller." Promoting the national aspirations of others could not but be a political act for a German unable to secure his own political ideals. In 1823 the censor was to forbid publication of Müller's hymn on the death of another radical, nationalist hero, Rafael del Riego, the executed Spanish general who had defended the short-lived constitutional government dissolved by the Quintuple Alliance. "Aber die Freiheit," Müller wrote, "wer kann sie morden?" (But who can murder freedom?).

The second volume of *Rom, Römer und Römerinnen*
is prefaced by a letter to an old companion from Müller's
sojourn in the Eternal City, the Swedish poet Per Daniel
Atterbom. One of the most revealing things Müller wrote
on the subject of politics, its sentiments only confirm that
emotional seesaw between unhappy resignation and a
desire for action which possessed so many in this political
Eiszeit (ice age):

And so I greet you, in your ancient and holy
Fatherland—not in the style of this book here, whose
author has already become a stranger to me, joking
and playing; no, earnestly and in brief; for the great
Lent of the European world, that Easter week of suffering, anticipating and awaiting salvation, will not
tolerate an indifferent shrug of the shoulders or flighty
excuses and apologies. He who cannot act in this time
can only be quiet and mourn.

Over the coming years, Müller was to have quite a few
more run-ins with the censors in Austria and the German
states. In the second volume of the *Waldhornistenlieder,*
in which *Die Winterreise* found its final home in 1824,
he included some *Gesellschafts- und Trinklieder* (Songs
for Clubs and Drinking) with a political edge, some of
which had been banned in Dessau. Müller's admiration for
Byron resulted in his translation of an English biographi-

cal piece on the radical Englishman which was published in the *Taschenbuch Urania* for 1822. It was on account of this piece that *Urania* was given the ban, or "damnatur," by the Viennese censors in 1822. The first twelve poems of *Die Winterreise* were part of the following, 1823 issue of the same periodical. Müller's winter cycle, found by Schubert in a suspect publication, has an intensely radical context.

Back to our charcoal burner then, finally. We can see now, for the first time, why he's there; we can decode what he signifies. He's not only an artisan plying his lonely trade, doomed by the harsh winds of socio-economic change, he's also one of the Carbonari, literally "charcoal burners," the secret society whose black and red were feared by the Hapsburg regime and so much a part of the Italian landscape of the 1820s which Müller had obliquely celebrated. His "engem Haus" is the *baracca* (shack, hut, hovel) in which the members of this secret society met to perform the obscure rituals which bound them together. The exiled Byron had joined the Carbonaro lodge in Ravenna in 1820; for Müller and for Schubert the Carbonari would have represented a commitment to constitutional government, and resistance to the reactionary project which the Holy Alliance and its confederates were pursuing throughout Europe. They are those who, as in Müller's letter to Atterbom, can act, can strike out;

the *Winterreise* of both Müller and Schubert is part of that
quiescent mourning which was all that was left to those
who could not act.

Reading the last words of "Rast" again, singing them,
they emerge with a new, rebellious ferocity, testament to
the repressed energy and pain of those who did not dare
to act:

> *Auch du, mein Herz, im Kampf und Sturm*
> *So wild und so verwegen*
> *Fühlst in der Still erst deinen Wurm*
> *Mit heißem Stich sich regen.*

> You too my heart, in battle and storm
> So wild and so daring,
> You feel in the stillness for the first time your worm
> Stirring with hot pang.

| II |

FRÜHLINGSTRAUM

DREAM OF SPRING

Ich träumte von bunten Blumen,
So wie sie wohl blühen im Mai,
Ich träumte von grünen Wiesen,
Von lustigem Vogelgeschrei.

Und als die Hähne krähten,
Da ward mein Auge wach;
Da war es kalt und finster,
Es schrieen die Raben vom Dach.

Doch an den Fensterscheiben
Wer malte die Blätter da?
Ihr lacht wohl über den Träumer,
Der Blumen im Winter sah?

Ich träumte von Lieb' um Liebe,
Von einer schönen Maid,
Von Herzen und von Küssen,
Von Wonne und Seligkeit.

Und als die Hähne krähten,
Da ward mein Herze wach;
Nun sitz' ich hier alleine
Und denke dem Traume nach.

Frühlingstraum · Dream of Spring

I dreamt of colourful flowers
That blossom in May,
I dreamt of green meadows,
Of joyful bird calls.

And when the cocks crowed,
My eyes woke up;
It was cold and dark,
The ravens shrieked from the roof.

But there on the windowpane
Who painted those leaves?
You're surely laughing at the dreamer
Who saw flowers in winter?

I dreamt of love returned,
Of a beautiful maiden,
Of cuddles and kisses,
Of joy and bliss.

And when the cocks crowed
My heart woke up;
Now I sit here alone
And think about my dream.

Die Augen schließ' ich wieder,
Noch schlägt das Herz so warm.
Wann grünt ihr Blätter am Fenster?
Wann halt' ich mein Liebchen im Arm?

I close my eyes again,
My heart still beats so warmly.
When will you turn green, leaves on the
    window?
When shall I hold my beloved in my arms?

Many of the phenomena of Winter are suggestive of an inexpressible tenderness and fragile delicacy.

—HENRY DAVID THOREAU, *Walden* (1854)

*T*HE FIRST DECISION to make in this song is how to play the piano introduction. We're in the illusory major again, that mode of sweet dreams and memories of the past, like that which opens "Der Lindenbaum" ("I dreamt so many sweet dreams in its shadows") or insinuates itself into the middle of the frantic escape of "Rückblick" ("How differently you once welcomed me, a town named Inconstancy"). The repetitive, obsessive rhythmic sweetness of the piano underlay in the last verse of "Der Lindenbaum," repeated as many as twelve times—"Nun bin ich manche Stunde entfernt von jenem Ort" (Now I am many hours from that place)—can inspire a sort of music-box, trancelike, mechanistic approach to both playing and singing (the rhythm is the basis, of course, for the triplet rhythm in the next song, "Wasserflut"). The sweet, even saccharine, opening of "Frühlingstraum" is very different in the way it is achieved, but it is again tempting to latch on to its music-

box, chocolate-box qualities, especially in contrast to the
darkness of what has gone before: the staccato first note;
the dancelike 6/8 time signature; that graceful leap of
a sixth; those repeated twiddly turns; the sighing leaning appoggiatura that begins the second bar. It all invites
parody; and when the reigning mood in performance is
expressionistic, exaggeration may seem the right way to
go, to make clear both to oneself and to one's audience that
none of this is for real. The hint, after all, is already there in
the poem: the dream may be of fields and flowers and May
and birds, but the word to describe the birdsong is (reminding us of the battle between the lark and the nightingale in
"Rückblick") unsettling. *Geschrei*—shrieking, screaming,
screeching—is not a peaceful word. On the other hand, it
may sometimes seem too much to point the parody which
Schubert has already written. Or, out on the farther side
of interpretation, one might even want to preserve a more
naïve, warm, touching dream, unironised, one which
points back to all those love tokens from previous songs—
the May of "Gute Nacht" with its many flowers, the happy
fields remembered in "Erstarrung." Different performers,
the same performers in different performances, will come
up with different solutions, different journeys.

The song's structure involves three musical sections
which are then repeated to set all six verses: "etwas
bewegt" (somewhat moving), piano and pianissimo, for
the dream; "schnell" (quick), moving from piano to forte

for the waking up; and "langsam" (slow) and pianissimo
for the aftermath. "Frühlingstraum" is one of those songs
in which the repetition of the same music allied to different words presents both problems and opportunities.

The music of the first verse is already sweet enough; for
its return in verse four, there is an intensification of sweetness, of sensuality in the words—love that is returned, a
beautiful girl, kissing and cuddling (*Herzen*), joy (*Wonne*)
and bliss (*Seligkeit*). At that last word I always want to
linger a little, stretch out that arpeggio which animates the
last syllable. It's not exactly a self-quotation (like Mozart
putting a bit of *Figaro* into the operatic medley in *Don
Giovanni*'s banquet scene), but the very word *Seligkeit*
does put me in mind of Schubert's song of the same name
and the dancing, quasi-spiritual rapture (teetering on the
edge of parody) which it embodies:

| 247

> *Freuden sonder Zahl*
> *Blühn im Himmelssaal,*
> *Engeln und Verklärten,*
> *Wie die Väter lehrten.*
> *O da möcht' ich sein*
> *Und mich ewig freun!*
>
> *Jedem lächelt traut*
> *Eine Himmelsbraut;*
> *Harf und Psalter klinget,*

Und man tanzt und singet.
O da möcht' ich sein,
Und mich ewig freun!

Lieber bleib' ich hier,
Lächelt Laura mir
Einen Blick, der saget,
Daß ich ausgeklaget.
Selig dann mit ihr,
Bleib' ich ewig hier!

Joys without number
Bloom in heaven's chamber,
Angels and enlightened ones
As the Fathers taught.
O to be there
And to be always rejoicing!

Each one is dearly smiled upon
By a heavenly bride;
Harp and psaltery sound,
There's dancing and singing.
O to be there
And to be always rejoicing!

I would rather stay here
If Laura smiled at me,

With a look that said
That my troubles were over.
Blessed then with her
I would stay here forever!

The waking up from the dream into the hell of reality is
then all the more agonising. The false consolations of the
third and the sixth verse—the ice flowers on the windows, the closed-eye withdrawal into the self—return,
brilliantly, into the major key. As so often in Schubert's
music, in the piano and chamber music without words as
much as in the songs, the major key is even more heartbreaking than the minor.

The harsh music of the second verse, full of dissonance and a certain violence of expression, very clearly
suits the words—the cock crowing, the ravens shrieking
(marked fortissimo, an extreme dynamic for Schubert).
When the same music returns for verse five, the poetic
narrative moves from the outside to the inside, from the
eye to the heart, the realisation that the wanderer is alone.
On reading the poem, the idea of waking up, realising
you're alone, and thinking about the dream you've just
had, might suggest something reflective; certainly there is
nothing violent suggested by Müller's prosody. Schubert's
music retains the violence he has set up before—the same
notes are repeated and the dynamic markings remain
exactly the same. The noisy awakening, part of the objec-

tive world, is being replayed; but its intense horror is drawn into the self, and the wanderer's recognition of solitude and the loss of the past is as shattering as the shrieks and screams of the birds outside the hut.

The last verse of the song is one of the lowest points of the cycle as the wanderer shuts his eyes, nurturing the echo of his excitement encoded in his heartbeat. "Wann grünt ihr Blätter am Fenster?" (When will you turn green, leaves on the window?) can be half spoken, barely sung. The voice reaches up achingly to the F-naturals in the phrase "Wann halt ich mein Liebchen im Arm?" (When shall I hold my beloved in my arms?). The resumption of the piano motif ends in an utterly dispirited, spread, exhausted, but also somehow brutal A-minor chord. The next song, "Einsamkeit," emerges pale and dull from this reckoning.

WATER IS AT ONCE the most ordinary and the most extraordinary of substances. Life emerged from water, as both myth and science tell us; we cannot live long without water; and we largely consist of it. We experience water on Earth in all its physical forms: solid, liquid, and gas; ice, water, and steam. Hot water is special: liquid water has a high specific heat capacity and a very high vaporisation heat, allowing it to perform a crucial role in

Earth's climate. Cold water, too, is out of the ordinary: unlike other substances, when it becomes a solid, and freezes, it expands rather than contracts, becoming less, rather than more dense. Icebergs float. The beautiful, various, and overabundant crystalline forms in which frozen water exists have been seen by many as a sign of divine intelligence at work in the universe. The great seventeenth-century astronomer, renowned discoverer of elliptical planetary orbits, Johannes Kepler, believed that the soul of water created snow crystals. In his pioneering work of microscopy, *Micrographia* (1665), Robert Hooke interpreted the complex and individuated structure of the snowflakes he saw through his instrument as tokens of the divine at work in the world:

Snowflake crystals by Wilson Bentley, c. 1902

In the twentieth century the American Wilson Bentley, working in a shed at his farmstead in Vermont, was the first to conduct an extensive photographic survey of snow crystals, creating over five thousand images during his lifetime.

"Under the microscope," he wrote, "I found that snowflakes were miracles of beauty; and it seemed a shame that this beauty should not be seen and appreciated by others. Every crystal was a masterpiece of design and no one design was ever repeated. When a snowflake melted, that design was forever lost. Just that much beauty was gone, without leaving any record behind." He died in 1931 after walking six miles home in a blizzard.

The multiform beauty of crystalline water, so evident in the microscopic realm of the snow crystal, is made manifest to the naked eye in the way in which ice can uncannily mimic natural, organic forms. Frost or ice "flowers" exist in all shapes and sizes. The most eerily botanical are probably those which form when thin layers of ice are extruded from long-stemmed plants, forming curling patterns which resemble petals and flowers. In polar regions, great meadows of frost flowers grow and, with the advent of global warming, are becoming more common: fragile ice crystals containing salt which grow to a height of ten to thirty millimetres on the surface of young sea ice.

Ice flowers on a windowpane

The most familiar ice flowers in literature are those which grow on a window during wintertime, when the air outside is very cold and the air inside is reasonably moist.

Charlotte Brontë's novels are full of the imagery of snow, frost, and ice. "I am hot," declares Jane Eyre to Mr. Rochester, "and fire dissolves ice." Earlier in the book Jane as a girl falls "to breathing on the frost-flowers with which the window was fretted, and thus clearing a space in the glass through which I might look out on the grounds, where all was still and petrified under the influence of a hard frost." Through the window, just as she has "dissolved so much of the silver-white foliage veiling the panes as left room to look out," she sees the arrival

of her terrible, ice-hard enemy-to-be, the schoolmaster
Mr. Brocklehurst.

German literature is suffused with the notion of *Eis-blumen*, ice flowers, which figure in books and poems by
authors as diverse as Ludwig Tieck, Thomas Mann,
Robert Walser, and Rainer Maria Rilke. In Mann's
Doctor Faustus his composer antihero, Adrian Leverkühn,
is drawn to these strange formations. It is their ambiguity, their liminality, their mineralogical imitation of the
organic that fascinate him.

The roots of the obsession are philosophical, part of
the sort of physico-theology which inspired Hooke or
Kepler's interest in snowflakes, but which continued into
the eighteenth and even the nineteenth century. In 1732,
the satirist Christian Ludwig Liscow, mocking the learned
but superstitious endeavours of the Lübeck-born theolo-
gian and naturalist, rector of the Katharineum in Lübeck
(where Thomas Mann was to go to school), Heinrich
Jacob Sivers, published his Swiftian tease *Vitrea fracta
oder des Ritters Robert Clifton Schreiben an einen gelehrten
Samojeden, betreffend die seltsamen und nachdenklichen
Figuren, welche derselbe den 13. Jan st. v. 1732 auf einer
gefrorenen Fensterscheiben wahrgenommen* (Broken Glass
[slang for rubbish in Latin], or Sir Robert Clifton's writings to a learned Eskimo, concerning the strange and
thought-provoking shapes, which were descried on a
frozen windowpane on the 13th January 1732). Mount-

ing his own satirical attack on Swedenborgian mysticism
and contemporary speculative metaphysics in his *Dreams
of a Spirit Seer* (1766), Immanuel Kant referred back to
the business of mystical frost patterns on windowpanes in
wintertime, ridiculing

> that rare play of imagination which so many other
> collectors have found in the plays of nature, when,
> for example, in spotted marble they make out the
> Holy Family, or in stalactite formations they make
> out monks, baptismal fonts, and church organs, or
> even as the banterer Liscow discovered on the frosted
> window-pane the number of the beast and the triple
> crown, all of which nobody else sees but he whose
> head is filled with it beforehand.

One of the most interesting discussions about the
meaning and metaphysics of ice flowers took place
between Goethe and his intimate friend the poet and
translator Karl Ludwig von Knebel. In 1788 Goethe was
off travelling in Italy, enjoying the warm delights of "das
Land wo die Citronen blühn" (the land where the lemon
trees blossom), as he famously called it in one of the
Mignon songs from his bildungsroman *Wilhelm Meisters
Lehrjahre*. Knebel wrote to him playfully reminding him
that if the South had its charms, the cold North had its
compensations. On his window, for example, he could see

Eisblumen which might well be compared with "echten Pflanzen," true plants, with leaves, branches, vines, even roses. He praises their beauty, sending his friend a few drawings of them which display their marvellous delicacy of form.

Yet, at a period in his life when establishing himself as a credible scientist was even more important than the maintenance of his literary fame (he was to publish extensively on what was called *Naturphilosophie:* on geology and mineralogy; on plant morphology and the so-called *Urpflanze;* and most famously contra Newton in his *Farbenlehre*, his theory of colour), Goethe took this opportunity to overreact to Knebel and ridicule any notion that there might be a connection between the realms of the organic and the inorganic. Goethe was happy, he wrote in an issue of Wieland's literary periodical, *Der Teutsche Merkur,* in 1789, "that my friend in the North can at least get a little harmless enjoyment from other natural phenomena" while he himself was tasting the delights of the South and its luxuriant vegetation. On the other hand, it worried him that there might be any confusion here— "you seem to give too much significance to these natural effects; you seem to want to make these crystallisations part of the vegetable realm." The pleasure of a sensuous walk through an orange grove, Goethe ends up saying, is entirely different from the momentary appreciation of something as ephemeral as one of these crystalline "apparitions." That might seem obvious to anyone—and Knebel was rather offended by Goethe's heavyhanded response to his letter—but what Goethe is anxious to do is to separate the poetical realm of metaphor, his native realm, from that of the scientific and objective, where the close observation of differences between phenomena is opposed to the naïve and casual accumulation of superficial and striking similarities. Living stuff is one thing, inanimate matter another, and the uncanniness of the ice flowers must be, for Goethe, no more than a poetic conceit. Anything else is to allow backsliding into "bequemen Mystizismus" (comfortable mysticism) and the old-fashioned Renaissance idea of a harmoniously ordered universe structured by metaphor and similarity, a chain of being.

That this often-exasperated fascination with the liminal properties of crystals on the windowpane continued on into the era of Wilhelm Müller and Franz Schubert is evident from a passage in Schopenhauer's *World as Will and Representation*, first published in 1819:

> The ice on the window-pane forms itself into crystals according to the laws of crystallisation, which reveal the essence of the force of nature that appears here, exhibit the Idea; but the trees and flowers which it traces on the pane are unessential, and are only there for us. What appears in the clouds, the brook, and the crystal is the weakest echo of that will which appears

more fully in the plant, more fully still in the beast,
and most fully in man.

Schopenhauer's take is, as one would expect, metaphysical, and he does not entirely dismiss the idea that the
crystalline imitation of organic form may be a faint echo
of the will which lies at the root of all phenomena in his
philosophical system; at the same time, he is clear that
those patterns in the frost are "unessential, and are only
there for us," metaphors not actualities. Writing a very
different sort of account in 1840s America, Henry David
Thoreau could afford to be more lyrical. For Thoreau,
looking at the "melting frost on the window" and seeing
"the needle-shaped particles . . . bundled together so as
to resemble fields waving with grain," it is a "fact that
vegetation is but a kind of crystallisation."

Lying behind the passing reference in "Frühlingstraum" to frost flowers painted on the window of the hut
in which the wanderer has taken refuge is, then, a whole
slew of cultural baggage and reference. Having unpacked
some of it, the resonances for *Winterreise* emerge as
complex and overlapping, and not all of them need to
be spelled out. In a cycle which is much concerned with
the place of man in Nature—does he belong, is he the
eternal outsider, a creature of value stranded in a valueless
cosmos?—*Eisblumen* are the uncanny tokens of that slippery boundary between the living and the unliving, part

of a cast list that includes crows, falling leaves, and ignes fatui. For Thomas Mann in *Doctor Faustus,* they were to seem proof of the oneness of living and unliving nature, an image of life in death. They are also the residuum of a supernaturalist worldview which held them to be evidence of the operation of spirit or divinity in the world. Poetically it is the fragility of the frost flowers, and the recognition that they are no more than images of natural life, that together fuel the devastating irony of their last appearance—"Wann grünt ihr Blätter am Fenster?" They will soon melt; they will never turn green.

We don't see *Eisblumen* so much anymore, what with double glazing and central heating and global warming. If they were more of a feature of German than of English literature and philosophy, it may not have been only for intellectual reasons but also for purely material ones— harsh continental winters were a fact of life in Central Europe around the turn of the eighteenth into the nineteenth century.

The historical irony about this debate is that all Goethe's concern for science and differentiation, for the separation between the living and the unliving, for the boundaries between the realms of Nature ("ein Salz ist kein Baum, ein Baum kein Tier"—a salt is not a tree, a tree is not an animal), turned out to be an intellectual blind alley. Vitalism—the doctrine that living stuff has some sort of spark or élan vital which distinguishes it from brute matter—may have lingered on to the end of the nineteenth century, but the impact and tendency of evolutionary theory from Darwin's *Origin of Species* in 1858 on was to break down the barriers between life forms and ultimately between the living, the organic and the inorganic. What material factors, we are now compelled to ask, came together to create life itself out of nonliving matter? In modern terms, this is to ask how the first non-organic replicators came into existence, however simple they may have been, kicking off the whole process of natural selection which eventually led to RNA, DNA, and the first true organisms.

| *261*

One of the most fascinating of these theories of "abiogenesis" is that proposed by the organic chemist and molecular biologist Graham Cairns-Smith in the 1980s. It depends upon the capacity of mineral structures to encode information for primitive proto-organisms—as DNA does, at an infinitely more complex level, for organisms all the way from the simplest bacteria to Homo sapiens. It is crystals—not ice crystals, but the tiny silicate crystals in clay—which Cairns-Smith postulated as the first replicators. In the mineral world, before the arrival of organic molecules, only these crystals had the complex, information-bearing structure to seed life. As he puts it in his wonderful popularisation of his scientific work:

The first organisms had genes in them. These genes were, in all probability, microcrystalline, inorganic and mineral. They crystallised continuously from water solutions that were being maintained slightly supersaturated, over long periods of time, somewhere near the surface of the Earth.

In the end, organic machinery and the whole edifice of RNA and DNA took over what the crystals had started; but that much-ridiculed hunch that crystals could embody some sort of life turns out not to have been quite so ridiculous after all.

| 12 |

EINSAMKEIT

LONELINESS

Wie eine trübe Wolke
Durch heitre Lüfte geht,
Wenn in der Tanne Wipfel
Ein mattes Lüftchen weht:

So zieh' ich meine Straße
Dahin mit trägem Fuß,
Durch helles, frohes Leben,
Einsam und ohne Gruß.

Ach, daß die Luft so ruhig!
Ach, daß die Welt so licht!
Als noch die Stürme tobten,
War ich so elend nicht.

Just as a sombre cloud
Drifts through clear skies,
When in the tops of the fir trees
A feeble little wind blows—

Just so do I take my path
With dragging foot
Through bright, cheerful life
Alone and without any greeting.

Oh, that the air is so still!
Oh, that the world is so full of light!
When the storms were still raging
I wasn't half so wretched.

Edvard Munch, Two People, the Lonely Ones, *1899*

No one to feel the other's grief, no one to understand the other's joy! People imagine they can reach one another, but in reality they only pass one another by. Oh misery for him who realises this!

—SCHUBERT, DIARY ENTRY, MARCH 27, 1824

*E*INSAMKEIT" was the conclusion to Schubert's original, twelve-song version of *Winterreise*. This "ur-*Winterreise*" has its own aesthetic integrity. I have performed it many times, very often in harness with the Benjamin Britten winter cycle, *Winter Words*, and the juxtaposition is a rewarding one. There are connections of key (both pieces set out in D minor), of poetic mood (the mingling of the cosy and the cosmically depressing in Thomas Hardy's verse has its Biedermeier antecedents), and of musical method (as a song composer, Britten was a Schubertian through and through). By performing these twelve *Winterreise* songs as a unit, with the tiny differences of key and melodic contour which are to be found in the manuscript, one loses the power of the whole twenty-four-song colossus, missing out on some of the most famous songs ("Der Leiermann," the last song, above all) and the sheer sublimity of the work as finally presented, teetering on the edge of unreason. Nevertheless, it's an interesting experiment. In both versions, the short and the long, whether it sits at the end of the cycle or midway through, "Einsamkeit" remains some sort of endpoint.

Schubert did change the key of "Einsamkeit," and not, apparently, for reasons of tessitura on this occasion. The original manuscript's D minor was a return to the key of the opening song and a form of closure; the eventual published version, a third down in B minor, opened the cycle out in a formal sense. This also allowed for a change of shape in the final vocal phrase. In the first version the words "War ich so elend, so elend nicht" (I wasn't half so wretched) are repeated to the same music, creating a sort of dispirited fizzling out after the bravery of the quasi-orchestral piano tremolos; in the second, the repeated "so elend nicht" is transposed up a minor third, so that the phrase reaches up to a keening F-sharp. It sounds at the same time more conclusive, paradoxically resisting closure, and more desperate.

What is undeniable is that after "Einsamkeit" the next song, the first of part two, "Die Post," with its "etwas geschwind" (somewhat fast) major-key triplets and its jaunty posthorn call, registers as a new beginning and the offer of a refreshed, if unstable, mood. "Einsamkeit" is a low point. The tiredness which was resisted in "Rast" takes over, and the slow quavers in the piano drag, with their mournful sonority of bare, open fifths. These don't

recur in the cycle until the end of part two and the hurdy-
gurdy man's appearance on the scene. They were always,
apparently, part of the composer's conception of how to
end his cycle, twelve songs or twenty-four: with a musical
gesture which sounds hollow or empty.

What should we imagine in our mind's eye for this
song? A sliver of impoverished narrative seems possible
at this moment in the cycle. The two preceding numbers
are fairly clear stages on our wanderer's journey, easy
to conjure up. In "Rast" he seeks refuge in the charcoal
burner's hut and falls asleep. In "Frühlingstraum" he is
woken from his dreams, sees ice flowers on the windows,
but realises that, like the leaves on the window, his dreams
will not come to life, and that he has somehow lost the girl
he loved. If the succeeding song is to be the last, then we
can only imagine him back in the town, with spring on the
way or at least some change in the weather. The world is
no longer dark, the wind no longer blows, and he walks
"durch helles, frohes Leben, / Einsam und ohne Gruß"
(Through bright, cheerful life, / Alone and without any
greeting). The painful alienation from the world, from
humanity, from social intercourse, from life in the city,
from the possibility of happiness, is underlined by the very
etymology of the German word *einsam*. *Ein* is the German word for "one"; -*sam* is a suffix derived from the old
High German word for "same." *Einsam* is a word which

embodies the lonely reflexivity of the isolated individual, a oneness which is the same as itself. Schubert certainly plays with the word in the peculiarities of emphasis which his melody insists upon. He shifts the natural stress of the first words—"Wie eine trübe Wolke" (Like a sombre cloud)—to underline the loneliness of the single cloud, placing the musical stress on the first syllable of the word: "*ein*e." And when he sets the word *einsam* itself, a few lines later (*"Einsam und ohne Gruß"*), the musical shape and the emphasis are weird and alienating, drawing attention to the word and making it strange.

If this is to be the end of the cycle, we are left with a grim conclusion. Only the love left behind at the beginning of the story, and recalled in the dream of the eleventh song, can give us the feeling—the illusion?—that the isolation of oneness can be transcended. "In the sea of life enisl'd," as Matthew Arnold put it a quarter of a century later in his poem "To Marguerite," "we mortal millions live *alone*." This is quite the opposite of John Donne's famous assertion in his *Devotions* that "no man is an Island." What had disappeared for Arnold, and was fast disappearing for Schubert and Müller's generation, was the spiritual, metaphysical, divine underpinning which, for the likes of Donne, could guarantee the reality of the human community. The wanderer's hope of love has withered, and so has his connection with the world in which he has hitherto lived.

If "Einsamkeit" is not the end of the story, on the
other hand, then we will understand its setting as being
more in the wanderer's mind than in reality. He hasn't
actually returned to town, but he remembers how he
felt when he was a town dweller. He is the sort of man
who doesn't feel at home in society, the alienated individual, and always has been. This pushes us, margin-
ally, towards an interpretation of "Gute Nacht," the
first song, in which the wanderer wasn't rejected in
love but rather unable to cope with its consequences.
Doubt on that front remains, though; and what is crucial
about the continuation of the cycle is the way it allows
Schubert, having reached the impasse of "Einsamkeit,"
having allowed his wanderer to embrace loneliness and
radical separation, to move out from the wound which
animates and initiates the cycle—lost or abandoned
love—to a more existential quest which builds on those
resonant passing assertions of the first song: "Fremd bin
ich eingezogen, fremd zieh ich wieder aus" (I came a
stranger, a stranger I depart"), "Ich kann zu meiner Reisen nicht wählen mit der Zeit" (I cannot choose the time
of my journey). By the time we reach the end of part
two, the love affair of the first song is a million miles
away. What might have been no more than a simple love
story progressively deepens to become something more
nuanced and complex, in terms of both social relations
and metaphysical engagement. How do we live in the

271

world and relate to others? Where is God? What can we
know of the divine?

LIKE WANDERING, loneliness—or rather *aloneness*—
is a recurrent theme in the poems Schubert set to music,
and he approached it in myriad and multifaceted ways.

The most lavish treatment is in the unusual, sectional
song, virtually a cantata for voice and piano, also called
"Einsamkeit." Its six stanzas move from the solitude of
the young man immured in a Gothic abbey—"Give me
my fill of solitude"—through his excursions into the real
world. He encounters, successively, busy activity, good
fellowship, the bliss of love, and battle, arriving finally at
the consummation of solitude destined for the old man in
the evening of life. The poem is by Schubert's close friend
Mayrhofer, but it lacks the verve of his shorter lyrics, of
which Schubert set more than forty. The suspicion is that
it was written expressly for Schubert to set: a new ven-
ture in songwriting in the form of a compact, continuous
cycle to vie with Beethoven's *An die ferne Geliebte* (To
the Distant Loved One). The latter, Beethoven's only
song cycle, had appeared not long before Schubert started
working on "Einsamkeit" while tutoring the Esterházys
in Zseliz in summer 1818. Writing to his close friend
Schober, Schubert declared that he was "composing like a

god." Mayrhofer's "Einsamkeit," he reported, "is finished, and I believe it to be the best thing I have done, for I was without a care." The concept is ambitious, allowing Schubert's musical imagination to range over the various scenes and emotions of the text; this very strength may also be a weakness, with its attendant lack of emotional focus. The song does demonstrate that, regardless of personal circumstance—and this was, after all, a happy period in Schubert's short life—the paradoxes of solitude and aloneness were a cultural preoccupation for the artists of his generation.

"Der Einsame" (the solitary one, the loner, the lonely one?) is one of the composer's most popular, most anthologised, and most performed songs: laconic but untroubled, it is almost nonchalant in its approach to being alone. The prevailing tone of the song, in words (by Karl Lappe) and music, embroiders a sort of cosiness. To be alone is not to be lonely, but to set oneself apart from the busy, silly world and all its vanities; in the end, sitting by the fire, listening to the chirruping of the cricket—so beautifully characterised, if not imitated, in the piano part— "bin ich nicht ganz allein," I'm not completely alone.

At the other extreme is one of the three songs which Goethe gives to the cursed and blind Harper in his bildungsroman *Wilhelm Meisters Lehrjahre*. Schubert set these as his *Gesänge des Harfners* (Songs of the Harper), published as his op. 12 in 1822 (though this opening song and the third of the trilogy were written as early as 1816). The musicologist Alfred Einstein described them perceptively as the composer's first song cycle; they have often been regarded as precursors of *Winterreise*. Goethe's poem is worth quoting in full:

> *Wer sich der Einsamkeit ergibt,*
> *Ach! der ist bald allein;*
> *Ein jeder lebt, ein jeder liebt*
> *Und läßt ihn seiner Pein.*
> *Ja! Laßt mich meiner Qual!*
> *Und kann ich nur einmal*
> *Recht einsam sein,*
> *Dann bin ich nicht allein.*
>
> *Es schleicht ein Liebender lauschend sacht,*
> *Ob seine Freundin allein?*
> *So überschleicht bei Tag und Nacht*
> *Mich Einsamen die Pein,*
> *Mich Einsamen die Qual.*
> *Ach, werd ich erst einmal*
> *Einsam in Grabe sein,*
> *Da läßt sie mich allein!*

He who gives himself up to solitude,
Ah! He is soon alone;
Others live, love,
Leaving him to his own pain.
Yes! Leave me to my torment!
And if I can just once
Really be lonely,
Then I'll not be alone.

A lover creeps softly listening,
Is his loved one alone?
So by day and night creeps over me,
Solitary, the pain,
Solitary, the torment.
Ah, were I just once
To be alone in the grave,
There it would leave me alone.

Translating this haunting text—intensely set by
Schubert, with a melancholy instrumental prelude, impro-
visational in character just as Goethe's text requires—is
tricky because of that poetic playing with the concepts of
solitude, solitariness, lonesomeness, loneliness, aloneness.
Goethe teases out all the Romantic paradoxes which by
1816 had become so familiar, absorbed into the Byronic
cult of celebrity which we ourselves have inherited

(so famous and yet so, so alone). The poet or the composer
writing of the depths of human loneliness, of the isolation of the self is nonetheless speaking and singing to an
audience which he hopes to engage. The Harper wants to
be alone, while at the same time he complains of solitude
as much as he longs for and embraces its torments. The
word for one, *ein*, needles its way through the poem like
a refrain, rhyming at the ends of lines and within them—
*Einsamkeit, allein, ein, ein, Pein, meiner, einmal, einsam,
sein, allein, ein, seine, allein, Einsamen, Pein, Einsamen,
einmal, einsam, sein, allein*—colonising the mind with
that locked-in notion of a necessary oneness which cannot
be escaped.

The *Winterreise* "Einsamkeit" has the same complex
attitude towards being alone. It is a long way from the
happy progression of the Mayrhofer setting, in which life
achieves a fulfilling shape through the final retreat of the
aged into solitary reflection. It does lend the wanderer the
trappings of a sort of Romantic heroism in his loneliness,
his oneness, amplified by the grandeur of those quasi-
orchestral tremolos we hear in the piano part as he sings of
how he was less wretched when the storm was raging.

There is an affinity here with the sort of sublimity we
find in the paintings of Caspar David Friedrich, often
with an ecclesiastical tint reminiscent of the Mayrhofer
"Einsamkeit," but also with a bleakness more akin to

the Schubert of *Winterreise*. Take Friedrich's so-called *Monk by the Sea* (not the artist's title), for example, widely accepted to be a depiction of Friedrich himself, and originally paired with a painting in which the painter imagines his own funeral procession:

Of more direct relevance to *Winterreise,* take the pair
of paintings from 1807–8, *Summer* (now in Munich) and
Winter (now destroyed). Foregrounded in the soft, green
landscape of the former, a couple in an arbour embrace;
nature welcomes them and echoes their cosy, intertwined
duality, with a pair of doves perching on the sinuous
ivy, and two auspicious sunflowers at the entrance to the
bower. "Der Mai war mir gewogen" (May was good to
me) indeed:

In "Winter" all is, by contrast, jagged and overcast, blasted, ruined, largely (one must imagine from the black-and-white photograph) monochrome. In the foreground, dwarfed by ruined masonry, a bent, lonely figure in a habit crosses the snowy ground with the aid of a stick:

Another visionary mendicant, he is again an image of the artist himself. Friedrich was to imagine himself in a chalk drawing of 1810 as a monkish loner with a demonic gaze: working in the monastic solitude of a cell-like studio, never at home even when at home, "self-concealed, withdrawn and tragically eccentric" as the art historian Joseph Koerner has put it, "a purgatorial wanderer."

The happy, loving couple of *Summer* are genre figures: they seem to emerge from and belong to the landscape they inhabit, and the composition in which they participate expresses a notion of Edenic ease. This is the lost world of the past, lost to Schubert's wanderer as much as to Friedrich's. The artist, like his protagonist, searches among the ruins, alone.

Friedrich's wanderers do not inhabit their landscapes: they are moving through or moving on, taking it all in but not being absorbed by it: "Fremd bin ich eingezogen, / Fremd zieh ich wieder aus" (A stranger I came, a stranger

I depart). The people in a landscape must, the philosopher Friedrich Wilhelm Joseph von Schelling wrote in his *Philosophy of Art* in 1802, be either "indigenous"—like the loving couple in *Summer*—or else "they must be portrayed as strangers or wanderers recognisable as such by their general disposition, appearance, or even clothing, all of which is alien in relationship to the landscape itself." Hence the wandering monkish types, and also, in many of Friedrich's paintings, those oddly well-dressed wanderers so far removed from their natural orbit. The most famous of all, composite poster boy for lone Romantic strivings Byronic and Nietzschean in equal measure, *Wanderer above the Sea of Fog* (1818), is in the Hamburg Kunsthalle.

The setting is utterly sublime, the figure ambiguously heroic; but I have always wondered what it is that the wanderer is wearing. His outfit is, the art historians suggest, a sort of uniform, that of the Freiwillige Jäger (Volunteer Hunters), called into service (like Wilhelm Müller) by Frederick William III of Prussia to fight against Napoleon in the Wars of Liberation. There is even a tradition that Friedrich's wanderer (not Friedrich's actually, as he did not give the picture the title by which it is generally known) is an identifiable individual, one Colonel Friedrich Gotthard von Brincken of the Saxon infantry, though there is confusion as to whether Brincken went on to become a forestry officer or fell in battle in

1813. The presence in this picture of a reference to the heroes of 1813–14, celebrated in verse and song, would have given it a controversial edge. By 1818, German opinion was already divided between those who, like Wilhelm Müller, felt that they had fought in a struggle for freedom as part of a national community, a war for liberty; and those who followed the official line, encapsulated in the formula "Der König rief und alle, alle kamen" (The King called and all, all came). To insist upon the popular character of the anti-Napoleonic campaigns was to put yourself at odds with authority; and the notorious student commemoration of the Battle of Leipzig at the Wartburg in October 1817 was one of the unruly events of the immediate postwar years which culminated in the promulgation of the Carlsbad Decrees in 1819 and the clampdown on liberal and radical activity.

As a teenager Schubert had met the most famous of these insurrectionary patriots, the poet Theodor Körner, who spent time in Vienna in 1812, the year before his enlistment (he worked at the Burgtheater and became affianced to Antonie Adamberger, daughter of Johann Valentin Adamberger, for whom Mozart wrote the role of Belmonte in *Die Entführung aus dem Serail* [The Abduction from the Seraglio]). The pair attended a performance of Gluck's *Iphigénie en Tauride* together with Schubert's dear friend Joseph von Spaun; they then dined together,

Caspar David Friedrich, Wanderer Above the Sea of Fog, *1818*

Georg Friedrich Kersting, On Sentry Duty, *1815*

sharing a mutual distaste for some professors sitting
nearby who were mocking the singers. Körner was killed
in battle the following August at the age of twenty-one;
buried under an oak tree, he became a potent symbol of
the German yearning for nationhood, celebrated as such
into the twentieth century. An inspirational figure for his
generation, he had been something of a firebrand, insistent that the war was not one "that crowns know of" but
rather a "crusade" and a "holy war." He was famously
depicted in a commemorative painting of 1815, *On Sentry
Duty* by the artist and fellow volunteer Georg Friedrich
Kersting; the same Kersting who had painted Caspar
David Friedrich at work in his studio in 1812, and whose
kit and uniform as a volunteer had been partly paid for
by Friedrich, too old to fight but still keen to participate
somehow. Three degrees of separation, then—Friedrich
to Schubert, via Kersting and Körner.

The year after his son's death in 1813, the grieving
Christian Gottfried Körner published a collection of
thirty-six patriotic poems which Theodor had written
between 1811 and his death. He called it *Leyer und Schwert*,
Lyre and Sword: "Denn was berauscht die Leyer vorge-
sungen, / Das hat des Schwertes freie Tat errungen"
(What the lyre sang, intoxicated, / The free deed of the
sword has accomplished). The most famous of them is
"Lützows wilde Jagd" (Lützow's Wild Hunt), a vigorous

paean to the most celebrated of the Jäger volunteer companies, to which Körner himself belonged, the Lützowers. Schubert set twenty Körner poems to music in all, most of them in one year, 1815, the year of German victory. Half a dozen were from the *Leyer und Schwert* collection. Most are love songs, but warlike rhythms and sentiments also manifest themselves: not the Schubert we know, whose only famous war song, "Kriegers Ahnung" (Warrior's Foreboding) from his last collection, *Schwanengesang* (Swan Song), is full of foreboding; they seem to reflect the naïve enthusiasm of the youthful patriot who identified with the struggle for freedom that had been waged by the young hero with whom he had actually broken bread.

The only absolute masterpiece among the Körner songs, the harmonically daring "Auf der Riesenkoppe" (On the Riesenkoppe), dates from the era of growing postwar disillusionment, written in the same year as Friedrich's *Wanderer above the Sea of Fog* was painted, 1818. The poem is alive with patriotic feeling, sure enough, to which the music responds; but we are far away from war, treasuring from the summit of the Riesenkoppe a view of flowering meadows and shining towns, the poet and composer together blessing the home of their loved ones. The title of the poem could easily be mistaken for that of a Friedrich canvas—*Sonnenaufgang auf der Riesenkoppe* (Sunrise on the Riesenkoppe). Schubert begins the song with a rising, climbing gesture in the piano, opening into a vista in D minor which introduces a determined recitative passage celebrating this peak, this "Himmelanstürmerin" (heaven stormer): a worthy companion for Friedrich's monumental composition.

If "Auf der Riesenkoppe" is a retreat from the martial and amatory enthusiasm of 1815, a return to the poetry of Körner but in a more reflective mode, Schubert's farewell to heroism is beautifully and definitively encoded in a setting of a translation of Anacreon which he wrote in the winter of 1822–3, "An die Leier" (To the Lyre). The poet takes up the lyre but can, to his frustration, only sing songs of love, not martial prowess. It is difficult not to imagine that Theodor Körner was in his thoughts as he set the words "So lebt denn wohl, Heroen"—Farewell you heroes.

LOOKING AT FRIEDRICH'S PAINTINGS while thinking about Schubert helps us to understand the political and social roots of even the most determinedly metaphysical, heaven-storming art in this period. This is not to deprive Schubert's or Friedrich's wanderers of their aesthetic autonomy, or to deny their offer of, or even potential for, some sort of transcendence, but rather to accept that they were created in history, and not in a world set entirely apart. The desire to be alone or to retreat into oneself can have personal, psychological dimensions; pursued systematically in art or philosophy, it inevitably has roots in social and political realities.

This Friedrich picture, in Dresden, dating from 1819–20, has been given the title *Two Men Contemplating the Moon:*

It generates a sort of metaphysical aura, a mysterious poetry; it might indeed be an illustration for Goethe's sublime "An den Mond," twice set (both times miraculously) by Schubert:

Selig, wer sich vor der Welt
Ohne Haß verschließt,
Einen Freund am Busen hält
Und mit dem genießt,

Was, von Menschen nicht gewußt
Oder nicht bedacht,
Durch das Labyrinth der Brust
Wandelt in der Nacht.

Happy he who shuts himself away from the world
without hatred, holds one friend to his heart, and with
him enjoys that which, unknown and unthought by
men, nightly wanders through the labyrinth of the
breast.

But the picture could be understood and meant in quite
a different way. In 1820, the Dresden poet Karl Förster
took the famous Nazarene painter Peter von Cornelius to
visit Friedrich's studio. The arrogant, fashionable Cornelius was dismissive of the middle-aged has-been; but
Förster admired the way in which Friedrich's arrangement
of figures within a landscape summoned up what he called
the "contemplation of the infinite." Friedrich showed
them a picture of "two cloaked men embracing each other
as they gazed enraptured at a landscape with a moon,"

surely a supreme example of what Förster was appreciating. Friedrich's self-exegesis pointed in another direction: " 'They are plotting demagogic intrigues,' said Friedrich, with teasing irony, as if in explanation." That phrase "demagogische Umtriebe" is precisely how the Carlsbad Decrees had characterised and condemned the student and liberal stirrings which they sought to repress.

Friedrich was at odds with the political stagnation which he witnessed around him after the victories of 1815, something he expressed in words as well as images. Returning from a trip to Italy in June 1816, he likened living in Germany to "burying oneself alive," something "my whole being revolts against." His pictures made his allegiances more or less clear, and increasingly so. In *Ulrich von Hutten's Grave* of 1824 the names of resisters and reformers can be deciphered on the masonry: Jahn, Stein, Görres, Scharnhorst, Arndt.

It was Ernst Moritz Arndt, an old friend of Friedrich's and a fellow Pomeranian, who had encouraged the wearing of the so-called *altdeutsche Tracht* (traditional German costume). For men, this consisted of a long, tight-fitting coat with a widely opened collar, loose-cut trousers, and often a large velvet beret. It had originated as a symbol of resistance to the tyranny of French fashion and French rule, but soon became associated with liberalism and reform. A sort of uniform for the student *Burschenschaften*, it was, along with those societies, banned by the Carlsbad Decrees in 1819: Karl Ludwig Sand had donned the *Tracht* preparatory to his murder of August von Kotzebue in that year, the trigger for Metternich's clampdown. In many, many of Friedrich's pictures both before and after 1819, the *altdeutsche Tracht* appears: in *Two Men Contemplating the Moon*, shown above, for example; *Moonrise over the Sea* (1822); *Evening* (1820–1), and countless others.

To return to the wanderer on his mountain eminence, that green velvet frock coat (and the rather unrobust footwear) have a certain elegance; they are certainly, as Schelling had recommended, in stark and pointed contrast to the natural grandeur of the surroundings. He is neither a local—if such an imagined and imaginary mountainscape could possess such a thing—nor a pioneering mountaineer. The mise-en-scène is a peculiarly hybrid one: has this almost dandyish figure been somehow airlifted into the mountains, or are the misty peaks an emanation of his singular imagination? He might be read as a figure straight out of the drawing room: if so, Friedrich's version of the domestic sublime is well matched to the genre at play in *Winterreise*, an equally sublime frozen journey for reenactment in the intimacy of a Biedermeier salon. He certainly does not seem to me to be military. Epaulettes, frogging, contrasting colours, weaponry, boots are identifying features in contemporary illustrations of soldiers, volunteer and otherwise; look, for example, at Kersting's painting *On Sentry Duty* (page 284), and at what Körner and his companions are wearing. The "uniform" Friedrich's wanderer wears is that of the liberal and radical opposition, a version of the *altdeutsche Tracht*. He stands alone, high above the misty landscape, and the meanings of his solitariness are manifold and

ambiguous. As a visionary, he may be looking through the mists into what the future holds. As a lone figure on a mountain peak he may seem to triumph over the pettiness of what goes on below. But like Müller and Schubert's wanderer in *Winterreise*, he may also be the denizen of this Biedermeier *Eiszeit*, lonely and alone because political association is forbidden him, because he must hide within himself, because he is not at home in his own country.

LONELINESS IS A PERENNIAL FEATURE of the human condition; it has been and is a fairly universal subject for art in all forms and all cultures. In Romantic art, though, with its emphasis on human subjectivity, it gained a particular salience. Another of Jean-Jacques Rousseau's works (we met him in song one, with *La Nouvelle Héloïse*) was especially influential on the development of Romantic attitudes. Unfinished at his death, *The Reveries of a Solitary Walker* was published posthumously in 1782. "I am now alone on earth," he wrote,

no longer having any brother, neighbor, friend, or
society other than myself . . . Everything is finished
for me on earth. People can no longer do good or evil
to me here. I have nothing more to hope for or to fear
in this world; and here I am, tranquil at the bottom of
the abyss, a poor unfortunate mortal, but unperturbed,
like God Himself.

With that last characteristic note of bizarre, pathological grandiosity—"like God Himself"—Rousseau managed to bequeath to following generations the Romantic
schizophrenia about solitude, its pains and its pleasures,
its abasement and its heroic nobility (the wanderer in the
mountains, those tremolos in Schubert's piano). We see
the preoccupation reflected in art forms as disparate as
Schubert's songs, Byron's narrative poems, and Friedrich's paintings. "These hours of solitude and meditation,"
Rousseau declared, valorising loneliness,

are the only ones in the day during which I am fully
myself and for myself, without diversion, without
obstacle, and during which I can truly claim to be what
nature willed.

The period after the Napoleonic wars, as we have seen,
gave another twist to this Romantic discourse of solitude,
a political one in which the inward-looking bourgeois self

mourned its inability to reinvent the political community
in the face of authoritarianism and repression. Müller's
poetry, Friedrich's compositions, were fraught with coded
dissenting messages; Schubert's choice of Müller for his
deepest adventure in song reflected his own political leanings, as well as many other aesthetic predispositions.

Solitariness, always a subject for Schubert the song-
writer, immersed as he was in a poetic milieu fascinated by
its perils and its possibilities, had an especial attraction for
Schubert after 1822, as he lived in the shadow of syphilitic
illness, producing an extraordinary stream of masterpieces
under the pressure of impending incapacity and dissolu-
tion. "Pain sharpens the understanding and strengthens
the mind," he declared in 1824. Between 1823 and 1828,
Schubert was in a hurry to set down his musical legacy;
but he also lived the horrors of isolation which syphilis
imposed. "They greatly praise Schubert," Beethoven's
nephew Karl wrote in the composer's conversation book
in August 1823, "but it is said that he hides himself." In
March 1824 the horror of his isolation, intensified by the
shame and regret, pressed in on him with renewed force,
and he wrote an agonised letter to his friend the painter
Leopold Kupelwieser, in Rome:

> I feel myself to be the most unhappy and wretched
> creature in the world. Imagine a man whose health

will never be right again, and who in sheer despair
over this ever makes things worse and worse instead
of better; imagine a man, I say, whose most brilliant
hopes have perished, to whom the felicity of love and
friendship have nothing to offer but pain, at best,
whom enthusiasm (at least of the stimulating kind) for
all things beautiful threatens to forsake, and I ask you,
is he not a miserable, unhappy being?

| *295*

Sociability was at the core of a good deal of Schubert's
art in this period—of the dances he wrote, and of many of
the songs. The very same day that the first part of *Winterreise* was published by Haslinger in Vienna, January 14,
1828, Greiner in Graz published the "Grätzer Galoppe"
for four hands and the "Grätzer Walzer" for piano solo.
For those last five or so years Schubert continued to live
and to work and to socialise. He lodged, intermittently,
in the house of his friend Franz von Schober; he attended
reading parties, late-night gatherings at taverns, and
some of the social gatherings known as *Schubertiaden* at
which his music was performed. Often, though, in these
last years, his friends and companions were disappointed:
"Schubert kept us waiting in vain." Some of the time he
was in quarantine; sometimes he was too ill to go out. If
Schubert was a moody character, his illness can only have
intensified this, both when its symptoms were on the ram-

page (or the symptoms of the mercury treatment he underwent, losing his hair or suffering appalling headaches) and
when the well-known and ravaging long-term effects of
the disease possessed his imagination. Up and down, like
the music: like the piano sonatas with their characteristic
and sudden outbursts of rage; or *Winterreise* itself with
its happy memories, cutting sarcasm, dancing rhythms,
and profound misanthropy. "He was most amiable and
talkative," wrote Sophie von Kleyle to Ferdinand Walcher
in June 1827, "but escaped suddenly, before anyone had an
inkling."

| **13** |

DIE POST

THE POST

Von der Straße her ein Posthorn klingt.
Was hat es, daß es so hoch aufspringt,
Mein Herz?

Die Post bringt keinen Brief für dich:
Was drängst du denn so wunderlich,
Mein Herz?

Nun ja, die Post kommt aus der Stadt,
Wo ich ein liebes Liebchen hatt',
Mein Herz!

Willst wohl einmal hinübersehn,
Und fragen, wie es dort mag gehn,
Mein Herz?

A posthorn sounds from the road.
What makes you leap up so high,
    My heart?

The post doesn't bring any letter for you,
Why do you throb so strangely,
    My heart?

Now, yes, the post comes from the town,
Where I had a beloved love,
    My heart!

Do you really want just once to have a look,
And ask, how things are going there,
    My heart?

Logo of the (privatised) German postal service

Across the world, postal services are being altered
like this: optimised to deliver the maximum amount
of unwanted mail at the minimum cost to businesses.
In the internet age private citizens are sending
less mail than they used to, but that's only part
of the story of postal decline. The price of driving
down the cost of bulk mailing for a handful of big
organisations is being paid for by the replacement
of decently paid postmen with casual labour and the
erosion of daily deliveries.

—JAMES MEEK, *London Review of Books* (2011)

*W*INTERREISE IS A LONG WORK, performed without interval. When I was singing it some years ago with the pianist Leif Ove Andsnes, on tour, he pointed out that it involved sitting continuously at the keyboard longer than for any solo or orchestral work in his repertoire— seventy minutes at least. There are various ways in which the cycle can be broken up in performance. The songs can be gathered into groups. Different architectures can articulate the presentation of the same musical material.

Most song recitals are made out of smaller musical units: groups by different composers, for example; or smaller cycles by one composer (Schumann's *Dichterliebe*—Poet's Love—for instance, or Britten's Hardy cycle, *Winter Words*). The greatest challenge is to make a whole evening out of individual songs by one composer—Schubert, say, or Brahms, or Hugo Wolf. A song recital will have a dozen or so songs in each half, and they will tend to fall into groups—by mood, by poet, or by theme. Very often, one song will flow quite seamlessly into the next; sometimes there will be some sort of pause, more or less extended. A rhythm will emerge—now forward movement, now stasis—which can enhance the audience's reception of each song, as well as creating a larger drama, both internal and external. The drama of narrative and of poetic emotion is enhanced by the play of musical juxtaposition and of physical reengagement for pianist and singer. When most songs run swiftly into each other, the creation of an intervening silence can have enormous impact. New meanings are created.

The alternative is to present each song as an individual, self-contained experience. Some performers do indeed find the near-overlapping of songs, the fusion of their musical stuff, to be a denial of the this-ness of each individual piece. That is not how a song recital works for me, and I would call *Winterreise* in aid here as the paradigm. In constructing an evening of Schubert song, the example of *Winterreise* is compelling. It uses variation of key, near and distant, major and minor, to great effect—implying, for example, physical proximity and distance between some of the songs on this long journey. A short, fast song can form a bridge between two longer, slower songs (something another great song composer, Francis Poulenc, learnt from in his cycles); and, as we have seen earlier in the piece, motivic connections can create an elective affinity between certain songs (the way the impetuous triplets of

"Erstarrung" segue into the rustling triplets of "Der Lindenbaum"; the way the repetitive, nagging dotted figure of the last verse of "Lindenbaum" is transmuted into the opening of "Wasserflut"). Solutions will be different for different singers, on different occasions, for different audiences, with different pianists, in different halls, after the challenges of a day that will always have been somehow unique. That multivalency is part of the fascination of *Winterreise*.

To give an example from another great cycle: the opening song of Robert Schumann's *Dichterliebe* famously refuses to resolve at the end, the music left hanging in an indeterminate tonal space, without closure. I had always followed the common practice and used this failure to close as a bridge into the next song, which forms the resolution of its predecessor: no gap then. I was recently performing the cycle at Carnegie Hall with the composer Thomas Adès, in the context of a programme which also included Liszt's transcription of Wagner's "Liebestod." Tom suggested pausing significantly before the second song. The effect on the rest of the cycle was palpable, recreating unfamiliarity and renewing for us and for the audience the original sensation of radicalism and daring.

MY FIRST SCORE OF *Winterreise* (the Dover reprint of the Breitkopf & Härtel edition edited by Eusebius Mandyczewski) splits the cycle in two, heading them Part One and Part Two. The familiar (and slightly earlier) Peters edition, edited by Max Friedländer, has no such division. The manuscript of the cycle, again in two parts (the first in rough, the second in fair copy), reflects Schubert's discovery of a further twelve songs after completing his "ur-*Winterreise*" (the first twelve)—so "Einsamkeit" has

"FINIS" written under it and "Die Post" continues the cycle. Tobias Haslinger published the work in two volumes, part one in January and part two in December 1828, after Schubert's death. On his deathbed, as we know, Schubert was correcting the proofs. In what sense did the composer intend the piece to have a bipartite structure? We know from the manuscript that he characterised the second twelve songs as a "continuation." We also know that he changed the key of "Einsamkeit," the twelfth song in the first part, not for vocal reasons but almost certainly to prevent the sense of closure that a return to the key of the very first song would imply. We cannot claim to know how Schubert wanted to have the cycle performed, if only because we are not even sure that he conceived of it as a concert entity at all. He did perform the songs to his friends, privately; but Schubert's *Winterreise* was as much a poetic work of the imagination, to be read, played, and half-sung along to at home, as a concert-hall colossus. The comparison might be with a Byronic or Shelleyan drama as opposed to a Shakespearean play. It was not until

much later in the century that it began to be performed
complete in concert halls (nineteenth-century practice
is surprising: it comes as a shock to discover that Clara
Schumann performed extracts from *Dichterliebe* in concert
after Schumann's death, a work he so clearly intended as a
whole). There is in that sense no "authentic" performing
tradition.

Still, "Die Post" feels like a new beginning, as indeed
it is—Schubert was so seized by the possibilities of the
new *Winterreise* poems he had discovered that he could
not but set them. The low mood of "Einsamkeit," and that
dark final minor chord, are lifted by what can be imagined as revolving carriage wheels (a repeated descending
arpeggio) and a punchy posthorn call in the piano. I used
to pause significantly before "Die Post," to make a nod
towards the two parts as published, to allow myself and
the audience a moment of gathering, and to permit (if necessary) a sip of water. I increasingly find that too much of
an interruption; the lift of "Die Post"—which also introduces a new and more visionary musical world—works
much better if it is not too much separated from what has
gone before. Still, the choice is open.

THE HORN CALL—last heard in "Der Lindenbaum"—is
such a feature of the Romantic imagination that it is not
surprising to come across it again on our journey. Charles

Rosen in his *Romantic Generation* cites a famous and
sonorous line from a poem roughly contemporaneous with
Winterreise, Alfred de Vigny's "Le Cor" of 1826: "J'aime
le son du cor, le soir, au fond des bois" (I love the sound
of the horn, in the evening, from the depths of the wood).
Vigny goes on in the poem to tell us of the farewell of the
huntsman "que l'écho faible accueille, / Et que le vent
du nord porte de feuille en feuille" (that the feeble echo
welcomes, / And that the north wind carries from leaf to
leaf): the link with Schubert's "Lindenbaum" is almost
eerie. Vigny's evocation of "les airs lointains d'un cor
mélancholique et tendre" (the distant airs of a melancholy
and tender horn) is a poetic embodiment of a trend in
German Romanticism which blended the aesthetic, the
antiquarian, and the philosophical.

The seventeen-year-old Robert Schumann made a telling aside to his diary in May 1828, some six months before
Schubert's death: "Schubert is Jean Paul, Novalis and
Hoffmann expressed in sound." For Schumann's beloved
Jean Paul (1763–1825), arch-Romantic novelist and story
writer, sound and, by extension, music had a special significance, a metaphysical quality which outran the capaci-
ties of visual art or literary prose:

> Music . . . is romantic poetry for the ear. Like the beau-
> tiful without a limit, this is less a delusion of the eyes,

of which the boundaries do not fade away as indeterminably as those of a dying sound. No colour is as romantic as a sound, since one is present at the dying away only of a sound but not of a colour; and because a sound never sounds alone, but always threefold, blending, as it were, the romantic quality of the future and the past into the present.

The very fragility of sound, its onset, its resonance, its decay, somehow, even before musical organisation has embraced it, connect the human sensorium to the mystery of time. Again:

> The Romantic is beauty without limit, or beautiful infinity, just as there is a sublime infinity . . . It is more than an analogy to call the Romantic the undulating hum of a vibrating string or bell, whose sound waves fade away into ever greater distances and finally are lost in ourselves, and which, although outwardly silent, still sound within. In the same way moonlight is both image and instance of the Romantic.

Romantic song, and Schubert song in particular, delights in moonlight (the sublime settings of Goethe and Hölty, for instance) and in the sound of bells (the tolling bells of "Das Zügenglöcklein" and of "Abendbilder").

The acoustic qualities of particular instruments, in Jean Paul's reckoning, mediate that particular tonal relationship between movement and moment: "the extension of tone into ideal space, the resolution of future and past into the present [which] results in the unlimited expansion of time within a single instant of the temporal continuum," as the musicologist Berthold Hoeckner has described it. The bell, for example, "calls the Romantic spirits," as Jean Paul puts it, because of its long reverberation time, as well as the distance at which we often hear it. Jean Paul puts this to use in his stories: "The distant bells of the village were recalling, like beautiful, dying away times, over into the dark shouting of the shepherds in the fields." The horn, similarly, carries, etiolated, over long distances. And it was Schubert's beloved Novalis—philosopher and poet, whose "Hymns" the composer set to music, whose prose he imitated in the fragment "My Dream"—who put his finger on the Romantic character of distance. "In the distance," he wrote, "everything becomes poetry." So, when we hear a distant horn call imitated in the piano in "Der Lindenbaum," we are absorbing a Romantic leitmotif; the encounter with memory and with loss that the poem suggests is given affective, symbolic, audible form.

The horn, real or impersonated, will not always be heard at a distance; but the meanings it has accumulated, and continued to accumulate over the course of the nineteenth and into the twentieth century, give it a remarkable capacity to evoke what Charles Rosen called "distance, absence and regret." Benjamin Britten's *Serenade for Tenor, Horn and Strings*, a profoundly Romantic work (Britten saw himself as a Romantic manqué), plays most beautifully with these elements, both in the natural-horn prologue and epilogue, the latter played outside the hall, as distant as possible; and in the second movement proper, where the horn itself imitates the dying fall of Tennyson's bugle in "The Splendour Falls."

German Romantic literature, as well as its music, is saturated with atmospheric horns. Here is Joseph von Eichendorff: "I sat with the porter on the bench in front of my house and enjoyed the warm air and the gradual darkening and disappearing of the merry day. Presently the horns of the returning hunters sounded in the distance, answering one another from the opposite hills." And again, as the same protagonist in *From the Life of a Good-for-Nothing* sits in a tree on a hillside, "from far away came the sound of a posthorn over the wooded hilltops, at first hardly discernible, then louder and clearer." It inspires him to sing to himself a melancholy song about homesickness: "it seemed . . . as though the posthorn in the distance was playing the accompaniment . . ." (It was later set to music by Hugo Wolf.)

Clemens Brentano's influential but eccentric and capricious Romantic bildungsroman, *Godwi, oder Das steinerne Bild der Mutter—Ein verwilderter Roman* (Godwi, or

The Stone Image of the Mother—An Overgrown Novel;
1800–01), has some notable passages of horn atmospher-
ics, here reminiscent of some 1960s acid trip:

> Here Godwi took up a small silver hunting horn from
> the wall and gave a few bright blasts upon it . . . [T]he
> notes are a wondrous living breath of the darkness, I
> said, as if everything were murmuring and living and
> speaking to us in this secret chamber, through which
> the sounds shoot like glowing pulse beats. The tones
> are the life and form of Night, Godwi said, the token
> of all that is invisible, the offspring of desire.

To the Lieder aficionado, Brentano is most familiar
as co-compiler (with Achim von Arnim) of *Des Knaben Wunderhorn* (The Boy's Magic Horn), the collection
of German folk poems and songs. The magic horn in
question is most obviously a cornucopia, since the volumes themselves are a treasury akin to a magical horn
of plenty—"What miraculous riches are here!" the title
seems to say.

Yet the horn is also, and obviously, the magical instrument calling to us from the depths of the dark forest,
where myths and mysteries have their home. Volume one
has a horseback rider waving his horn aloft; but while
this may remind us of the postillion with his posthorn, it

Des Knaben Wunderhorn, *vol. 2, title page, 1808*

is in fact the magical receptacle-cum-instrument of the opening poem in the collection, "Das Wunderhorn," full of gold and jewels, with a hundred golden bells engraved upon it which, when touched by the empress in her castle, will "sound sweetly, / As no harp has ever been played, / And no lady has ever sung." Bells, harp, voice, horn— all the Romantic musical tropes in one. Schubert's friend Moritz von Schwind illustrated the Wunderhorn less ambiguously, with a painting of 1848, now in Munich, for which he made a wonderful sketch, and in which the horn is clearly placed to the lips of the languorous youth dreaming in the woods:

That's a lot about horns, but it should be enough to establish that when we hear them in *Winterreise*, as we hear them in "Der Lindenbaum," there is a lot of cultural baggage in play. The horn is deeply embedded in German Romantic culture, and since the Lied tradition, virtually created by Schubert, is the place where Romantic music and Romantic poetry meet, the horn's appearance has a crucial significance. The historical connotations are telling too. As in Vigny's poem, the main body of which is a retelling of the legend of Roland, hunting horns evoke the past, a feudal past, the world we have lost. They smell of violence and masculinity, of course, though this is less at issue in *Winterreise* than in *Die schöne Müllerin*, where the "Saus und Braus" (roar and rush, literally) of "Der Jäger" (The Huntsman) and the braying horn of "Die böse Farbe" (The Evil Colour) threaten the miller boy's very existence as his pretty songs and dances for children, played on a reed pipe, have to compete with the feral swagger of the huntsman. But they also summon up an idealised past, with the *Waldhorn*, the valveless hunting horn, sounding from the depths of the immemorial German forest, source of German myth, of German values, and almost, one might say, of German nationhood. Add to that all those connotations of resistance to Roman legionaries and the roots of Gothic architecture in the forest glade, good German trees reimagined in stone to set against the tyrannical marble, and the rationalising urge of classical architecture.

More immediately, the horn hangs over *Winterreise* as a motto because Müller's verses were first published in full in the second volume of his *Gedichte aus den hinterlassenen Papieren eines reisenden Waldhornisten* (Poems from the Posthumous Papers of a Travelling Hornplayer). Müller was a great friend of both Brentano and Achim von Arnim, and his title borrows for the collection a typically Romantic air, co-opting the suggestive sound of the horn to his purposes, drawing on the aura to which Brentano had contributed; but also winking with a sort of playful mystery. Who is this travelling hornist? Why is he travelling? Does he go from court to court as an outdoor player? Does he travel from city to city as an ensemble player? Surely he is not one of the celebrated players of the eighteenth century who made great careers from their virtuosity with the hand-stopped natural horn? How are we to imagine him? Is he a figure out of the past? Certainly by the 1820s, travelling virtuosi were out of fashion; and the natural horn, while still the dominant instrument, was on its gradual way out with the slow adoption of the valved horn from the 1820s on: a victim of industrial progress.

. . .

THE HORN THAT SOUNDS in "Die Post" may remind us of horns gone by, of Romantic myth, of the reverie of the lime tree. In itself it has a quite different character, one which is busy, urgent, and excitable—present, and not distant. These are the calls so familiar to the early-nineteenth-century traveller, signalling arrival or departure at the post station, or simply warning pedestrians on the road to watch out. If, in "Der Lindenbaum," the wanderer was tempted by images of the past or deathly longing, he is now confronted by a resonant, sounding image of modernity.

The posthorn itself may be ages old, but the mail coach of the 1820s which it summons up here was an agent of modernisation, a form of speedy, purposeful, efficient transport which stands in stark and deliberate contrast to the aimless wanderings on foot of *Winterreise*'s protagonist. This is a confrontation with the busy world to which he does not belong.

The Stockton and Darlington Railway, the first publicly subscribed passenger railway, opened in 1825, too late to have had much impact on Wilhelm Müller or Franz Schubert; passenger steam railways were first built in Germany and Austria in the mid-to-late 1830s. Conventional wisdom would have it that it was the coming of the railways that revolutionised communications in the nineteenth century, annihilating time and space. Speedy and reliable transport links shrank the world. It was the railway with its speed and use of timetables that gradually imposed a universal standard of time on the world, a process only accelerated by the advent of the telegraph, the telephone, radio, and television. The spectacular, glamorous advance that the railway represented makes it easy to forget that the mail coach came first. "In purely mathematical terms," as the historian Wolfgang Behringer avers, somewhat provocatively, "the increase in speed between 1615 and 1820 was greater than the increase between 1820 and the modern day." In the early years of the nineteenth century, in which both Schubert and Müller reached maturity, passenger-carrying postal services were the wave of the future.

It had been a slow process. First the delivery of mail on horseback, using relay stations to facilitate speed. Then, in the seventeenth century, the introduction of postal vehicles running according to timetables, which were also available to the wider public as a form of socialised transport. The mail coach is a familiar feature of eighteenth-century literature Europe-wide, but it was in the 1820s that the system reached its apogee. The coaches remained horse-drawn, of course, but within that constraint every effort was now made to remove organisational obstacles to speedy and reliable service. Express post was introduced in Prussia in 1821, Austria in 1823, Saxony in 1824, and Bavaria in 1826.

Contemporaries spoke of the "entirely new life" which had been given to "the vehicular post in Germany" (1825). Commentators were impressed: "The reform of the vehicular post that has been carried out in Germany in this century is novel, grand and admirable" (1826). The road network was expanded, and surfaces improved hand-in-hand with developments in carriage suspension, which gave passengers the feeling that they were "gliding along." Lengths of stops at post stations were cut down; conductors using clock and logbook ensured that advertised times were adhered to, penalties for slacking expressed no longer in hours or quarter-hours but in minutes. Journey times were slashed—Berlin to Magdeburg from two and a half days to fifteen hours. Frankfurt was now only two and a half days distant from Berlin, and ninety-three rapid post vehicles made the journey every week in the 1830s. The coordination of timetables involved a new and standardised conception of time itself. In 1825 the main Prussian post office in Berlin installed a "standard clock." All mail coaches were to carry a portable timekeeper conveying that standardised time to the sleepiest corner of the postal network.

By the standards of the railway locomotive, let alone the automobile, and in comparison to the achievements of the succeeding decades, this may seem small beer. To contemporaries, however, even the speed of the coach itself, horse-drawn as it was, had a physical impact. The

impassioned prose of Thomas de Quincey was to recall
in 1849 the lost glories of the English mail coach, declaring
that "through velocity at that time unprecedented . . .
they first revealed the glory of motion." The whole
system, relentless in its demands for punctuality, speed,
and efficiency, robbed travel of a leisureliness which it
would never again regain. The new way of travelling was
"nothing short of a horror," wrote one observer in 1840;
"the tyrannical punctuality, which may be of advantage
to the generality, is a torment to the individual." Journeying
from Berlin to Hamburg in 1830, Therese Devrient
felt like a piece of merchandise, robbed of her "sight and
hearing." August von Goethe, nervous son of a more
adventurous parent, travelling to Italy in the 1820s, was
so troubled by speed that he gave up his mail coach for a
more sedate private vehicle from Basel onwards, "posting
quickly, but not too quickly, through these glorious
regions." The mail coach in Germany and Austria
in the 1820s was no Pickwickian piece of nostalgia and
romance; it was less poetic than practical. The confrontation
between Schubert's alienated wanderer and this
contraption of commercial society has a brilliant dramatic
intensity about it; the two very different sorts of horn
call, that from the forest of memory, and that of the
mail coach careering down the road, underline his
outcast state.

. . .

LETTERS ARE A CRUCIAL DEVICE in Romantic literature. The word "Romantic" has a wealth and welter of meanings and connotations, but at least one of them derives from the French word for novel, *roman*. To be Romantic is, somehow, like living in a novel, making the connections and meanings that create narrative from disorder. Many of the iconic novels from the eighteenth century through into the Romantic period were epistolary in form, their tale told through the exchange of letters. And in a period during which the post as a technology made great advances, this makes sense; the individuals whose subjectivity the novel was born to explore are bound together by the possibility of regular and reliable epistolary communication. Here is one locus classicus for this emotive weapon in the novelistic armoury:

| *319*

> How was I tormented in receiving the letter which I so impatiently expected! I waited at the post-house. The mail was scarce opened before I gave in my name, and began to importune the man. He told me there was a letter for me—my heart leaped—I asked for it with great impatience, and at last received it. O Eloisa! how I rejoiced to behold the well-known hand! A thousand times would I have kissed the precious characters, but

I wanted resolution to press the letter to my lips, or
to open it before so many witnesses. Immediately I
retired; my knees trembled; I scarce knew my way; I
broke the seal the moment I had passed the first turning; I ran over, or rather devoured, the dear lines . . .
I wept; I was observed; I then retired to a place of
greater privacy, and there mingled my joyful tears
with yours.

Thus Saint-Preux to Héloïse in Rousseau's supremely
influential *La Nouvelle Héloïse*. A love affair conducted
by letter had its own very special rhythm of expectation (when will it arrive?), disappointment (not today),
and joyful fulfilment. That fulfilment then had its own
emotional layers: the physical letter itself, folded paper
thick with anticipation; the handwriting, "well-known,"
as Saint-Preux says, but also with the character of the
moment it was undertaken, be it agitated, dreamlike, or
firm of purpose; and then the content, again uncertain,
and to be read and read over and over. And so on. This is
the emotion which is synthesised in the first verse of "Die
Post." Disappointment will ensue—there can be no letter
for him—but the posthorn is an involuntary reminder of
all those obsessive epistolary emotions. His heart leaps up
because the mail coach comes from town, where she lives,
so he tells us; but it also palpitates because the posthorn is

a sign for the mail coach and the mail coach means letters, and all the emotions of receipt are set in train. We hear all this in the vocal line, as it rises to a high A-flat. It is the oxytocin rush that modern researchers have identified with the use of social media and electronic messaging services; a love affair conducted by instantaneous text message, with that much-anticipated buzz or ringtone as the message arrives, has the same hormonal surges, but a very different texture and rhythm from one mediated by the postman.

If the little quizzical gap in the punch line of the first verse can read as real puzzlement—"Die Post . . . bringt keinen Brief für dich" (The post . . . doesn't bring any letters for you), that "Nun ja" in the second verse— "Of course, how could I forget, the post comes from town"—is a moment of recognition, but also of self-mockery. She has been out of his thoughts, more and more, as he had feared from the outset: "An dich hab' ich gedacht" (I thought of you), he insists in the first song; "Wenn meine Schmerzen schweigen / Wer sagt mir dann von ihr?" (When my sorrows are silent, who will speak to me of her?), he worries in the fourth. Now this sudden reminder. Will he go back to the house and spy on her, stalk her a little more? The tone of the verse and of the music suggests that he is beyond all that; and sets the scene for the remainder of the cycle, in which the visionary and the existential trump the emotional and the everyday. With a dazzling sureness of touch, Schubert uses a pat device in the last few bars in the piano to crush Romantic longings with a little bathos, and prepare us for the dark ironies of the next song.

DER GREISE KOPF

THE OLD MAN'S HEAD

Der Reif hatt' einen weißen Schein
Mir über's Haar gestreuet.
Da glaubt' ich schon ein Greis zu sein,
Und hab' mich sehr gefreuet.

Doch bald ist er hinweggetaut,
Hab' wieder schwarze Haare,
Daß mir's vor meiner Jugend graut—
Wie weit noch bis zur Bahre!

Vom Abendrot zum Morgenlicht
Ward mancher Kopf zum Greise.
Wer glaubt's? Und meiner ward es nicht
Auf dieser ganzen Reise!

The frost had scattered a seeming whiteness
Over my hair.
So I believed I'd become an old man
And I rejoiced greatly.

But soon it melted away,
And I had black hair again,
Such that I shuddered at my youth.
How far still till I reach the funeral bier!

325

From red of dusk to light of dawn
Many a head has become old.
Who'd believe it? And mine hasn't achieved that
On this whole journey!

The first time I saw her majesty, after the unfortunate catastrophe of the Varennes journey, I found her getting out of bed; her features were not very much altered; but after the first kind words she uttered to me, she took off her cap, and desired me to observe the effect which grief had produced upon her hair. It became in one single night, as white as that of a woman of seventy . . . Her majesty shewed me a ring she had just had mounted for the princesse de Lamballe; it contained a lock of her whitened hair, with the inscription, *bleached by sorrow*.

—MADAME CAMPAN, *Memoirs of the Private Life of Marie Antoinette* (PHILADELPHIA, 1823)

I FIND IT DIFFICULT to say at once why this song is musically so arresting, so new, so different. To my ear it sounds, simply, weirder than anything that has gone before, more dissociated, more alienated, more strange. The great meditative and painful pianistic arch with which the song starts presents an enormous contrast to the pulsating nervous energy of the preceding song, "Die Post." But it is not as if there have not already been moments of stasis and reflection in the cycle. Up to this point in the journey, much of the tension has been between the past and the present, between revisiting the past, picking at the psychic wound, and trying to move forward in a hostile environment. The last teasing psychological offer of return at the end of "Die Post" ("Willst wohl einmal hinübersehn . . . ?"—Do you just want to have one more look to check how she is . . . ?) has been clearly rejected by that pat ending in the piano. What we have now is a brute, bleak confrontation with the emptiness of life. And also an unsettling and eerie objectification founded in a sort of lie.

We have all had that moment of catching ourselves unexpectedly in a mirror and seeing ourselves as others see us—older, fatter, thinner, distracted, dismayed, happy, sad, but, above all, Other. The idea here is first cousin to such an epiphany: the wanderer doesn't exactly mistake himself for somebody else, but does make a similar-category error. He sees himself as an old man, because the frost has turned his hair white. All this is bathed in the irony of which Müller is such a master and his wanderer such an adept. How does the protagonist see himself thus transmogrified? There's no mirror out here, and the rivers, the ponds, the puddles are frozen.

The central conceit is not out of the question—we are quite accustomed to pictures of polar explorers transformed into ancient seers by ice crystals.

But the wanderer—and this is one of his great virtues as the cycle moves into its bleaker regions—typically clothes his distress in absurdity, an absurdity which gives the cycle its Beckettian resonances. It's all a bit of a joke, if at the same time a tragic one. The music explores the spaces which open up beneath the irony.

There are technical ways of giving a harmonic description of the piano's opening bars.

To be as brief as possible, the song is in the key of C minor, which is where we start, with the initial low C of that voice in the upper clef (the rising arc of black notes) rooted in a C-minor triad in the lower clef (the cluster of white notes). As the musicologist Susan Youens puts it, the introduction has "a tightly encapsulated initial harmony that expands outward and then contracts." From the first whole bar to the third, intensity increases, and we end up with what can be defined in the lower clef as a dominant ninth against a tonic bass—that bottom C in the chord which has been insisted on in each bar but which seems increasingly at odds with what is going on above it. From the point of view of the craftsman musician it is a sublime piece of technical wizardry. It takes the harmony somewhere unexpected, and piles on the tension, allowing for the exhausted resolution in the fourth bar, with its forlorn little turn in the upper voice. In the bottom clef, the notes stack up—first three, then four, then five—crowding the tonal space with dissonance. It is uncomfortable and (like the horror-movie clusters that borrow from it) surely meant to speak of terror.

Being a singer, I tend to overinvest in the singing line the piano plays over these chords, especially since it is a singing line which is repeated (with a tiny modification) by the singer when he or she joins in in the fifth bar. Harmonically it is uninteresting in itself, and could indeed have been harmonised in several banal ways by any of Schubert's less talented contemporaries. For a singer, though, the "melody" is striking in its stretch over nearly an octave and an augmented fourth (twenty semitones) from top to bottom. What is more, the last stage in the punishing upward trajectory is from D to A-flat, a tritone. In the context of the harmony, that is ordinary enough. In the context of a "melody" it is more striking. For a singer it is an awkward interval, not a natural constituent of a grateful singing line; and, what is more, it is the interval known from the Middle Ages on as the diabolus in musica, the devil in music. There are plenty of other examples of composers using it to insinuate discomfort or uncanniness of some kind (as I write this, I am learning Britten's church opera *Curlew River* and it seems quite natural to him in that piece to use a downward tritone to characterise the word "strange").

I am not educated in the finer points of harmony and counterpoint—like most listeners—but if from the very outset "Der greise Kopf" seems to be a new adventure in alienation and distress, it is because of that musical structure. The crazily stretched, effortful singing line in the piano (of which every listener will be conscious) and the underlying uncomfortable harmony (which in performance will operate less close to the surface, more a matter of both representing and operating upon the unconscious mind—"hidden mastery," as the pianist and Schubert scholar Graham Johnson has called it) collude to extraordinary effect.

| *331*

The opening does, as Youens says, seem to offer us the song in miniature, and its gestures recur throughout in truncated form. Music is open to many meanings, and different listeners will find different things in the same sequence—different images, different connotations and constructions. But Youens's notion that the story recounted in the first four bars of "Der greise Kopf" is a matter of "expanding hopes and . . . disillusionment" doesn't make much sense to me. As I listen to the piano

introduction, participating in it emotionally as the prelude
to the act of singing, I don't feel it "ascending to joy, and
then descending to disillusionment." That crux in bar
three, with the tritone in the melody and the dominant
ninth with the tonic bass as harmony, is a confrontation
with horror. The voice repeats the piano phrase, without
quite stretching across that tritone—it peaks on an F
instead of an A-flat. What follows, after this stretchy, can-
tabile singing, this great arc, ideally if painfully achieved
in one breath, is much more conversational, and the effect
is bathetic after the sublime terror of the opening. Complicated ironies then. To turn suddenly into an old man
should be the stuff of horrible nightmares, that is what we
hear at the beginning; but for the wanderer it is accepted
casually, as a not unexpected gift. After all, has he not
suffered enough on his journey to deserve the hastening
of his physical decline? And wouldn't the shortening of
such a painful life span be oh so welcome?—the triplets
which go with the words "I rejoiced greatly" mimic a sort
of laughter.

I'm not sure that, in the end, "Der greise Kopf" tells a
coherent emotional story. It seems too odd and dissociated
for that. The wanderer's mind lurches between tragedy
and self-mockery. Casual, conversational passages, laps-
ing into recitative (with characteristic piano-arpeggiated
punctuations) confront oppressive cantilena, but are themselves interrupted by a stab of pain in the piano.

The laughing triplet figure—"und hab mich sehr gefreuet" (and rejoiced greatly)—is later attached to the words "auf dieser ganzen Reise" (on this whole journey). First time round those words are introduced with breathtaking breeziness—"Wer glaubt's?" (Who'd believe it?), and the phrase, high in the voice, with no dynamic markings to make it emphatic, retains a whisper of the self-mocking joviality which it had originally possessed. Immediately repeated, low in the voice and with loud piano chords underneath, it has a very different effect, bitter but dispirited.

| *333*

Even the words "Wie weit noch bis zur Bahre" (How far to the grave—repeated) have an unexpected effect in performance. Expressed for the first time, they are charged with their primary meaning—I wish death was closer. The second time, more meditative, looking at the listeners in front of you, the secondary meaning acquires force—death will come when it will come, perhaps sooner than you think. "When do you think you'll be dying?" is the thought, eyeballing the spectator: a moment of extraordinary etiquette-shattering intimacy. The wanderer's longing for death is not a simple one; it co-exists in him, as it does in us all, with fear of that consummation. As he wrote this song, Schubert's syphilitic predicament would surely have made these words all too ambiguous.

Müller indulges a little word play in the poem to heighten the ironic tone. The word *Greis*, "old man," has its etymological origins in much older words which mean "grey"—like the French or High German *gris*. A *Greis* is one whose hair has turned grey, as in the German phrase "Ich lasse mir über das keine grauen Haare wachsen" ("I'm not losing any sleep over that"—literally "I'm not growing any grey hair about that"); but here the process is apparently even more dramatic, for the wanderer's hair has turned white. Such a transformation was a Romantic trope. Walter Scott's *Marmion* (1808):

> For deadly fear can time outgo,
> And blanch at once the hair.
> Hard toil can roughen form and face,
> And want can quench the eye's bright grace;
> Nor does old age a wrinkle trace.

Wilhelm Müller's favourite Byron, in his *Prisoner of Chillon* (1816), plays more ironically with the Romantic gesture:

> My hair is gray, but not with years,
> Nor grew it white
> In a single night,
> As men's have grown from sudden fears.

Accounts of the phenomenon are legion, one of the earliest being from the Chronique d'Arras of 1604:

A young gentleman of the court of Emperor Charles
V, becoming in love with a young lady, went so far,
that partly from love, partly by force, he plucked the
flower of her virginity: which having been discovered
he was imprisoned, especially because the act was
committed on the premises of the Emperor, and he
was condemned to lose his head. Then, having been
informed that evening that his life would be ended on
the following day, this very same night was for him
so fearful and had such an effect on him, that the next
morning leaving the jail to appear before the judge to
hear his death sentence, nobody recognised him, not
even the Emperor, because fright had so changed him
that instead of having as yesterday a fine red color,
blond hair, pleasant eyes and a face to be looked at
with pleasure, he had become like an unearthed corpse
and had the hair and beard as white as a septuagenar-
ian. The Emperor, suspecting that another criminal
had been substituted, ordered an inquiry, how came
this wonderful and sudden change. His desire of just
vengeance changed to that of pity and he pardoned the
young man, saying that the prisoner had already been
sufficiently chastised.

As one medical authority, Pierre François Rayer,
explained in 1812 in his *Dictionnaire des Sciences médicales*,
"paroxysms of rage, unexpected and unwelcome news,

335

Alexander Littlejohn, first-class steward on the Titanic,
before the disaster and six months after, 1912

habitual headache, over indulgence in sexual appetite
and anxiety have been known to blanch the hair prema-
turely." The wanderer in *Winterreise* has, one suspects,
been a prey to all these mental states. The debate as to the
causes of sudden whitening of the hair, a well-attested but
at the same time disputed phenomenon, continues to this
day. The most plausible explanation of this seems to be as
an "acute episode of diffuse alopecia areata in which the
very sudden 'overnight' whitening of hair is caused by

the preferential loss of pigmented hairs in this supposedly immune-mediated disorder" (Trüeb and Navarini in a submission to *Dermatology*), a process now thought to be unrelated to mental stress or disturbance. Someone with speckled, pepper-and-salt hair more or less suddenly loses all the darker hairs, an autoimmune response of some sort, and is left white-headed.

Whatever the physical reality, the image Müller uses lends his poem, and Schubert's song, a tone of grotesque playfulness. The musical confrontation with terror is not all it seems.

| 15 |

DIE KRÄHE

THE CROW

Eine Krähe war mit mir
Aus der Stadt gezogen,
Ist bis heute für und für
Um mein Haupt geflogen.

Krähe, wunderliches Tier,
Willst mich nicht verlassen?
Meinst wohl bald als Beute hier
Meinen Leib zu fassen?

Nun, es wird nicht weit mehr gehn
An dem Wanderstabe.
Krähe, lass mich endlich sehn
Treue bis zum Grabe!

A crow came with me
Out of the town
And till today steadily
It has flown over my head.

Crow, strange beast,
Won't you leave me?
Do you really mean to take
My body here as carrion, soon?

Now it's not much further to go
With my walking stick.
Crow, let me see at last
Fidelity to the grave.

Tippi Hedren in a publicity still for Alfred Hitchcock's The Birds *(1963)*

Schubert, Franz, crowed for the last time, 26 July 1812

—written by the choirboy Schubert in his alto part
of Peter Winter's Mass in C

*T*HE SPATIAL GESTURE in the music which connects the previous song to this one is irresistible.
"Der greise Kopf" ends at the bottom of that pianistic arc
described in the last chapter. Now "Die Krähe" carries us
high up into the air. Weightless, hallucinatory, the high
end of the piano used to brilliantly disorientating effect.
We all look up, and there is the bird; but we're also up in
the air with it, borne aloft by its music.

When I made a film of the cycle with the director
David Alden back in 1997, he created an image which
redoubles that sensation. At first sight we are given the
crow's point of view, the wanderer observed from the sky;
but with his black coat spread out like wings, and with the
twirling vertiginous dance of the camera, the objective
and the subjective, observer and observed, seem to merge.
The wanderer becomes the crow; we all become the crow.

Montage from David Alden's film of Winterreise
made for the centenary year, 1997

This seems to me in retrospect (I'm not sure I appreciated it fully at the time) to reinforce something already in the poem, which the music itself heightens—that hazy loss of identity, of a clear distinction between self and other.

The man is shadowed by the crow, circling overhead, eager for carrion. If man is prey, though, has he not also been hunter, stalking the hind: finding his way in the darkness guided by animal tracks in the snow in "Gute Nacht"; looking for *her* traces in "Erstarrung"? Doesn't his closeness to the crow, to whom he speaks so familiarly ("Wunderliches Tier"), betray a certain identification, a breaking down of barriers heightened by the slight wooziness invoked by the music? He's up there with the bird, looking down, dizzy; and we are with him.

This painting by Lucian Freud, an early self-portrait, seems to thrive on the same sort of mysterious affinity. The white feather and the hatted figure framed by the window are beautifully opposed, of course, white and black—the feather strangely optimistic in itself (bright and upright), the man somehow threatening. We have one sliver of autobiographical information—Freud tells us that the feather was given to him by his lover. But it is the bird in the background that is interesting here. I'm not positive it is a crow, though it looks like some member of the corvid family (the black-and-grey colour-

ing suggests a hooded crow); but it does echo the subject
in the foreground, his blacks and his greys, and with the
white feather a whole complex of meanings are set bounc-
ing off each other: man as bird; man against bird; vulner-
ability; cruelty; awkwardness.

The crow is a notorious creature of ill omen in both
literature and art. Caspar David Friedrich's *Woman on
the Edge of an Abyss* (1803) is a woodcut of terrifying
bleakness, probably created as a frontispiece for a book
of his own poems.

It shows us a figure who could be the female counterpart
of *Winterreise*'s male protagonist, alone in a bleak land-

scape, surrounded
by emblems of tran-
sience, isolation,
and death—craggy
peaks, ragged trees,
two crows. Only
the snake marks her
fate out as a pecu-
liarly feminine one;
self-destruction
seems to await her.

At first glance
Friedrich's paint-
ing *The Chasseur in
the Forest*, begun in

summer 1813 and shown in March of the following year, in an exhibition of patriotic art in Dresden, might seem a Romantic piece typical of the artist—the wanderer in the forest, the so-called *Rückenfigur* (figure seen from behind, a Friedrich speciality) in the snow. But there is that crow sitting on the stump in the foreground, ominous and expectant. The man is clearly lost and he is a *chasseur,* a French soldier—if it is 1813, he is more than likely on the long retreat from Moscow, isolated in the German forests. What the crow is expecting and, by its very presence predicting, is the soldier's death in the snow. Here is how the picture was described by its first owner, Prince Wilhelm Malte of Putbus: "It is a winter landscape; the rider, whose horse has already been lost, is hastening into the arms of death; a raven is crowing a funeral dirge after him." The bird will presumably feast on the corpse, which makes for a gruesome bond between them. Being vulnerable to such a horrifying fate, the soldier is himself reduced to an animal, whose tracks in the snow signal his status as prey.

Prince Wilhelm Malte, from an old Slavic-Rügen family, was effective ruler of Rügen under Prussian suzerainty from 1815, and Caspar David Friedrich's local prince and patron. Wilhelm Müller, intriguingly, did make an extensive visit to Rügen in 1825, publishing his influential poetic cycle *Muscheln von der Insel Rügen* (Shells from Rügen Island) in 1827. It is not unlikely, therefore, that he saw the picture, though we cannot know.

Caspar David Friedrich, The Chasseur in the Forest, *1814*

The thematic connections between song and picture are tantalising.

WHAT IS A CROW? The crow family are the *Corvidae*, itself part of the order *Passeriformes,* the songbirds or, more correctly, perching birds. A large subset of the *Corvidae,* around a third, are the so-called true crows— rooks, ravens, jackdaws, and crows, the genus *Corvus.* As even the more formal nomenclature suggests, the distinctions are not always so clear, especially as between crows and ravens. Ravens are members of the crow family; crows are, conversely, members of the genus *Corvus,* a Latin word usually translated as "raven." Bigger or smaller, social or less social, with varying styles of flight and characteristic calls: "practically every inhabited land has a black-feathered creature of the Crow genus," as the American naturalist Frank Warne observed in 1926. "Though differing in size and habits to some extent," he continued, "in various localities, climates and amid varying surroundings, these birds are, as a rule, true to colour—a glossy black—and whether they are locally known as Crows, Ravens, Jackdaws or Rooks, their instinctive sagacity, alertness, intelligence and resource- fulness mark them out."

Modern study of the crows has revealed them to be

quite remarkably intelligent: in terms of brain size relative
to body size, they are more akin to primates than to other
birds. As early as Pliny the Elder, corvid cunning, ability
to mimic speech, and problem-solving talents were being
noted; his tale of a crow dropping stones into a bucket to
raise the level so it could drink, was taken up by Aesop.
Crows have lived close to human settlements since time
immemorial, and their presence in myth reflects this,
whether it be in the Bible—Noah sends a raven from the
Ark as a messenger, Elijah is fed by ravens—or in Norse
lore. The native peoples of North America formed tribes
in the crow's name. Alexander the Great foolishly ignored
the soothsayers when met by a dying flock of crows before
the gates of Babylon. All cultures seem to have this resi-
due of crow stories and crow wisdom. Most impressive of
all in its antiquity is the cave painting at Lascaux in which
a dead hunter is represented with what is, in all probability, a crow's head.

Two raven or crow myths have most relevance to
Winterreise. Odin had two such birds, Hugin and Munin,
perching on his shoulders and flying far and wide to
gather intelligence for the father of the gods. Their names
mean "thought" and "memory." Even closer to home,
Ovid tells how it was a crow that supposedly told Apollo,
the musician god, that his lover Coronis had been unfaith-
ful. He killed her and then, full of remorse, "in his fury

black'd the raven o'er, /And bid him prate in his white plumes no more." The carrion crow is, in a nod to Ovid, classified as *Corvus corone*.

Battlefields and the gallows have had a particular association with the crow and the raven, and death is a close companion. Christopher Marlowe tells us in *The Jew of Malta* (Wilhelm Müller translated his *Doctor Faustus*) of

| *351*

> The sad-presaging raven, that tolls
> The sick man's pass-port in her hollow beak;
> And, in the shadow of the silent night
> Doth shake contagion from her sable wing.

A flock of ravens was an "unkindness," an assemblage of crows a "murder." In nineteenth-century literature the most famous raven is Edgar Allan Poe's, in his poem of 1845. A mourning lover is visited by a raven whose only word, "Nevermore," drives him into insanity. "My soul," the poem ends, "from out that shadow that lies floating on the floor / Shall be lifted—nevermore!"

Whether Wilhelm Müller or, in turn, Franz Schubert, made a clear and properly ornithological distinction between crows and ravens is unimportant (ravens are, for what it is worth, bigger, louder, more soaring in the air, more "dignified," as one commentator puts it). Corvids make a couple of other appearances earlier on

in *Winterreise:* as the comical dislodgers of snow from
the roofs onto the wanderer's head in "Rückblick" ("Die
Krähen warfen Bäll und Schloßen / Auf meinen Hut von
jedem Haus"); and as the unkind and raucous morning
call in "Frühlingstraum" ("Es schrieen die Raben vom
Dach"). The crow in this song is very clearly solitary, a
carrion crow, *Corvus corone*. A whole complex of meanings attach to him, and they deepen our experience of the
wanderer's plight. The bird is self and other; lonely lover
and treacherous betrayer; portending death and mocking fidelity. Crows are vermin, and this bird is, above all,
an outsider, just like the wanderer; he focuses our sense,
as the cycle continues, that this almost nameless alienation is what is at issue. At the end, in another form, he
returns. The "wunderliches Tier" (strange creature) is
echoed by the "wunderlicher Alter" (strange old man) of
"Der Leiermann," whose playing is just as ugly, no doubt,
as the crow's characteristic caw. Maybe that's what we
hear in that nasty dissonance, D-flat in the voice against
D-natural in the piano when the poet talks at the end of
the song of finally seeing fidelity. From there on, voice
and piano descend to earth from the unearthly register
with which the song began and we feel that the connection
has gone. The crow has vanished and the bitter conclusion is redoubled by the music. Even the faithful crow
disappoints.

| 16 |

LETZTE HOFFNUNG

LAST HOPE

Hie und da ist an den Bäumen
Manches bunte Blatt ʒu sehn,
Und ich bleibe vor den Bäumen
Oftmals in Gedanken stehn.

Schaue nach dem einen Blatte,
Hänge meine Hoffnung dran;
Spielt der Wind mit meinem Blatte,
Zittr' ich, was ich ʒittern kann.

Ach, und fällt das Blatt ʒu Boden,
Fällt mit ihm die Hoffnung ab,
Fall' ich selber mit ʒu Boden,
Wein' auf meiner Hoffnung Grab.

Here and there on the trees
There is many a colourful leaf to be seen,
And I stay before the trees
Often, deep in thought, standing.

I look at one leaf,
I hang my hopes on it;
If the wind plays with my leaf,
I tremble, as much as I can.

Ah, and if the leaf falls to the ground,
Hope falls with it,
I fall too,
Cry on the grave of my hope.

It is statistics that first demonstrated that love follows psychological laws.

—WILHELM WUNDT (1862)

l (a

le
af
fa

ll

s)
one
l

iness

—E. E. CUMMINGS

*A*FTER SO MUCH DIGRESSION, I was tempted to leave it with this bare juxtaposition: a poem by E. E. Cummings and a masterpiece of typographical poesy. The word "loneliness" is broken up into two pieces by the storyline "a leaf falls." The letters fall down the page. And "loneliness" becomes l, the number one, and "oneliness," 1-liness, something Cummings points up by making sure that the l of "oneliness" has its own line below "one." And so on. You can find "a" and "le," English and French particles of singularity, the indefinite and definite articles; "soli," from the Latin. Just four words.

If I were to digress—which I shall try to resist—I would want to talk about probability. The weirdness of these songs, their palpable peculiarity (which I noted in relation to "Der greise Kopf") is at a premium here. How very strange they must have seemed to contemporaries: no wonder Schubert's friends didn't really like them. The initial oddness of "Letzte Hoffnung" is achieved with mis-

placed accents, and it even looks odd on the page. Within
the classical constraints of a two-page song in a perfectly
normal time signature, 3/4, the impression is given of
unpredictability. The accents, those > signs, are always
out of kilter with the 3/4 meter:

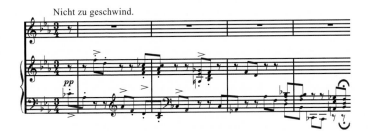

When the voice enters, it is at odds with the implied
rhythm and we don't quite know where we are, an
impression intensified by the ziggy-zaggy, unsatisfy-
ing, emotionally dissociated nature of the music in the
piano—clearly, at one level, supposed to represent the
phenomenon of falling leaves. When I first heard the
song, in the recording by Daniel Barenboim and Fischer-
Dieskau, I was a virtual musical illiterate and couldn't
imagine how this improbable music had been lifted off the
page. Now, after nearly twenty years of Schubert—and of
Britten and Adès and Henze—it sounds less singular, if
no less extraordinary. An unlikely comparison in modernist music might be with those moments of rhythmic

unpredictability (for the listener) throughout Stravinsky's noisy and extravagant *Rite of Spring*. The experience of the well-seasoned orchestral player or the conductor who knows what is coming must be very different; the audience, even if they know the piece well, are almost always discombobulated.

The relationship between music and the unexpected, music and probability, has gone further and deepened in the twentieth century, into the byways of music composed by probabilistic methods, and music performed under probabilistic constraints (both specialities of that archmodernist John Cage). Schubert's song is, of course, classical in form and formally regular in its construction but, in its realisation of Müller's poem, effects an atmospheric meditation on probability and determinism. Pick a leaf, any leaf, and then, which will it be that falls? One will certainly fall, but we cannot know which. A dialogue between the individual and the normative is suggested: here is my life, in all its uniqueness, but it is part of a natural world in which the final outcome is inevitable, the fall of the leaf, while the pathway and timing is uncertain. Which leaf will it be, when will it fall?

The traditional view of chance had been that it was mere superstition. The world might seem haphazard, but underneath apparent disorder lay immutable laws, the sort of laws about falling things (leaves as well as apples) that Newton had so triumphantly elaborated. The French astronomer and mathematician Pierre-Simon Laplace (the same Laplace who, asked by Napoleon where God's place was in his celestial mechanics, reputedly replied, "I had no need of that hypothesis") supplied, in 1814, and in a study of the mathematics of probability, the classic statement of determinism:

> An intellect which at a certain moment would know all forces that set nature in motion, and all positions of all items of which nature is composed, if this intellect were also vast enough to submit these data to analysis, it would embrace in a single formula the movements of the greatest bodies of the universe and those of the tiniest atom; for such an intellect nothing would be uncertain and the future just like the past would be present before its eyes.

This is the first appearance in print of the hypothetical intelligence known as Laplace's "demon."

The early nineteenth century was the period in which the development of statistical science—what the philosopher Ian Hacking has called "the avalanche of statistics"—began to undermine this determinism, which had dominated the so-called Age of Reason. The French Revolutionary Wars necessitated not only the *levée en masse* and the birth of the citizen army, but also the increasing collection of numerical data about such citizens. "The nation-states," Hacking writes, "classified, counted and tabulated their subjects anew." The statistical patterns which emerged from such data—and increasingly from data about deviant behaviours which the state apparatus wished to police, such as suicide, crime, vagrancy, madness, prostitution, and disease— came to have increasing explanatory force. From events that on the level of the individual seemed, and indeed were, random, statistical laws emerged and predictions could be made about the incidence, the ebb and flow, of suicide or madness within a society. The notion of the norm emerged, as did the idea of trying to conform to the norm. Hacking again:

> Social and personal laws were to be a matter of probabilities, of chances. Statistical in nature, these laws were nonetheless inexorable; they could even be self-regulating. People are normal if they conform to the central tendency of such laws, while those at the extremes are pathological, so "most of us" try to make ourselves normal, which in effect affects what is normal. Atoms have no such inclinations. The human sciences display a feedback effect not to be found in physics.

The paradox, then, was that from the accumulation,
tabulation, and analysis of random events (although
that element of feedback would come to infiltrate their
randomness), regularities and social "laws" emerged.
This tendency was to dominate the development of
nineteenth-century science and culminate in the extension
of statistical laws to thermodynamics, the study of heat,
and even, by the early twentieth century, to the ultimate
understanding of physical law through the development of
the quantum theory. Looking at it in its grand historical
sweep, it is interesting to note that the feedback problem
Hacking notes in the development of the social sciences
has its analogue in the physical sciences with the notion
(expressed in Niels Bohr's Copenhagen interpretation of
quantum mechanics) that observation may be an intrinsic
component of our conception of physical reality.

This may all seem a long way, indeed it is a long way,
from Schubert and Müller and that falling leaf. But *Winterreise*'s historical moment was a crucial one, on the cusp,
as it were, between an old intellectual world and a new
one. I would argue that this is one reason for its deepening
cultural impact from its birth in 1827–8 into the modern
age. It is not the case that in "Letzte Hoffnung" in particular, or *Winterreise* in general, Schubert or Müller meant
to make a reasoned contribution to a burgeoning debate
about determinism and statistical inference—that would

be a ludicrously implausible suggestion—but the poem
and the song do draw strength from an intellectual climate
in which probability and providence were in dispute.

Even more importantly, the idea of normality—which
was coming to birth in the 1820s—cannot but have an
impact on any modern performer of or listener to *Winterreise*. Is the wanderer of interest to us because he or she is
everyman or everywoman, or because he or she is a pathological study, an outsider? As I make my way through
Winterreise it is one of the questions that return again and
again. Do we identify with him, or seek to separate ourselves from him? Is he sympathetic or repellent? Insight-
ful or embarrassing? Weird? Normal? These discomfiting
responses are what make *Winterreise* so compelling.

The song is dominated by austere and chancey sounds.
I mustn't forget that little jokey comment, typical of the
wanderer's mordant wit, "Zittr' ich, was ich zittern kann,"
amplified by Schubert's setting—I tremble, as much as I
can tremble, since I'm actually frozen with cold. But the
song ends with an outburst which is exactly on the edge,
right between genuine grief and self-mockery, an awareness of how ridiculous it all is. There's no written change
of tempo here—"Wein' auf meiner Hoffnung Grab"
(Cry on the grave of my hope)—and the fact that it is a
leaf, however symbolically freighted with meaning, that
is being mourned suggests a mocking tone. But genuine

pain pierces through and the crucial ambiguity, the tragic
absurdity, remains.

POSTSCRIPT

Chance aside, there is a scientific explanation for why,
if not exactly when, leaves fall from trees. Deciduous
trees—from the Latin *decidere,* to fall down—use their
green, chlorophyll-rich leaves to soak up sunlight in the
summer to effect the photosynthesis which is at the heart
of their metabolism. In the autumn or fall, the chlorophyll
is drained away, and the leaves turn yellow or even red,
as chemicals to repel insect infestation are produced in the
leaves. At the base of each leaf the so-called abscission
zone contains cells which, once the fall is under way, swell
and cut off the flow of nutrients from tree to leaf. A tear
line forms, and eventually the leaf falls or is blown away.
A protective seal then forms around the wound, prevent-
ing both the evaporation of water and the depredations of
insects. Only in the past ten years have scientists begun to
uncover the complex genetic pathways by which abscission takes place.

| **17** |

IM DORFE

IN THE VILLAGE

Es bellen die Hunde, es rasseln die Ketten.
Es schlafen die Menschen in ihren Betten,
Träumen sich Manches was sie nicht haben,
Tun sich im Guten und Argen erlaben:
Und morgen früh ist Alles zerflossen.
Je nun, sie haben ihr Teil genossen,
Und hoffen, was sie noch übrig ließen,
Doch wieder zu finden auf ihren Kissen.

Bellt mich nur fort, ihr wachen Hunde,
Laßt mich nicht ruhn in der Schlummerstunde!
Ich bin zu Ende mit allen Träumen—
Was will ich unter den Schläfern säumen?

The dogs bark, the chains rattle.
People sleep in their beds,
Dreaming of many things that they don't have,
Consoling themselves with good things and
    bad things:
And early in the morning, it's all vanished.
Even so, they've enjoyed their share,
And hope what is still remaining
Still to find on their pillows.

Bark me away, you watchful dogs,
Don't let me rest in the hour of sleeping!
I'm at an end with all dreams—
Why should I linger among the sleepers?

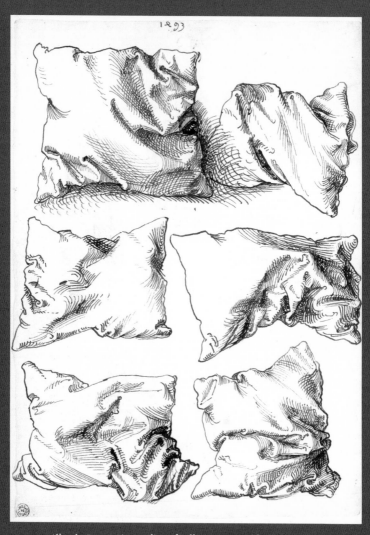

Albrecht Dürer, Six Studies of Pillows, *pen and brown ink, 1493*

*T*HIS IS ONE OF THOSE SONGS in which Schubert's protean way with musical motifs is at its most creative. A sort of rumbling in the piano sets off, each time ending with a clipped accented note approached by a little upward ornament in the bass. The gesture is repeated another five times before the singer joins in. It gets louder, harmonically a little more threatening, and then again more distant and relaxed. Surely it's meant to be something—what could it be? Here, the singer tells us, is the answer: "Es bellen die Hunde," the dogs are barking. You can hear the snarling, the sense of threat in the harmonic tension, the whole thing is almost Disney-like in its clarity of purpose. But no, it's something else too: "Es rasseln die Ketten," the dogs' chains are rattling, and yes, those rattling semiquavers in the bass line of the piano are graphic. Then we're offered another image to go with the sound—"Es schlafen die Menschen"—people are sleeping. Schubert changes Müller's original "Die Menschen schnarchen" (People are snoring). He had to reverse the word order to get the repetitive effect he was looking for ("es bellen . . . es rasseln . . . es schnarchen/schlafen"), and *schnarchen* is too clotted and consonantal a word to suggest what *schlafen* can—those sleepy people yawning, a notion somehow amplified by the seesawing extension of the vocal line: "Es bellen die Hunde, es rasseln die Ketten, / Es schlafen die Menschen in ihren Betten."

Yet again, in the midst of *Winterreise*'s gloom and existential darkness, Schubert strikes sardonic sparks to light our way. The tone remains lightly amused, detached from this essentially bourgeois scene of sleepy wish fulfilment. This may be a different settlement, and a smaller one (it's a village), than the town he left his girl in, but we are surely reminded of her family's wish to acquire her a suitable husband—she's a "reiche Braut," a rich bride, we remember from "Die Wetterfahne" (though whether she offers riches to her suitor or will attract them from him has been left tantalisingly unclear). The dreams—dreams of riches for many, no doubt—burst like a bubble come morning. All that seemed solid, to paraphrase Karl Marx, vanishes into thin air, the whole nocturnal feast has been but a baseless fabric. Like a puff of smoke, it vanishes on the *floss* of "zerflossen" (vanished). The ritardando before "zerflossen" paints the picture of a reluctant yielding to reality; and the hissing *tz* sound of *zer* whisks us away.

Schubert then ups the satirical ante, repeating those connecting words of Müller's, "Je nun, je nun" ("well now," or "even so," a little condescending in tone), and the word "hoffen" (to hope) and giving us a repeated single pitch in the piano part, an insistent D-natural. In Schubert's first song cycle, *Die schöne Müllerin,* a repeated F-sharp throughout a whole song, "Die liebe Farbe" (The Beloved Colour)—and there are a remarkable 532 of them)—meant the deathly longing of disappointed passion. Here, a nagging obsession is gracefully rendered, pretty-pretty almost, the dance of bourgeois life from which the wanderer has absented himself. That hairpin crescendo and decrescendo on the D implies a little surging forwards and back which can be exploited to point that sense of gently poking fun at the banality of material longing. The passage ends with a sort of twisting and extended curlicue in the piano, a little ridiculous somehow, the needle seems to have stuck; and then we're back outside and the dogs are warning our traveller to keep away from human habitations, just as he said they would in the first song. The vocal line achieves its own, authentic dreaminess as he repeats that he is at an end with dreams, with that wonderful upward reach; and then stillness, stasis, again contradictory, as he tells us that he won't linger— a long, long note on "säumen" (linger), even though he doesn't mean to stay; but underneath it in the piano part, in octaves, is a dotted figure. It is a distinctly antique, ecclesiastical gesture—a syncopated musical genuflection, an ironic amen—irresistibly mocking in tone, surely, like similar churchy echoes, more or less teasing, which we shall notice in subsequent songs.

ONE OF THE LASTING ATTRACTIONS of *Winterreise*, and one of the keys to its depth, is its ability to leaven existential anxiety—the absurdity of existence, that Beckettian riff—with political or social engagement. This is partly, as we have seen, a matter of intention on the part of the co-creators of the cycle, poet and composer. Müller and Schubert both lived in a postrevolutionary period, fearful of reform, in which the discontents of the educated middle classes, their sense of repression and experience of a reactionary regime, were palpable. Whether or not these were particularly salient themes in the work of either artist, both undoubtedly had moments in their creative lives when they felt the bonds of repression and kicked against them. Coded political messages found their way into Müller's work, despite his official position as privy councillor and ducal librarian in Dessau. Schubert's choices of material to set to music point to a degree of disaffection with the current order of things; his ability to read Müller's subversive codes, if even we, two hundred years later, can read them, is not to be doubted.

Hence Schubert's *Winter Journey* confronts the winter we all face, the coldness we all experience, the coldness of life itself; but also obliquely challenges the social and political order from which it emerged and which, paradoxically, also made it possible. Schubert was not an agitator or a revolutionary; but, trapped within a way of living which so often frustrated his ideals, he rattled the bars of the cage. Like Müller, like all of us who live in society rather than retreat to the woods, he had to make compromises with things as they were, but sometimes became acutely aware of and alert to his own capacity for an estrangement from political, social, and economic arrangements. Schubert's particular difficulties were not those which prevail in our own age, and Metternich's Vienna is a long, long way from twenty-first-century London and its preoccupations. At the same time, it is difficult to sing *Winterreise* in modern-day London, or New York, or Tokyo, and not be struck by the irony of performing these particular songs in such spaces and to such audiences. We all, performers and audiences, enter into an aesthetic compact according to which we challenge, for an hour or so, our basic assumptions and our ways of living. The existential confrontation embodied in *Winterreise* is easy to recognise, maybe even to process or rationalise; the political charge is easier to miss, but it cannot be historicised out of existence. We have hints of discomfort throughout the cycle, with that rich bride and her family in the second song, and the poverty-stricken charcoal burner of the tenth. It is here in the seventeenth song that a self-satisfied bourgeois world is directly confronted, a world that lives on dreams of possessing new things, a world that makes as much sense to us—creatures of debt and inhabitants, even prisoners, of a succession of financial bubbles—as it did to the men and women of the 1820s. There is something uncannily visionary about this song; yet one might dismiss it as a passing fancy were it not for the unalloyed power of its successor the twenty-fourth, "The Hurdy-Gurdy Man"—and I don't want to anticipate too much here—which presents us with a poor, old outsider and the notion that this crabbed figure, cold and despised and outcast, is a victim of a careless society and, even more scarily, might one day be us. The last song of the cycle, aesthetically sublime, makes at the same time an unmistakeable plea for social solidarity.

There is a political undertow to *Winterreise*, one which is not a matter of textual archaeology and fine-grained historical context, but one which hits me, viscerally, every time I reach "Im Dorfe" in the red plush halls of the classical tradition. The question that intrudes is one of good faith. One feels these feelings, and passes on, out into the street, into the taxi or the train, back home, back to the hotel, to the airport. What are those feelings there for? We confront our anxieties in *Winterreise*, and

our purposes may be cathartic or even existential—we
sing of our absurdity only to rebut it, pulling ourselves up
by our musical-poetic bootstraps. But when we hear the
social protest embedded in the cycle, are we just playing
with the idea of a retreat to the woods, or the embrace of
the outsider? It was easier, perhaps, in previous generations to believe in the power of what the 1960s generation
called "consciousness raising," the 1820s "sympathy." Is
Winterreise, dangerously, one tiny part of the scaffolding
of our complacency? If the point of philosophy is not only
to interpret the world but to change it, what is the point
of art?

DER STÜRMISCHE MORGEN

THE STORMY MORNING

Wie hat der Sturm zerrissen
Des Himmels graues Kleid!
Die Wolkenfetzen flattern
Umher im mattem Streit.

Und rote Feuerflammen
Ziehn zwischen ihnen hin.
Das nenn' ich einen Morgen
So recht nach meinem Sinn!

Mein Herz sieht an dem Himmel
Gemalt sein eignes Bild—
Es ist nichts als der Winter,
Der Winter kalt und wild!

Der stürmische Morgen · The Stormy Morning

How the storm has torn
The grey garment of the sky!
Cloud-shreds dance about
In dull dispute.

And red fire-flames
Go among them.
That's what I call a morning,
Just how I like it.

My heart sees in the sky
Its own image painted—
It's nothing but winter,
Winter cold and wild.

The shock of the morning artillery attack . . .

S OME SONGS IN SONG CYCLES make sense only in terms of the whole structure, its rhythms and emotional narrative. However much it was the nineteenth-century practice to take songs out of cycles and perform them on their own, however long it took for the practice of performing whole song cycles in concert to establish itself as the norm, starting from the 1850s and 60s, it is quite clear that this brutal song can only have life as connective tissue, as a bridge and also as a jolt. The aggression and energy it embodies is new to the cycle, and it is both necessary and enabling. It allows the journey to continue, galvanising performers and audience members alike. It wakes us up from the dreaminess at the end of "Im Dorfe," the pull of bourgeois illusion. It disrupts the dangerous stasis which seems about to set in, despite the wanderer's "Why should I linger?"

The marking is "ziemlich geschwind, doch kräftig" (somewhat fast, but forceful) and the full power of the song can only be unleashed if it doesn't rush, except in the virtuosic descending triplets in the piano which finish off the first and last verses. All sorts of rhythmical devices pull us back—accents, staccatos, staccatissimos, forzandos (sudden loud notes or chords). *Ffz* is a marking of unparalleled violence in the cycle so far, matched by the hammering repetition in the piano which accompanies, or competes with, the singer's repetition of the words "Es ist nichts als der Winter" (It's nothing but winter). It is in a minor key, it is full of pain and of frustration, but also wild in its exaltation.

| *383*

As already described, one of the crucial decisions to be made in the performance of any set of songs, be it a song cycle or a group assembled by the performers themselves, is how much time to leave between each song. All sorts of considerations, practical and aesthetic, coalesce. Faced by the desire to create an emotional arc, to assert a unity of conception (and to confound those who might want to cough between songs), I tend to want to connect songs, to push them close together so that contrasts and affinities are fully exposed by juxtaposition. The occasional longer silence before a song can then achieve a sort of sublimity, or at least a greater impact, and can exist as a musical experience in itself rather than as a moment of nothingness or mere embarrassed waiting for the musical parade to move on. An even succession of songs is, on the whole, to be avoided.

The end of "Der stürmische Morgen" is special because it is the only place in *Winterreise* where I feel that there should be no palpable gap before the next song. One should precipitously tip into the other, with a lurch into the mad dance that is "Täuschung." Two sorts of physicality are juxtaposed here: the galumphing, stamping, noisy, clumsy rhythm of the stormy morning (particularly striking in that regard are the false accents in the piano which mispoint the words "*um*her *in* matt*en* Streit" and "*ge*mahlt *sein* eig*nes* Bild") and the whirling, heady, disembodied dance of illusion. March time and waltz time collide.

| 19 |

TÄUSCHUNG

DELUSION

Ein Licht tanzt freundlich vor mir her;
Ich folg' ihm nach die Kreuz und Quer;
Ich folg' ihm gern und seh's ihm an,
Daß es verlockt den Wandersmann.
Ach, wer wie ich so elend ist,
Gibt gern sich hin der bunten List,
Die hinter Eis und Nacht und Graus
Ihm weist ein helles, warmes Haus,
Und eine liebe Seele drin—
Nur Täuschung ist für mich Gewinn!

A light dances in a friendly fashion before me,
I follow it this way and that.
I follow it gladly, well aware
That it lures the wanderer from his path.
Ah, anyone as wretched as I
Willingly gives himself up to colourful wiles
That behind ice and night and horror
Show him a bright, warm house,
And a beloved soul within.
Only delusion is the prize for me!

| *387*

Detail from the frontispiece to Thomas Wilson's
Correct Method of German and French Waltzing *(1816),*
showing the nine positions of the waltz

SOME TWENTY-FIVE YEARS before *Winterreise*, in
1802, Schubert's great Viennese predecessor Joseph
Haydn painted, in *Die Jahreszeiten* (The Seasons), a picture
in music of a wanderer in a winter landscape. The tenor,
Lukas, describes his predicament:

Here stands a traveller now bewildered and perplexed,
not knowing which way to turn. In vain he seeks the
road, but finds neither path nor track. Vainly he tries
to struggle, and wades through the deep snow; only to

find himself more lost than ever. Now his courage ebbs away, his heart is gripped by the fear of seeing daylight disappear and being paralysed by weariness and cold.

It is all too reminiscent of our *Winterreise* wanderer, but the outcome, as one would expect from an oratorio dedicated to the virtues of social cohesion and divine purpose, is very different. After the doubts and confusions, after the angst, comes salvation as "suddenly his eye is caught by the glimmer of a light nearby."

This light, unlike Schubert's or Müller's, is not an illusory one. For just at hand is a cottage where the wanderer will be able to take refuge; a cottage, moreover, whose warm room is full of villagers gathered sociably together, "im trauten Kreise," in a cosy circle, telling tales, drinking, singing. Everything that is fugitive and unreal about "Täuschung" is here made solid and consoling, but socialised. Haydn's wanderer is gratefully reabsorbed into sociability.

"TÄUSCHUNG" takes us back to the will-o'-the-wisp, the *Irrlicht*, but the presiding spirit is that of the dance—a lilting, graceful Viennese waltz, an echo of urbanity, but at the same time with something crazy about it, and poised perilously on the edge of unreason. Looking at the charming picture at the head of this chapter, it is difficult to take on board the exaggerated anxieties of contemporaries surrounding the craze for the new dances and their "rotatory motion." "Ten to eleven thousand deaths," wrote one, "occur annually in Vienna. The cause of death for about one-fourth of these is consumption which can be brought on by immoderate waltzing." This was a matter of ballroom dust swirling up and damaging the lungs. But the hallucinogenic, almost pharmacological properties of the waltz—the swooning and hysteria which we sense in "Täuschung"—were also routinely condemned. Donald Walker, author of *British Manly Exercises* and *Exercises for Ladies*, could aver in 1836 that "vertigo is one of the great inconveniences of the waltz":

> The character of this dance, its rapid turnings, the clasping of the dancers, their excited contact, and the too quick and too long succession of lively and agreeable emotions, produce sometimes, in women of a very irritable constitution, syncopes, spasms and other accidents which should induce them to renounce it.

The playwright Heinrich Laube described this scene at the Sperl dance hall in Vienna at a Johann Strauss concert in 1833:

> In bacchantic abandon the pairs waltz . . . joyful frenzy is on the loose, no gods check it . . . [T]he dance itself

begins with whirling rapidity and the couples hurl
themselves into the maelstrom of gaiety.

In 1840, dancing masters were still relying on health
officials to intervene when inexperienced young men and
women danced too quickly.

The great public dance halls of Vienna—the Sperl and
the Apollosaal—had opened in 1807 and 1808, respectively, and the dancing craze was only intensified by the
atmosphere and opportunities of the Congress of Vienna.
By 1820, the police were concerned:

> Dancing establishments have mushroomed, and
> with them all kinds of disorderly conduct and other
> excesses, all to the detriment of nocturnal peace and
> quiet.

Schubert loved dancing (though whether he loved to
dance is another matter), and he wrote reams of dance
music—five hundred compositions on paper to add to the
many that he apparently improvised in the company of
friends and acquaintances. The different types of dance
were legion: cotillions, galops, Deutschers, waltzes,
ecossaises, polonaises, allemandes, anglaises, ländlers,
minuets, contredanses, quadrilles, and mazurkas.

Here Schubert's friend Franz von Hartmann describes
a typical evening of Schubertian entertainments—one of

the so-called Schubertiads—in December 1826. I quote
at length to give some taste of what Viennese boho-
bourgeois sociability in the Metternich epoch was like:

> I went to Spaun's, where there was a big, big Schubert-
> iad. On entering I was received rudely by Fritz and
> very saucily by Haas. There was a huge gathering.
> The Arneths, Witteczek, Kurzrock and probationer
> Witteczek: Dr. Watteroth's widow, Betty Wanderer,
> and the painter Kupelwieser with his wife, Grillpar-
> zer [the Austrian playwright], Schober [Schubert's
> dissolute friend and companion], Schwind [painter],
> Mayrhofer [poet and censor] and his landlord Huber,
> tall Huber, Derffel, Bauernfeld [playwright], Gahy
> (who played gloriously *à quatre mains* with Schubert)
> and Vogl [opera singer], who sang almost thirty splen-
> did songs. Baron Schlechta [poet and amateur singer]
> and other Court probationers and secretaries were also
> there . . . When the music was done, there was grand
> feeding and then dancing . . . At 1230 after a cordial
> parting we . . . went to the "Anchor" where we still
> found Schober, Schubert, Schwind, Derffel and Bau-
> ernfeld. Then home. To bed at 1 o'clock.

Dancing was part of the deal, and Schubert was often in
command, animating activity from the keyboard, but not,
apparently, participating himself.

Another telling dance anecdote from the Schubert circle, dating from around 1821, is to be found in the memoirs of the Viennese actor Heinrich Anschütz. Schubert and some other friends came round to Anschütz's place and "soon the conversation turned to dancing":

> Schubert, who had already given us a few piano pieces, sat down at the instrument himself, in the gayest of moods, and struck up for dancing. The whole company is waltzing round and round, there is laughter and drinking. Suddenly I am called away, a strange gentleman wishes to speak to me. I go into the ante-room.
>
> "In what way can I be of service, Sir?"
>
> "You are having a dance?"
>
> "It could be called that; the young people are jumping around."
>
> "I must ask you to stop it, we are in Lent."
>
> "What has that got to do with you, may I ask?"
>
> "I am police inspector X."
>
> "Indeed? Very well then, inspector, what am I to do? Do you expect me to send my guests home?"
>
> "I rely on your word that there won't be any dancing."
>
> When I returned to the drawing-room with the bad news and mentioned the police, they all scattered in mock terror. But Schubert said, "They do this to me

on purpose, because they know I like playing dance music so much."

Dancing was viewed by the authorities as a possible occasion of disorder; dancing in Lent was an act which might be interpreted as seditious. It was only a year or so before that Schubert and his companions had been involved in the Senn affair, which had ended in arrests, imprisonment, and deportation. Schubert clearly felt himself picked on, with a sense that he was being harried by the authorities. Anschütz's vignette points to Schubert's particular love of dancing, but also tells of the repressive atmosphere which he lived and breathed.

THE PREVAILING FEELING in this song is that of being slightly tipsily out of control, elevated by exhaustion perhaps; another example of how various the tones and attitudes demanded by the cycle are. It is not just a succession of gloomfests. Spilling over from the last song into this is one trick; the other is to find a tempo that seems just a little too fast and reckless. In the piano introduction the rhythm repeats itself in the right hand, upper stave, the pitch rises, and then somehow the whole thing excitedly flips, overflows neurotically into the next harmony.

Schubert achieves a wonderful moment of abandon

in the way the minor middle section of the song ("Ach, wer wie ich so elend ist"—Ah, one as wretched as I) is connected to the renewal of the major-key dance in the last section by a giddy musical enjambement. The singer sings "Die hinter Eis, und Nacht und Graus / Ihm weist" (That behind ice and night and terror / Shows him) and the tension grows with rising pitch only to be released into the renewal of the dance on the word "weist" (shows); the horrible reality is succeeded by the lovely fugitive vision of "ein helles, warmes Haus"—a bright, warm house.

| *395*

It is easy in the swirling impetus of this song to miss that rather shocking word *Graus*, horror. When the notion of horror is introduced into another late and very famous Schubert song, "Der Doppelgänger," a setting of Heinrich Heine's equally famous poem, the musical response is extreme and terrifying. "Mir graust es, wenn ich sein Antlitz sehe" the poet sings, "Der Mond zeigt mir meine eig'ne Gestalt" (I'm horrified when I see his face / The moon shows me my own form)—and by the time we get to "Gestalt" the music, in voice and piano, is all horror. Here the word is smothered by crazy candyfloss, but amplified by it too. The wanderer's reminiscence of social pleasures, and more specifically of the waltz, which is both intimate (for two dancers who embrace each other) and public, underlines his horrible isolation, his inability to find the refuge which Haydn's traveller was able to discover. This very naturally takes us into the first question of the next song, metaphorically understood—"Was vermeid' ich denn die Wege / Wo die ander'n Wand'rer gehn?" (Why do I avoid the paths taken by others who wander?). But before the journey continues, after the heady dance, we pause for breath.

| 20 |

DER WEGWEISER

THE SIGNPOST

Was vermeid' ich denn die Wege,
Wo die ander'n Wand'rer gehn,
Suche mir versteckte Stege
Durch verschneite Felsenhöhn?

Habe ja doch nichts begangen,
Daß ich Menschen sollte scheun—
Welch ein törichtes Verlangen
Treibt mich in die Wüstenein?

Weiser stehen auf den Wegen,
Weisen auf die Städte zu,
Und ich wandre sonder Maßen,
Ohne Ruh', und suche Ruh'.

Einen Weiser seh' ich stehen
Unverrückt vor meinem Blick;
Eine Straße muß ich gehen,
Die noch Keiner ging zurück.

Why do I avoid the ways
Other wanderers go by?
Seeking out hidden paths
Through snowed-up rocky heights?

After all, I've done nothing
That forces me to shun other people—
What sort of a foolish longing
Drives me into the wastelands?

Signposts stand on the roads
Pointing to towns,
And I wander without measure,
Without peace, and seeking peace.

I see a signpost standing
Fixed before my gaze;
I must go a road
From which none has returned.

Emanuel Leutze's The Last of the Mohicans, *c. 1850, a German painter's view of James Fenimore Cooper's novel, with more than a touch of Caspar David Friedrich about it. Now in the American Museum of Western Art, Denver, Colorado.*

L IKE THE FIRST SONG, "Gute Nacht," "Der Weg-weiser" exhibits a "gehender Bewegung," a walking motion, with its steady tread of staccato repeated notes which persist through most of the song. A little touch of the antique emerges just before the voice comes in, an ecclesiastical turn akin to that we have heard with ironic force in "Im Dorfe." Now it is a heartfelt benediction:

As in "Gute Nacht," we have two voices in the piano, the one in the right hand joined by a lower imitation in the left: no longer a man and a woman as we feel they might be in the opening song, with that memory of lovely complicity, but perhaps instead the lonely questioner questioning himself. He questions, and he does that which

the Romantic lyric is so good at, and which Goethe so
well described in a poem set by Schubert, "Erster Ver-
lust" (First Loss). "Einsam nähr' ich meine Wunde"—
All alone I nurture my wound—Goethe writes, and that
is precisely what the piano does under the vocal line in
"Der Wegweiser," these turns followed by an expressive,
lingering accent:

But the piano also compels onward movement with
a sturdy rising dotted rhythm which is taken up in the
voice, repeated four times in all:

After the hectoring of the stormy morning and the
crazed dance of illusion, this is a long, slow song, the
longest so far in the second half, a moment of reflection,
though not of stasis. There is a tenderness about the opening, a warmth and a sense of genuine wonderment at the
compulsiveness of the wanderer's wandering. Why do I
do this to myself? Irony, bravado, hysteria, desperation

are stripped away, momentarily washed clean by the major
key which enters at "Habe ja doch nichts begangen / Daß
ich Menschen sollte scheun" ("After all, I've done nothing
to be ashamed of" is the force of what he says). Stabbing
accents underlying the phrase "Welch ein *tör*ichtes Verlangen / Treibt mich *in* die Wüsteneien?" (What a foolish
longing drives me into the wilderness) draw the voice out
and insist on a crescendo, but overall a sadness prevails, a
quiet and reverent one, and the outburst fades away.

| *403*

A tender minor key returns, but as the wanderer sings
of his longing for peace, the voice begins to keen with
urgency. "Und ich wandre sonder Maßen, / Ohne Ruh,
und suche Ruh" (And I wander without measure, / Without peace and seeking peace) is repeated, first with a leap
to a G-flat, and then two pleading high G's—"und suche
Ruh, und suche Ruh." Those repeated, plangent high
notes are on the word "und," and the unwieldy emphasis
on what would otherwise be an unimportant word gives
the cry an added desperation.

This outburst is followed by one of the most extraordinarily moving passages in the cycle, and in Schubert song
as a whole. The fixed signpost in front of the wanderer's
eyes, the imaginary pointer to the road from which none
has returned, is given a musical analogue in the repeated
unharmonised pitch G in the piano which is then taken up
by the voice.

It is a moment of intense stillness and intensity, and as

the lines are repeated the G now sounds an octave lower, while above it the piano line descends and below it, in the bass, ascends, a painful progression. As the great song accompanist Gerald Moore memorably describes it: "With those hypnotic monotones again in evidence the last verse is repeated, this time less in volume but made more ominous by the pincer movement closing in on the vocal line."

"DER WEGWEISER" is the moment in the cycle at which death is definitively engaged with for the first time; the terms of that engagement remain tantalisingly ambiguous. "Eine Straße muß ich gehen / Die noch Keiner ging zurück" (I must go a road / From which none has returned). We have had the whisper of death—as well as the whisper of memory—in "Der Lindenbaum"; we have had the fugitive vision of old age in "Der greise Kopf," the shadow of the carrion crow in "Die Krähe." The wanderer now seems to choose the path towards death, a choice reflected in the subject of the next song, "Das Wirtshaus," in which a graveyard is reimagined as an inn. At the same time, the wanderer as everyman is only saying what we all come to say to ourselves at some point, sooner or later, that which we must all acknowledge: the inevitability of a journey with no return. This is not a matter of choice; there is no freedom except the freedom of acceptance. The winter journey becomes an axis between the two Freudian poles, eros and thanatos, love and death; an education in renunciation, in reconciliation with the inevitable. This is how the novelist Paul Auster starts his 2012 memoir—and not for nothing is it called, with a half-conscious nod to Schubert and Müller, *Winter Journal:*

> You think it will never happen to you, that it cannot happen to you, that you are the only person in the world to whom none of these things will ever happen, and then, one by one, they all begin to happen to you, in the same way they happen to everyone else.

The first mention of the serious illness which was to dominate, with periods of remission, the last five years of Schubert's life, comes in a business letter concerning his opera *Alfonso and Estrella*, dated February 28, 1823: "The circumstances of my health still forbid me to leave the house." By August of the same year, Schubert's isolation was a matter for comment between Beethoven and his nephew Karl in one of his conversation books: "They greatly praise Schubert, but it is said that he hides himself." Although contemporary delicacy forbad any explicit mention of the nature of Schubert's illness in public, it is fairly clear and generally accepted that he was suffering from syphilis. Piecing the fragmentary evidence together, the composer's most punctilious biographer, Elizabeth Norman McKay, suggests November 1822 as the most likely period for the onset of syphilitic symptoms. Schubert left the house of his close friend Schober, where he had been lodging, and returned to his own family to be nursed through the highly infectious second stage of the illness. At some time in 1823, probably in May, he was admitted to the General Hospital in Vienna, where he wrote a part of *Die schöne Müllerin* (The Beautiful Miller Girl), his first song cycle to words by Wilhelm Müller, and also a poem, "Mein Gebet" (My Prayer). Deeply depressed by his physical state, he was no doubt also doubly in the grip of the depression which is symptomatic of this disease:

> See, abased in dust and mire,
> Scorched by agonizing fire,
> I in torture go my way,
> Nearing doom's destructive day.

By August he was well enough to travel to upper Austria with his friend, the singer Vogl, but was seeing his physician in Vienna, August von Schaeffer, regularly. On November 18, Johanna Lutz wrote from Vienna to her fiancé, Leopold Kupelwieser, in Italy that "Schubert is already well again." On December 24, Moritz von Schwind, his close friend, the painter, wrote to Schober:

Schubert is better, and it will not be long before he
goes about with his own hair again, which had to be
shorn owing to the rash. He wears a very cosy wig.

This optimism did not last long. In March of 1824,
Dr. Jacob Bernhard started a new treatment regime,
with a strict diet and copious tea drinking; but by the end
of the month Schubert was writing in utter despair to
Kupelwieser:

Imagine a man whose health will never be right again,
and who in sheer despair over this ever makes things
worse and worse, instead of better; imagine a man,
I say, whose most brilliant hopes have perished, to
whom the happiness of love and friendship have nothing to offer but pain, at best, whose enthusiasm (at least
of the stimulating kind) for all things beautiful threatens to disappear, and I ask you, is he not a miserable,
unhappy being?

In April he developed excruciating pains in his bones,
especially his left arm, and experienced aphonia, the loss
of the ability to speak. For a time he was able neither to
sing nor to play the piano. These symptoms had disappeared by July 1824. By early 1825 he was back in hospital,
by July well again. His health continued to fluctuate for
what remained of his short life, as did his mood.

The mercury treatment on offer at the time cannot have helped. Two of the medical men who looked after Schubert in his last years, Joseph von Vering and Ernst Rinna von Sarenbach, wrote books which dealt with the treatment of syphilis. Vering's two manuals, *The Treatment of Syphilis by the Inunction of Mercury* (1821) and *Syphilido-therapie* (1826), give us a painful sense of the torturous indignities Schubert suffered in addition to his syphilitic symptoms. No meat, no carbohydrates. No milk, coffee, or wine—only water and tea. A hot room (up to 29 degrees centigrade) with no open windows. No change of underwear or bedding, no washing except rinsing the mouth. The patient may not leave the room as long as the treatment continues. An unguent of lard and mercury was to be applied to various parts of the body every second day; the mercury would have been absorbed (topically, and in greater quantities if inadvertently, by inhalation) in concentrations which by present-day standards would be considered highly toxic. Vering gives case histories in which four cures were successful and one patient died—the result of disobediently changing his linen and drinking wine, according to the good doctor.

The last cycle of this grim journey seems to have commenced on September 1, 1828, when Schubert moved to his brother Ferdinand's apartment in the Kettenbrücken Gasse in what was then a suburb of Vienna, the Neu

Wieden. He went there on the advice of his other physician, von Sarenbach, and it seems that the layout of the flat made it especially suitable for the application of the recommended mercury treatment. Schubert was certainly unwell, and taking medicine. In early October, he and Ferdinand, with a couple of friends, took a trip walking to Haydn's grave in Eisenstadt, a distance of about forty miles there and back. Not surprisingly, Schubert felt unwell on his return, but long walks were often prescribed after a course of mercury inunction. On October 31, he ate some fish which made him feel sick, as if poisoned— something he had complained of before on more than one occasion. From this day on, according to his brother, he ate very little. He took a debilitating three-hour walk on November 3 and began counterpoint studies with the musician and teacher Simon Sechter on the fourth. On the ninth he had dinner at Schönstein's house, but on the eleventh took to his bed. Delirium and moments of lucidity seem to have alternated: he worked on his opera *Der Graf von Gleichen* and on correcting the proofs of the second part of *Winterreise*.

| *409*

On November 12, Schubert wrote his last letter:

Dear Schober,

I am ill. I have eaten nothing for eleven days and drunk nothing, and I totter feebly and shakily from my chair to

*bed and back again. Rinna is treating me. If I ever take
anything, I bring it up again at once.*

*Be so kind, then, as to assist me in this desperate
situation by means of literature. Of Cooper's I have read*
The Last of the Mohicans, The Spy, The Pilot, *and* The
Pioneers. *If by any chance you have anything else of his, I
implore you to deposit it with Frau von Bogner at the coffee-
house for me. My brother, who is conscientiousness itself,
will most faithfully pass it on to me. Or anything else.*

*Your friend
Schubert*

It was in Schober's company and under his influence
that Schubert had, it is generally assumed, caroused himself into the syphilis which had laid him low. "Schober," as
the greatest of Schubertian scholars, Otto Erich Deutsch,
laconically records, "stayed away, probably from fear of
infection, and did not visit that November."

A CRAZE FOR THE NOVELS of James Fenimore
Cooper—the first "representative" American writer,
according to one authority—swept Europe in the 1820s.
"In every City of Europe that I visited," wrote the painter
and inventor Samuel Morse, "the works of Cooper were
conspicuously placed in the windows of every bookshop."
The poet and journalist William Cullen Bryant asked a

traveller to fill him in on contemporary European life—
"They are all reading Cooper," he reported.

Goethe's fascination with America is well attested,
and was representative of a powerful strain in German
life. "If we were twenty years younger, we'd be sailing
for America," he declared in 1819. In the same year he
read Lewis and Clark's account of their expedition across
the American West; in 1823 he read Washington Irving's
Sketch Book. From 1824, translations of Cooper began
appearing in German, and Goethe was hooked. He made
notes on his reading:

| 411

> September 30th–October 2nd 1826, *The Pioneers*
> October 15th–16th, *The Last of the Mohicans*
> October 22nd–24th, *The Spy*
> November 4th, *The Pilot*
> June 23rd–27th, *The Prairie*
> January 21st–29th 1828, *Red Rover*

The attraction of America in general to Germans
in particular, and the appeal of James Fenimore Cooper's work, can be summed up in Goethe's lines from
his "Xenien" of 1827, "Den Vereinigten Staaten" (The
United States), with its characteristic geological reference:

> America, you have it better
> Than our continent, the old one,

You have no tumbledown castles
And no basalt.
You are not inwardly disturbed
In the present time
By useless remembrance
And vain strife.

A fantastical America could be a promised land, free of the constricting politics and locked-in habits of a has-been Europe. In Cooper's primeval forests, with their heroic natives and rough-hewn colonists, the so-called *Europa-müdigkeit* (European tiredness) of the time could find refreshment in an open and invigorating atmosphere. That illness of the times was in fact already pulling the young towards America. It was in 1817 that the great migration of Germans across the Atlantic had begun, and the family connections which this established also made for a fascination with the world which Cooper summoned up, pioneering and free. These reflections on Cooper, from the magazine *Literarisches Conversations-Blatt* (Literary Conversation Pages) of January 1825, are revealing:

The image of a strong life and a bold death, as thousands live it and which thousands have died—it is this that has lifted me out of the paralysis of my workaday life. It gave me, alongside the grumbling courage with

which I experience the slow destruction of my civic
life, a series of ideas that make me excited and happy.

Schubert reading *The Last of the Mohicans* on his
deathbed, in the midst of correcting the proofs for
Winterreise—this has always been a wonderfully human
picture for me. In the midst of illness, he sought distraction, of course; and what could have been more distracting
than to devour tales of the adventurous West, the successor novels and successor craze to the books of Walter
Scott, which Schubert had so loved and poetical parts of
which he had set to music? In relation to *Winterreise* in
particular, I think of the wanderer alone in his wilderness,
staring at the *Wegweiser*—signpost, but literally "path
teller"—and am reminded of the frontiersman Natty
Bumppo, hero of Cooper's so-called *Leatherstocking Tales*
(*The Deerslayer, The Pathfinder, The Pioneers*, and *The
Prairie*, in addition to *The Last of the Mohicans*). Born of
white parents, Natty grows up among Delaware Indians
and, immersed in their way of life, becomes as fearless and
deadly as his friend and companion the Mohican Chingachgook. Cooper may have moved on from the simple
idealisation of the Native American retailed by Chateau-
briand in popular novellas like *Atala* (1801), widely read
in Germany; but there remains an aura of Rousseau-esque
noble savagery about both Natty and Chingachgook, with

| 413

Hawkeye (one of Bumppo's many sobriquets) representing an ideal synthesis of natural and civilised humanity. He navigates his landscape—he owns it, is at one with it, and knows his way about in it. Not for nothing is one of his other nicknames Pathfinder. He stands in clearest opposition to the alienated European, to the outcast wandering about "sonder Maßen, / Ohne Ruh, und suche Ruh" (without measure, / Without peace, and seeking peace).

NOVEMBER 13, 1828

Two florins spent on a venipuncture.

NOVEMBER 14

Schubert asks some of his friends to play Beethoven's String Quartet in C-sharp, op. 131; he is so overcome with joy that his friends are anxious for him. A special nurse is hired.

NOVEMBER 16

The physicians Joseph von Vering and Johann Wisgrill consult about Schubert's illness; the diagnosis is apparently one of *Nervenfieber* (nerve fever).

NOVEMBER 17

Schubert weak but lucid. Towards evening delirious.

NOVEMBER 19, 3 P.M.

Schubert dies.

"It is enough," he said. "Go, children of the Lenape; the anger of the Manitto is not done. Why should Tamenund stay? The palefaces are masters of the earth, and the time of the red men has not yet come again. My day has been too long. In the morning I saw the sons of Unamis happy and strong; and yet, before the night has come, have I lived to see the last warrior of the wise race of the Mohicans."

| **21** |

DAS WIRTSHAUS

THE INN

Auf einen Totenacker
Hat mich mein Weg gebracht.
Allhier will ich einkehren:
Hab' ich bei mir gedacht.

Ihr grünen Totenkränze
Könnt wohl die Zeichen sein,
Die müde Wandrer laden
In's kühle Wirtshaus ein.

Sind denn in diesem Hause
Die Kammern all' besetzt?
Bin matt zum Niedersinken,
Bin tödlich schwer verletzt.

O unbarmherz'ge Schenke,
Doch weisest du mich ab?
Nun weiter denn, nur weiter,
Mein treuer Wanderstab!

To a graveyard
My journey has brought me.
I'll turn in here,
I thought to myself.

You green funeral wreaths
Could well be the signs
That invite tired wanderers
Into the cool inn.

Are in this house, then,
The rooms all taken?
I'm tired enough to collapse,
I am wounded even unto death.

O unmerciful inn,
You nonetheless turn me away?
On then now, only onwards,
My trusty wandering staff.

Franz Lachner, Schubert, and Eduard von Bauernfeld at Grinzing.

Pen and ink drawing by Moritz von Schwind, 1862

*I*LL AS HE WAS, periods of remission gave Schubert the opportunity to forget his sorrows with his friends. "Schubert is back," Bauernfeld wrote in his diary in October 1825. "Inn and coffee-house gathering with friends, often until two or three in the morning.

> *Wirtshaus, wir schämen uns,*
> *Hat uns ergötzt;*
> *Faulheit, wir grämen uns,*
> *Hat uns geletzt.*

The inn, we're ashamed to say, has delighted us; laziness, we're sorry to say, has refreshed us.

In the notes on Schubert which Bauernfeld wrote in 1869, he gives us a more circumstantial account of a trip to Grinzing (see picture opposite) which paints Schubert in his element:

It was a summer's afternoon and, with Franz Lachner [the composer] and others, we had strolled over
to Grinzing for the "Heurige" [new wine], to which
Schubert was especially partial, though I was quite
unable to acquire a taste for its acute tartness. We sat
over our wine, indulging in lively conversation, and it
was not until the dusk of the evening that we walked
back; I wanted to go straight home, as I was living in
an outlying suburb at that time, but Schubert dragged
me forcibly to an inn and I was not even spared the
coffee-house afterwards, at which he was in the habit
of winding up the evening, or rather the late hours of
the night. It was already one o'clock and an extremely
lively musical discussion had arisen over the hot
punch. Schubert emptied glass after glass and had
reached a sort of elated state in which, more eloquent
than usual, he was expounding . . . all his plans for the
future.

W. G. SEBALD, in a deft analysis of the opening of Franz
Kafka's last, unfinished novel *The Castle*, identifies its
mise-en-scène as falling into that mediaeval tradition
within which the dead assemble in an inn before descending into Hell. The Devil's tavern is the last stage on the
journey of the dead, on the borderland between two
worlds—hence one name by which it is known, the *Grenz-*

wirtshaus auf dem Passübergang ins Jenseits (the border inn
on the crossing pass into the beyond). "Das Wirtshaus"
plays with the same images, and the music which Schubert
then invents for this cemetery scene can be imagined
as a funeral march. The key is major, the tune is broad
and hymnlike, resembling the Kyrie of the Gregorian
Requiem, which would have been familiar to Schubert
from his schooldays and experience as an organist, and
which he paraphrased in the first movement (in the same
F major as this song) of his German Mass, D. 872,
written in 1827. The piano writing moves in blocks of
chords, evoking the rich and closely spaced harmonies
of music composed for brass ensemble. Another tradition
is summoned up, a specifically Austrian one, that of the
Aequalen, short and solemn pieces composed mostly for
trombone quartet and played before, during, or after the
obsequies. Beethoven wrote three such pieces for the All
Souls' Day ceremonies at Linz in 1812. They were performed in a version for male-voice quartet at Beethoven's
funeral, which Schubert attended as a torchbearer in
March 1827. Here, it is as if the wanderer has stumbled
upon his own funeral.

SOME DETAILS:
The piano introduction has a wonderful Schubertian
use of a conventional figure, a turn whose dissoci-

ated and energy-less execution—anything but a mere decoration—speaks of the desire to stop, just to stop.

The song is marked "sehr langsam," very slow, and slow it should be, so slow that the sentences have to be broken up.

The literary usage "allhier," which simply means "here," is beautifully exploited by Schubert's setting, as the pitch on "all," with its bright vowel, settles tiredly onto that of "hier," with its expressively languorous diphthong.

Green wreaths were to be found at the entrances to inns as well as on coffins. They provide the pretext for the extended fantasy of graveyard as public house.

In the second verse Schubert uses another ecclesiastical colour to sublime effect, as the piano sings, above the voice, a descant, an imaginary high trumpet part. This moment invites intent listening on the part of the singer, as he or she becomes an accompaniment and moves into the background: an exquisite rendering of the longing to sink into nothingness as well as an echo of ecclesiastical ceremonial.

"Sind denn in diesem Hause / Die Kammern all' besetzt?" asks the wanderer—Are all the rooms in this house taken? And at this moment the voice feebly stretches up as high as it will do in this song, to an F on the word "matt" (weary, feeble, subdued, faint), which is to be sung with a lingering exhaustion which then carries it down for the rest of the phrase—"Bin matt zum Niedersinken, / Bin tödlich schwer verletzt" (I'm tired enough to collapse, / I am wounded even unto death).

The imaginative space that a singer creates enhances the performance of song. The audience has no set or props to engage with—only the music, the instrument, the bodies of the performers, the face of the singer. Contrariwise, the singer has the auditorium into which he or she directs the force of a performance, and from which he or she drinks in an atmosphere. By reimagining that space—as vast or intimate, forested or bare, with castle walls, a river bank, the deck of a ship—a song is intensified, lived, and projected. Space comes alive for performer and audience alike. At this moment in *Winterreise* we enter the cemetery, a confrontation as sombre and intimate as art can manage, one prefigured in this cycle by that ambiguous, repeated question from an earlier song, "Der greise Kopf"—"How far is it to the grave?" The impropriety of addressing that question to another human being is matched here by the imaginarium within which each of the members of the audience in "Das Wirtshaus" has become, for the wanderer, a fantastical tomb. He longs to join them.

| *425*

He cannot.

The song ends with a heroic return to the opening music, a heroism which turns into the bravado of the next song.

| 22 |

MUT

COURAGE

Fliegt der Schnee mir in's Gesicht,
Schüttl' ich ihn herunter.
Wenn mein Herz im Busen spricht,
Sing' ich hell und munter.

Höre nicht, was es mir sagt,
Habe keine Ohren,
Fühle nicht, was es mir klagt,
Klagen ist für Toren.

Lustig in die Welt hinein
Gegen Wind und Wetter!
Will kein Gott auf Erden sein,
Sind wir selber Götter!

If the snow flies into my face
I shake it off.
If my heart speaks in my breast,
I sing bright and lively.

I don't hear what it says to me,
I have no ears;
I don't feel its moaning,
That's just for idiots.

Cheerfully out into the world
Against the wind and the weather!
If there's no God on earth,
We're gods ourselves!

Memorial to Friedrich Nietzsche in the city of his death, Turin

God is dead. God remains dead. And we have killed him. Yet his shadow still looms. How shall we comfort ourselves, the murderers of all murderers? What was holiest and mightiest of all that the world has yet owned has bled to death under our knives: who will wipe this blood off us? What water is there for us to clean ourselves? What festivals of atonement, what sacred games shall we have to invent? Is not the greatness of this deed too great for us? Must we ourselves not become gods simply to appear worthy of it?

—NIETZSCHE, *The Gay Science*, 1882

*O*NE OF MY VERY EARLIEST professional performances of *Winterreise* (though I don't think it was a paid gig) took place in the Conway Hall in the mid-1990s. Career-wise it was a very important event for me, if only in retrospect. Peter Alward, legendary A-and-R man at EMI Classics—my recording home for many years—came along to listen, and offered me the first of a long series of collaborations on the basis of what he heard and saw. It was under Peter's aegis that I was to record *Winterreise* with Leif Ove Andsnes in 2006.

At the time, performing this particular cycle in this particular hall was especially piquant, it seemed to me, because of the history and nature of the building itself. Conway Hall—25 Red Lion Square, right in the centre of London, a stone's throw from the British Museum and the Inns of Court—had been since 1928 the seat of the South Place Ethical Society (renamed the Conway Hall Ethical Society in 2012). It claims to be the oldest organisation in the world devoted to the promotion of free thought, having grown out of a dissident nonconformist congregation which refused to subscribe to the orthodox doctrines of hellfire and eternal punishment. This group acquired premises in Bishopsgate in 1793, a dangerous year for radicalism, as a reactionary British government began to clamp down on anything that smacked of French free-thinking and the horror of revolution (habeas corpus was suspended the following year). By 1817, the congregation had become Unitarian and appointed William Johnson Fox as minister; under his leadership, a chapel was built in South Place in Finsbury. Fox was editor of the journal of the Unitarian Association, the *Monthly Repository,* whose list of contributors reads like a who's who of Victorian cultural life: Tennyson, Browning, John Stuart Mill, Harriet Martineau, Leigh Hunt, Henry Crabb Robinson. It was under the leadership of Stanton Coit, in 1888, that the South Place Religious Society became the South Place Ethical Society. Coit, an American, was a disciple of Felix Adler, founder of the Ethical Culture movement in 1876, which was to become the American Ethical Union in 1889. The South Place Ethical Society retained what one writer has characterised as a "somewhat religious tone" well into the twentieth century, but actual belief in God was no longer on the agenda. The driving force behind the ethical society movement, in England as in the States, was opposition to dogmatic doctrinal assumptions and a challenge to the idea that only religious people could be properly moral. The ethical core of religion might be retained and even refurbished, stripped of the superstitious and irrational penumbra which surrounded it: if there's no God on Earth, we're gods ourselves.

Hazy memories had convinced me that I had performed *Winterreise* on a Conway Hall stage whose proscenium arch bore the motto "There is no God." What is written is, in fact, the Shakespearian nostrum "To thine own self be true." There are hidden ironies here—the phrase is delivered by the fussy old bore Polonius in the course of a longwinded and platitudinous speech of advice to his son, Laertes, as he prepares to leave Elsinore for Paris—but the ideological thrust remains essentially humanistic. We can rely on ourselves.

SCHUBERT WAS BORN IN 1797, just as the intellectual and institutional antecedents of the South Place Ethical Society were beginning their long march from heterodoxy to humanism. He lived his life in a period of intense and intensifying crisis for the nature of religious belief. Bienpensant philosophers in the eighteenth century had moved away from the certainties of revealed religion to a view of the divine grounded in the works of nature, a deism rather than a theism, and one guaranteed by the argument from design. By the beginning of the nineteenth century, study of the Earth was undermining biblical chronology, establishing a notion of deep time which would eventually enable Darwin's devastating blow against teleology and the old doctrines of creation as well as the argument from design.

Established religion suffered attacks in the 1790s by secular-minded, deistic, and even atheistic revolutionaries; but the final victory of the allied powers in 1815 resulted in the domination of European politics and diplomatic relations by a Holy Alliance of Catholic Austria, Orthodox Russia, and Protestant Prussia, whose founding treaty spoke explicitly "in the name of the Most Holy and Indivisible Trinity," and which was to base its policies upon "the sublime truths which the Holy Religion of our Saviour teaches." Radical religion and natural religion were alike condemned. The clock was to be turned back; only by restoring the old religious values were crown and people to achieve the security they yearned for and deserved. It was under the shadow of this precarious restoration that Schubert lived and wrote.

Schubert's own upbringing was conventionally religious. The son of a schoolmaster, he was educated at the Stadtkonvikt, or Imperial Seminary, as a choirboy, and played the organ in his local church. He wrote a slew of

religious works: most obviously his six liturgical masses,
but also, among other pieces, the German Mass to words
by Johann Philipp Neumann, who commissioned it;
four Kyries; five Salve Reginas; two Stabat Maters; five
Tantum ergos; a "Hymn to the Holy Ghost"; as well as his
unfinished oratorio *Lazarus*. Among the songs, there are
expressions of the profoundest Catholic piety. Schubert
lost his mother at the age of fifteen and, unsurprisingly,
Mary the mother of God makes several appearances in
songs ranging from the celebrated "Ave Maria" of 1825
(actually a setting of verses from Walter Scott's *Lady of the
Lake*, entitled "Ellens Dritter Gesang" —Ellen's Third
Song—on its original publication) to the less-well-known
but exquisite "Vom Mitleiden Mariä" (Of Mary's Compassion) of 1818. Taking a few other songs at random, one
might cite the famous "Litanei" (1816), a litany for the
Feast of All Souls, or the marvellous "Abendbilder"
(Evening Pictures, 1819), which ends with a vision of resurrection to eternal bliss. "Pax Vobiscum" by Schubert's
friend Schober (1817)—a man so often depicted as irrever-
ent and wild—is more interesting in its effort to reconcile
the modish quasi-pantheism at work in so much Schubert
song with a more orthodox inflection. It moves from a
celebration of the holy martyrs to the return of spring to
the beauty of nature, mediated by the repeated refrain
"Peace be with you" and the varied last lines of each

strophe—"I believe in you, great God . . . My hopes are
in you, powerful God . . . I love you, God of goodness!"

Schubert was a professional composer, living in a
devout society, and it is difficult to imagine that any
"classical" composer—well into the twentieth century
and perhaps beyond—would not have become involved
in the composition of sacred music. It has always been
a central task for the composer, and a central challenge,
regardless of personal beliefs—Gabriel Fauré, Giuseppe
Verdi, Benjamin Britten, John Tavener . . . Four of
Schubert's mass settings cluster around the years 1814–16,
three of them written for performance in his family's local
parish church. The fifth was written between November
1819 and the beginning of 1823, the sixth and last in 1828.
The first four, clustered together, might be viewed as the
outpourings of a naïve religious heart, as well as a special
tribute to Therese Grob, Schubert's preferred soprano
soloist. The passionate subjectivity of the fifth and the
solemn dark style of the sixth seem to reflect less a composer in search of a court or church position than an artist
seeking to rival the great masters of the past, using traditional forms to forge a new musical language, one which
greatly influenced later composers such as Bruckner. Yet,
overall, all six masses bear tantalisingly on our notions of
Schubert's religious understanding, since they consistently
and crucially omit the lines from the Creed which com-

mit the believer to the Catholic Church and a belief in the resurrection of the dead.

Musical analysis which seeks to forge a connection between inspiration and dogma—this section of the mass is better than that because Schubert's faith was engaged, and vice versa—seems unconvincing to me. Likewise, it would be unwise to judge Schubert's commitment to the content of any of the religious poems he set to music by the success or otherwise of the end product. It may seem reasonable to view Schubert's vast corpus of songs as a sort of diary, reflecting his interests and, up to a point, his sentiments. Sometimes, though, a song may have been composed to flatter or please a friend or acquaintance. In the case of the settings of words by the powerful church-man and patriarch of Venice, Johann Ladislaus Pyrker, this may have been more a case of cosying up to a possible patron/customer than of any singular consonance between Schubert's world view and that of Pyrker; his dedication of his op. 4 set of songs to the ambitious and reactionary cleric was surely intended in this spirit ("The Patriarch was good for 12 ducats," Schubert wrote to Spaun). Nevertheless, the resulting masterpiece, "Die Allmacht" (Omnipotence), is a superb expression of the sort of pantheistic afflatus which in all likelihood inspired the mood of the "Great" C major Symphony, written, like "Die Allmacht," in the midst of the majestic scenery

| 437

of Bad Gastein, where Schubert encountered Pyrker in the late summer of 1825. The song's pantheism is strictly orthodox, though, straight from the pen of the most conformist of clergymen.

On the subject of Schubert's religious constitution, it would seem best to consider him, as Keats considered Shakespeare, as an artist with a supreme capacity for what the English poet called "negative capability":

> that is, when a man is capable of being in uncertainties, mysteries, doubts, without any irritable reaching after fact and reason.

Schubert's songs, or even his religious works, do not express a reasoned theological standpoint; rather, they explore the modes and emotional force fields of the religious sensibility, from the most conventional or even hackneyed, to the mystical reveries of a poet-philosopher like Novalis. They are imaginative embodiments of differing apprehensions of the numinous, the spiritual, the divine.

So much for Schubert as an artist; as a man, it may have been his own lack of fixed conviction that enabled him to avoid that "irritable reaching after fact and reason." He could leave out bits of the mass he dissented from, but here he is, writing in more conventional mode to his father and stepmother in 1825:

My new songs from Walter Scott's *Lady of the Lake* in
particular had a great success. There was a good deal
of surprise too at my piety, which found expression in
a Hymn to the Blessed Virgin, which seems to have
moved all hearts and created quite a devotional atmosphere. I fancy that is because my religious feeling is
never forced, and I never compose hymns or prayers of
this sort unless I am involuntarily overcome by a sense
of devotion, and then the feeling is, as a rule, genuine
and heartfelt.

| *439*

This seems too discursive and detailed to be mere cant
for the benefit of a sometimes disapproving father. Yet, in
January 1827, a friend joshingly started a letter with the
incipit phrase from the Creed, "Credo in unum Deum,"
adding, "Not you, I know well enough, but you will
believe. . . ." In the lost diary for 1824, on the other hand,
religious orthodoxy seems to be in the ascendant:

28TH MARCH

Man comes into the world armed with faith, which is far
superior to knowledge and understanding: for in order
to understand a thing one must first of all believe in it.

A day later, he longed to be "safeguarded from so-called
enlightenment, that hideous skeleton without blood or
flesh."

. . .

WHAT, THEN, TO MAKE OF "Mut" and its battle hymn
of the unbeliever? First of all, we should note that this
is the only point in the second half of the cycle at which
Schubert moved away from simply composing Müller's
extra poems in the order in which he found them. Müller's
final order in 1824, in the complete *Die Winterreise*, made
"Mut" the penultimate poem. Following his normal practice, Schubert should have moved from "Das Wirtshaus"
to "Die Nebensonnen" to "Mut"; instead he swapped
"Mut" and "Nebensonnen" around. Why? My hunch is
that it was not only in order to unleash a burst of energy
between two slow songs, but also to encase and enfold the
brute heterodoxy of "Mut" between the religious sonorities of the preceding and succeeding songs. This lends its
outrageous defiance all the more power. Furthermore, a
fragment of what one might call narrativity is enhanced as
the rejection by the inn of death and the determination to
carry on whatever is succeeded by this bold outburst.

That suspension between two oases of instrumental
brass sonority is a fragile one. It is unclear where reality
bites. The pervading irony of *Winterreise*, and Schubert's
negative capability, will not allow us to decide one way
or the other. We cannot accept the wanderer's view of
a godless world in "Mut" at face value; neither can we

receive the benediction of those ecclesiastical sound
worlds which glow before and after without questioning
them. The issues raised by Müller's words and Schubert's
sounds dramatise the predicament of the human being
alone in the world, searching for meaning, whether it be in
the bosom of Abraham or within the human community
standing proudly self-sufficient (note how, for the first
time, the wanderer here sings about "we," identifying, if
only momentarily, with others). Schubert is experiment-
ing with a world in which not only love, but God and
meaning, are lost. This world is cold and empty, a winter's
journey beyond the frozen rivers and desolate landscapes,
the snow and the ice. It becomes then an anticipatory echo
of Nietzsche's anxious positing of the death of God—if we
accept His passing and the emptiness of the world, what
will become of us? Can we do more than mourn?

RELIGIOUS REFERENCES, musical and textual, are sprin-
kled through *Winterreise*, and were surely picked up by
contemporaries. They must have been received by them
as unsettling in their equivocation between satire and
fugitive consolation. A review of the cycle in the Leipzig
Allgemeinen musikalischen Zeitung for October 1829
notices, but is disconcerted by, the strange dislocation in
the very first song, "Gute Nacht," voicing dissatisfaction

that the music which very comfortably and appropriately accompanies and illustrates the notion of girls and mothers and marriage and moonbeams seems by the third verse ill suited to the notion of "Die Liebe liebt das Wandern, / Gott hat sie so gemacht" (Love loves wandering, / God made it so), these "truly blasphemous words," as the critic calls them, which bitterly anticipate the noisy blasphemy of "Mut." "A certain vulgarity of the melody," he writes, "allied to a sort of joyfulness seems to spill over into mockery." This was surely and brilliantly Schubert's intention, one of the fortuitous mismatches which strophic song can deliver to the cunning composer.

MÜLLER'S POEM IS CALLED "Mut!": note the exclamation mark. When Schubert set the songs "Halt!" (Halt!) and "Mein!" (Mine!) from *Die schöne Müllerin* (The Beautiful Miller Girl), he retained the emphatic punctuation; here he removes it, perhaps to suggest the illusoriness of this bravado, to underline the hollowness and sarcasm of it all. If "Mut" is the first song in which the plural first-person pronoun is adopted by the wanderer, it is also the first in which he actually tells us that he sings. If we accept this at face value, then the third verse of "Mut" is the very ditty which the singer bellows into the wind and snow, one which reaches a climax of hysteria in the piano just before the last vocal phrase. Here, the span from the lowest to the highest note, from left hand to right hand, achieves an unprecedented four octaves, shrieking at the very top of its percussive voice. Before this we have heard what sounds like crazed wedding bells ringing in the piano, replying solo to the opening vocal assault—more ecclesiastical tail-tweaking—and its companion military motif, a trumpet fanfare which replies to the last vocal phrase, which itself stretches up to a high A in the key of Schubert's manuscript version. The song ends with a repetition of the piano introduction, its two strong crotchet accents in the last bar drawing a firm and definitive line under all the extravagance that has gone before, allowing us to enter into the very different world of "Die Nebensonnen."

| 23 |

DIE NEBENSONNEN

THE MOCK SUNS

Drei Sonnen sah ich am Himmel stehn,
Hab' lang und fest sie angesehn;
Und sie auch standen da so stier,
Als wollten sie nicht weg von mir.
Ach, meine Sonnen seid ihr nicht!
Schaut Andern doch in's Angesicht!
Ja, neulich hatt' ich auch wohl drei:
Nun sind hinab die besten zwei.
Ging' nur die dritt' erst hinterdrein!
Im Dunkeln wird mir wohler sein.

I saw three suns standing in the sky,
I stared at them long and hard;
And they stood there, too, so fixed,
As if they didn't want to leave me.
Oh, you're not my suns!
Look into others' faces!
Indeed I did have three, just a while ago:
But now the best two have gone down.
If only the third would go too!
I'd be better off in the dark.

| 447

Sun dogs, Fargo, North Dakota (2009)

Following three pages: Letter to the Philosophical Transactions

of the Royal Society, 1735

52

IX. *A* Letter *from the Rev^d Mr.* Timothy
Neve, *Secretary of the* Gentlemen's Society *at* Peterborourg, *to* C. Mortimer, *Secr.
R. S. containing his* Obſervations *of two*
Parhelia, *or* Mock-Suns, *ſeen* Dec. 30,
1735. *and of an* Aurora Borealis, Dec.
11, 1735.

S I R,

I Send you an Account of two *Phænomena* which
I lately ſaw : The firſt was on *Tueſday* the 30th
of *December* paſt, as I was riding betwixt *Cherry
Orton* and *Alwalton* in the County of *Huntingdon,*
I obſerved two *Parhelia,* the firſt of which ſhone ſo
bright, that at firſt Sight I took it for the real Sun, till
looking a little farther on my left Hand, I was convinced of my Miſtake, by ſeeing the true Sun much
the brighteſt in the Middle, and a *Mock-Sun* on each
Side, in a Line exactly parallel to the Horizon. I
gueſſed their Diſtance to be about 40 Diameters of
the Sun, or, as they uſually appear, 23 Degrees. That
on the left Hand of the Sun, when I ſaw it firſt, was
ſmall and faint, but in about two Minutes time became as large and bright as the other, and appear'd at
once as two white lucid Spots on each Side the Sun,
Eaſt and Weſt, ſeemingly as big, but not ſo well de-
fin'd : In about three Minutes they loſt both their Colour and Form, and put on thoſe of the Rainbow ;
the Red and Yellow in both very beautiful and ſtrong
neareſt to the Sun, the other Colours fainter. They became

came as two Parts of an Arch, or Segment of a Circle, with the Concave towards the Sun, only round at Top, the Light and Colours streaming downwards, and tending towards a Point below. This continued for about four or five Minutes, when the Colours gradually disappearing, they became, as before two lucid Spots, without any Distinction of Colours. They lasted a full Hour, sometimes one brighter, and sometimes the other, according to the Variation of the Clouds and Air, as I supppose. When I first saw it, it was exactly a Quarter after Eleven. There had been a Frost in the Morning, which went away pretty soon with a thick Mist, and between 10 and 11 o'Clock clear'd up, leaving only a Haziness in the Air behind it: The Weather quite calm, Wind, as I thought, N. W.

These *Parhelia* commonly are seen with a Circle or Halo round the Sun, concentrical to it, and passing through the Disks of the spurious or *Mock-Suns*. But there was not the least Appearance of such a Circle here, it having only a Tendency towards one, when it was seen with the Rainbow Colours.

The other Phænomenon was that pretty common one of the *Aurora Borealis*, of which though you have so many exact and curious Accounts in your learned *Transactions*, yet I do not remember any one in the Manner I saw this of the 11th past. A little after five o'Clock, I observ'd the Northern Hemisphere to be obscured by a dusky red Vapour, in which, by Degrees, appear'd several very small black Clouds near the Horizon. I thought it seem'd to be a Preparation for those Lights which afterwards were seen; the first Eruption of which was within a Quar-

ter

ter of an Hour, full East, from behind one of the small
dark Clouds, and soon after several others full North.
These Streams of Light were of the same dusky red
Colour as the Vapour, just appear'd, and vanish'd in-
stantly. I saw eight or ten of these at once, about the
Breadth of the Rainbow, of different Heights, several
Degrees above the Horizon, and look'd like so many
red Pillars in the Air; and no sooner did they disappear, but others shew'd themselves in different Places.
In about half an Hour, this Colour of the Vapour gradually chang'd itself towards the usual White, and
spread itself much wider and higher; and after that, appear'd as common.   *I am, S I R*,

Peterborourg,   *Your most obedient*
Jan. 29, 1735-6.   *humble Servant,*

                                        Tim. Neve.

NEBENSONNEN—LITERALLY "besides suns," in the sense of extra, or parallel—have several names in English: mock suns, phantom suns, sun dogs (they dog or follow the sun), or the scientific-sounding "parhelia" (from the Greek *para*, next to, *helia*, suns).

Parhelia form as light is refracted through hexagonal-plate ice crystals which form high up in cirrus clouds. These prismatic crystals drift and float gradually downwards. Their faces are large and six-sided (see opposite page) and they lie almost horizontal as they descend. Sunlight enters one side (the thick yellow arrows) and emerges through another (the broken lines with yellow converging on the eye of the observer). From the observer's perspective, extrapolating the refracted ray back in a straight line (the broken black line)—just as happens when a spoon looks bent in a glass of water—the two characteristic images of the sun can then be seen on each side of the sun, as long as it is near the horizon and on the same horizontal

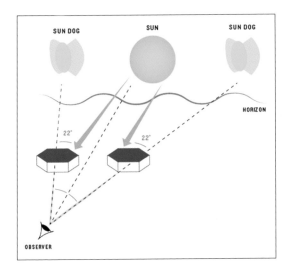

plane as the observer and the crystals. Since red light is refracted less than blue, the sides of the parhelia nearest the sun are tinted red. Rays passing through similar crystals in other ways create other sorts of halos.

PARHELIA HAVE BEEN A SUBJECT for philosophical comment since antiquity. Aristotle in his *Meteorology* writes of two which "rose with the sun and followed it all through the day until sunset," a beautiful conceit. The first approach to the modern scientific explanation emerged towards the end of the ingenious seventeenth century, in

France. René Descartes had mooted the bizarre mecha-
nism of a giant ring of ice in the sky, in his *Meteorology*
of 1637; but the correct explanation was arrived at by the
less celebrated Edme Mariotte, who published his *Essais
de Physique* between 1679 and 1681. The fourth treats of
colour both physically and physiologically, building on
the work of Newton and other savants (though Newton's
Opticks were not published until 1704), explaining optical
phenomena such as halos and parhelia in terms of refrac-
tion and reflection effected in the atmosphere by prismatic
ice crystals and water vapour. Some further advances were
made in explaining parhelia within Schubert and Müller's
lifetimes: the Englishman Thomas Young (one of the for-
mulators of the wave theory of light) in 1807, and the Italian Giambattista Venturi in 1814. The complete modern
theory was not laid out until 1845, when Auguste Bravais
published a paper in the *Journal de L'Ecole polytechnique*,
"Notice sur les parhélies à la même hauteur que le soleil"
(Note on Parhelia at the Same Altitude as the Sun).

MÜLLER'S USE OF MOCK SUNS as an image in this poem
reflects the intense Romantic fascination with such optical
phenomena. C. J. Wright, in an article for the *Journal of
the Warburg and Courtauld Institutes* published in 1980,
anatomises the popular vogue for halos and such like:

454 |

The journals, literary and political as well as scientific, were eager to print articles and correspondence on optical phenomena of all kinds. Whether it was a solar halo and parhelion lasting three-quarters of an hour seen between two and three at York, four parhelia seen between two and four at Arbroath, a circular ring seen round the sun at Greenwich, the rose-pink, light green and blue-grey colour of the sun viewed from Colombia over a period of two months, lunar haloes exhibiting the colours of the spectrum, the inversion of views along the Firth of Forth, or a large opening sighted in mountains near Baffin Bay due to the apparent junction of their peaks, the public was demonstrably interested.

One reason for this fascination was the lack of an adequate or agreed explanation. Mariotte's work had fallen into obscurity, and as yet no clear understanding of the relationship between air, water, and light in the atmosphere had emerged. New theories, even of the familiar rainbow, were being canvassed. The effect of the differing refractive indices of air at different temperatures was only now being grappled with, as was the phenomenon of the polarisation of light (in which light waves oscillate in a single plane).

The rainbow had had a theological significance since

time immemorial, as the seal of God's covenant with
man after the Flood. Other optical effects had something
equally uncanny, if less consoling, about them, despite the
efforts of "cold philosophy," as Keats put it, to "clip [the]
Angel's wings." Aside from the rainbow and the parhelion, the so-called "glory"—a body or a shadow surrounded by a halo—was especially potent in the Romantic
imaginings: Keats's Madeline in his *Eve of St Agnes* has
"on her hair a glory, like a saint." The most notorious
of these apparitions in real life was the "Spectre of the
Brocken," the Brocken being the highest peak of the Harz
Mountains, notorious haunt of witches and sprites, and
memorialised as such in Goethe's *Faust*. Wanderers on the
mountain reported observing a vast and shadowy figure
which would spookily move about and mimic their own
gestures. Coleridge made two, unsuccessful, attempts
to get a look at it in 1799. The phantom, still observable
today, is in fact just that: a haze or mist or cloud whose
constituent water droplets reflect images projected by
the sun, swollen to enormous apparent size by tricks of
perspective. The Spectre of the Brocken is, then, "but a
reflex of yourself," as de Quincey put it in his *Suspiria de
Profundis* (1845), making paradoxical Romantic use of the
scientific explanation by suggesting that "in uttering your
secret feelings to him, you make this phantom the dark
symbolic mirror for reflecting to the daylight what must

be forever hidden." This Doppelgänger (the title of one of Schubert's most famous late songs, to a text by Heinrich Heine), this "Dark Interpreter," mirrors and reveals our secret desires. Apparent objectivity is subjectivised: just like the mock suns, the Spectre of the Brocken may have a physical explanation grounded in optics and atmospheric science, but it retains its occult power as a subjective projection. Müller's poem further reflects this porousness of the boundary between the objective and the subjective, the feeling and the unfeeling, the living and the unliving, by employing the so-called pathetic fallacy, in having the wanderer fancy that, unlike the girl, the mock suns did not want to leave him.

BY CHOOSING A MYSTERIOUS ice-refracted optical phenomenon, first cousin to the Spectre of the Brocken and the rainbow, as a staging post on the wanderer's winter journey, Müller thus nods at a recognised Romantic trope. He also reaches out to the ice flowers of "Frühlingstraum" (the next poem in the final version of the poetic cycle)—mock suns are conjured into existence by ice crystals—and to the illusory lights of both "Täuschung" (Deception) and "*Das* Irrlicht" (*The* Will-o'-the-Wisp— Müller's original title). The wanderer's poetic universe is suspended between the alive and the only apparently alive; between the real and the imaginary; the objective and the subjective; between the natural and the supernatural. Schubert places this song cheek-by-jowl with another which seems to celebrate God's absence from the world ("Mut" or "courage"), and he cloaks it in music of sublime religiosity—with those brass sonorities and that same hymnic quality which we heard at work in "Das Wirtshaus" (The Inn). He thus intensifies the aura which hangs about Müller's parhelion, dramatising the Romantic equivocation between the desire for truth and the hunger for mystery. The power of the music in this song is itself mysterious and numinous, in seeming contradiction to the wanderer's sturdy denial of divinity in "Mut"; but the phenomenon in which it is grounded was on the very cusp of demystification and rational scrutiny.

IN 1849, ELLEN NUSSEY, Charlotte Brontë's best friend, made this laconic entry in her diary: "[July] Saw 2 suns of Haworth Moor 1847." Recalling the same event for a biography of Emily Brontë some thirty years later, the slim anecdote had become a full-blown piece of the Brontë myth—an echo of the Romantic poetic from which both Wilhelm Müller and, later in time, the Brontë sisters had emerged; a confirmation of their status as literary legends:

Once, at this time, when they were walking on the
moor together, a sudden change and light came into
the sky. "Look," said Charlotte; and the four girls
looked up and saw three suns shining clearly overhead.
They stood a little while silently gazing at the beautiful
parhelion; Charlotte, her friend, and Anne clustered
together, Emily a little higher, standing on a heathery
knoll. "That is you!" said Ellen at last. "You are the
three suns." "Hush!" cried Charlotte, indignant at the
too shrewd nonsense of her friend; but as Ellen, her
suspicions confirmed by Charlotte's violence, low-
ered her eyes to the earth again, she looked a moment
at Emily. She was still standing on her knoll, quiet,
satisfied; and round her lips there hovered a very soft
and happy smile. She was not angry, the independent
Emily. She had liked the little speech.

THE MYSTERY OF MÜLLER'S POEM, much commented
on—what are the three suns?—is at one and the same
time all mystery and no mystery at all. The wanderer's
three suns are the girl's eyes and the sun itself. He has
lost his love and would be better off dead. That is the
bald and clumsy reading of the image. Its very baldness,
though, its slight clunkiness, which may be a fault in

Müller's poetry, is what makes us seek for more, for deeper significance, which is its virtue here. We are helped first of all by Schubert's having inadvertently removed the poem from proximity to "Frühlingstraum" and its close emotional connection to the loss of love—"Wann halt' ich mein Liebchen im Arm?"—When will I hold my lovely one in my arms? By now, in Schubert's cycle, we are far away from such warm longing. Draped in music of such otherworldly affect, we cannot but feel that all these suns, metaphorical and otherwise, represent something inscrutable the wanderer has lost—much more than an unhappy love affair—and which leaves him fit only for the etiolated nonmusic of the next and last song. And that last line, "Im Dunkeln wird mir wohler sein"—it'll be better for me in the dark—has a wonderful poetic complexity and cadence.

DER LEIERMANN

THE HURDY-GURDY MAN

Drüben hinter'm Dorfe
Steht ein Leiermann,
Und mit starren Fingern
Dreht er was er kann.

Barfuß auf dem Eise
Wankt er hin und her;
Und sein kleiner Teller
Bleibt ihm immer leer.

Keiner mag ihn hören,
Keiner sieht ihn an;
Und die Hunde knurren
Um den alten Mann.

Und er läßt es gehen
Alles, wie es will,
Dreht, und seine Leier
Steht ihm nimmer still.

Wunderlicher Alter,
Soll ich mit dir gehn?
Willst ʒu meinen Liedern
Deine Leier drehn?

Der Leiermann · The Hurdy-Gurdy Man

Over there behind the village
Stands a hurdy-gurdy man,
And with numb fingers
He grinds away, as best he can.

Barefoot on the ice
He sways back and forth,
And his little plate
Remains always empty.

No-one wants to hear him,
No-one looks at him,
And the dogs growl
Around the old man.

And he lets it go on,
Everything, just as it will;
Turns the wheel, and his hurdy-gurdy
Never stays still for a moment.

Strange old man,
Should I go with you?
Will you to my songs
Play your hurdy-gurdy?

May ten thousand devils take all folklore! Here I am in Wales and oh how unlovely, a harpist sits in the lobby of every man of repute playing so-called folk melodies at you—that is to say, dreadful, vulgar, out-of-tune trash and simultaneously a hurdy-gurdy is tootling out melodies, it's enough to drive one crazy.

—FELIX MENDELSSOHN (1829)

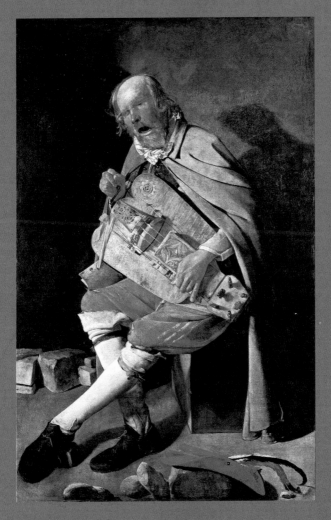

Georges de la Tour, Le Vielleur, *c. 1631–6*

*T*HERE IS A ROMANTIC IRONY embedded in the very title of this poem. The *Leier* in German, or lyre in English, was the most Romantic of instruments. When Schubert's friend Theodor Körner had a posthumous collection of his poems published by his father in 1814, after his death in battle, it was given a title which was meant to express the poles of his life and his poetic imagination: *Leyer und Schwerdt* (Lyre and Sword). One of Schubert's most famous songs, the "An die Leier" (To the Lyre) of Bruchmann (a translation of Anacreon), speaks to the poet's frustration at only being able to bend his lyre to gentle songs of love rather than songs of heroism and martial vigour. In another poem of Bruchmann's set by Schubert, "Der zürnende Barde" (The Angry Bard), the lyre is the very embodiment of mystical poetical power. The verses that Schubert set to create his *Lieder*—the poems which Wilhelm Müller wrote, and which he imagined transformed by music—these were

lyric poems, poems meant, in
fantasy at least, to be delivered
by a performer strumming a
lyre. Lyres were everywhere in
this period: embossed in gold
on the leather covers of the
commonplace books of teenage
girls; adorning innumerable
pieces of Biedermeier furniture
in respectable bourgeois estab-
lishments; and dignifying John
Keats's grave in the English
Cemetery in Rome.

So how fabulously apt it would have been to have
ended this cycle with a lyre song, how poignant, how
poetic, how decent. This, however, is no ordinary lyre;
or rather, it is an exceptionally ordinary and commonplace
lyre, no lyre at all but a vulgar, indecent hurdy-gurdy, a
Drehleier (a rotating or turning lyre), the chosen instrument of the musically unaccomplished beggar, the lowest
of the low.

The hurdy-gurdy is the fiddler's version of the bagpipe. The sound box can be that of a fiddle, a guitar, or
a lute, but the strings are neither plucked nor bowed.
Instead a wheel in the middle sets the strings vibrating
as it is turned by a crank at the end of the instrument.

This wooden wheel, coated in resin, acts as a sort of never-ending bow. The strings are of two types: the open strings, or drones, on either side of the sound box; and the melody strings, which are stopped by keys attached to rods, with projections which push against the string when pressed. A full scale is possible. The two melody strings are tuned in unison; the drones are tuned in octaves when there are only two of them, with the additional possibility of a fifth when there are more strings (that repeated fifth against which the etiolated melody is played in this song; with the characteristic sound of the drone starting under the pitch as the wheel gets going, something Schubert captures ingeniously with a grace note from below as the song sets off).

As a result, the hurdy-gurdy can be thought of as mechanised and dissociating—the perfect instrument for the expression of alienation, at the same time both modern and extremely ancient. For it is the wheel that actually does the work of sound creation, making the string vibrate, with the consequent loss over control of timbre or dynamics, and the associated lack of skill needed to play the instrument. Sound can be continuous, without breaks to pluck or bow; and the characteristic sound of the instrument, with its haunting and slightly exotic Asiatic aura, is that of the drone, a melody accompanied by an unvarying bass.

The hurdy-gurdy (without drone strings) first appeared in Europe in the tenth century and was known as the organistrum: we find it represented in high mediaeval art played by angels and mortals alike. By the time of the Thirty Years' War it had lost status and was usually described as a peasant instrument, often depicted in the hands of beggars or vagabonds. But in the same way as the bagpipe had started to appear in the fantastical pastoral entertainments of the French court, so too did the hurdy-gurdy, or *vielle à roue*, and elegant versions of the instrument can be seen in some of Watteau's *Fêtes champêtres*. We hear the drone effect at work in much pastoral music of the eighteenth century—in Handel's *Messiah* and *Acis and Galatea*, for example—but well before the end of the eighteenth century, the hurdy-gurdy and the bagpipe, the *vielle* and the musette, had returned to more insalubrious habitats, whose associations Müller draws on, mocking the poetic lyre with his clumsy *Leiermann*. It's a striking thought, nevertheless, that the "Pastoral" Symphony by Schubert's hero, Beethoven, starts up with a rustic melody played over a characteristic drone.

The old hurdy-gurdy, or *Drehleier,* was gradually replaced by the *Drehorgel* (wheel, or turning, organ) or barrel organ, in a process of transformation which left the vocabulary a little confused and overlapping. In English, hurdy-gurdy today often means a street organ. When Bertolt Brecht and Kurt Weill in their *Threepenny Opera* wanted to create an opera for beggars on the stage of a Berlin theatre in 1928, they launched it with a ballad sung in a cracked voice to the accompaniment of a *Leierkasten,* literally a lyre box or chest, actually a cheap street organ. I like to think of their ballad singer, whose "Ballad of Mack the Knife" I sometimes sing, as sinister first cousin to Schubert's *Leiermann*.

"DER LEIERMANN" is one of those magical, totemic pieces of music which seem to have a power and a resonance beyond all rational explanation. Somehow "dreadful, vulgar, out-of-tune trash," the sort of music which Mendelssohn later complained of, has been transformed into music of the utmost sublimity. It is, no doubt, partly a question of a song which is more anti-music than music and which comes at the end of seventy minutes of intense lyric utterance and vocal declamation. There's nothing to it, really: no flesh and all bare bones. Harmonically impoverished, it is largely composed of simple repetition. Like the "poor theatre" which the Polish theatre director Jerzy Grotowski advocated in the 1960s, Schubert gives us "poor music." There is nowhere for the singer to hide in this stark confrontation with emptiness.

I superstitiously try to avoid rehearsing this untouchable song. *Winterreise* is a piece which I know so well that one crucial aspect of preparatory rehearsal—the repetition which locks words and phrases into the back of the brain and the muscle memory—can usually be taken for granted. Nevertheless, the freedom which one ideally seeks in performance is best secured by running the piece through the night before singing in public, even with a pianist with whom one has performed the piece countless times. Yet, whoever I'm singing with, I bridle at singing "Der Leiermann" in rehearsal. It seems best to leave it out and await the inspiration of the moment of performance. It would surely be impertinent and unlucky to sing it outside the transformative context of actual reenactment, "the extreme occasion," as Edward Said called it.

·   ·   ·

THE SONG EXISTS IN TWO KEYS: B minor in the manuscript, A minor in the published version. Being a tenor, I
tend to opt for that original, higher version, as I do in the
rest of the cycle when alternatives are available. What's
more, the shift from the A major of the preceding song,
"The Mock Suns," to B minor seems more weird and
displaced and alienating than the more obvious kinship
between A major and A minor. I have often said to my
pianist collaborators, in the spirit of freedom or impro-
visation which I associate with the song, that they really
ought to choose the key in the moment, as the spirit moves
them. No-one has yet plumped for the lower key.

STYLES OF SINGING are convention-bound; they are
heard by listeners as "natural" or "mannered" only within
a context. The simple classical delivery of a folk song by
a "trained" voice may sound uptight and artificial to an
audience used to hearing "Barbara Allen" or "O Waly
Waly" in the nasal twang that has become associated with
an "authentic" folk voice. Crossing boundaries is perilous, and on the whole, opera singers sound as wrong in
pop music as pop singers do in German song. Prejudice is
at work here, and we are usually well advised to shed our
aesthetic prejudices; nevertheless, the mysterious constraints of style, so difficult to catalogue and so essential

(occasionally) to break, do crucial work in forming an engaged response to vocal music. We need the genres and subgenres of vocal music—classical, opera, "art song," Wagner, Puccini, rap, scat, soul, country—to sound different. At the same time, seepage across the boundaries, respectful borrowings, and outrageous thefts, do essential work in keeping any art form alive.

Admiring vocalism across the border—from Bob Dylan to Billie Holiday to Frank Sinatra—I have always thought that, in principle, one should be influenced by these extraordinary singers and their compelling way of bending melody to words and vice versa. Classical song and popular song should not be so far apart; they share a lot both in their subject matter and in their aesthetic of intimacy. Mostly, however, the influence has to be a subliminal one, for only then can it avoid self-consciousness or a certain archness. Doubtless, listening to popular music of all sorts can influence the singing of classical song; but we don't want it to be other than a subtle manoeuvre, barely conscious.

One of the rare times when I was conscious of somehow channeling another species of musical expression was in Moscow, at that same concert where I noticed an audience member in tears (see the chapter on "Frozen Tears"). I've often reimagined "Der Leiermann" as a sort of Bob Dylan song, best delivered outside the classical norms of singing.

In practice it had never seemed that easy to achieve the requisite vibe. On this occasion somehow it clicked; and it was definitely something to do with the space opened up by my particular reaction on that evening to the anger I had felt in "The Mock Suns" ("You're not my suns, why don't you go and look at someone else?"), and a connection made with the greatest Dylan love song performance on record, the bitter masterpiece "Don't Think Twice, It's All Right" on *The Freewheelin' Bob Dylan*. Schubert's "Hurdy-Gurdy Man" emerged as a song which was hardly sung at all: rasping and guttural by the standards of bel canto, but at the same time not impossibly at odds with what had gone before, and not a ridiculous intrusion of pop singing into the classical sound world—at least I hope not.

I HAVE NO IDEA IF BOB DYLAN was himself aware of *Winterreise*. Given his cultural eclecticism in the 1960s—swerving in imaginative intoxication between Rimbaud, Brecht, Elvis, and the Beat poets—it is not such an outlandish suggestion. There is a definite kinship between Schubert's hurdy-gurdy player and Dylan's tambourine man. This weary but not sleepy poet-wanderer talks of hearing "laughin', spinnin', swingin' madly across the sun"; of disappearing "far past the frozen leaves / The haunted, frightened trees." It's not a million miles from his jingle-jangle to Schubert's hurdy-gurdy.

. . .

IT IS UTTERLY APPROPRIATE to give the wretched
old hurdy-gurdy man "poor music," of course, though
Schubert's surefootedness in suggesting these grating
mechanical sounds takes the breath away. The raucous
third section of "Mut," two songs ago—"Joyfully out
into the world against wind and weather . . ."—was the
first intrusion into the cycle of notional real music, singing
aloud rather than the internal, symbolic sounds which have
emanated heretofore from the wanderer's mind. Now both
we and the wanderer hear someone else's music circulating in the frozen air. The confrontation with poverty
and another's exclusion which Müller arranges in his last
poem rouses a host of jostling feelings. Our wanderer's
existential misery is for the first time confronted with real
material distress, unchosen and stoically borne. The world
of Samuel Beckett collides with that of, say, Henry May-
hew, the Victorian cartographer and ethnographer of the
London poor, or of Sebastião Salgado, the documentary
photographer of contemporary Brazilian life; and we are
taken aback. Placing such a vision of true indigence at the
very end of the cycle is bound to raise at least a small question mark over the self-indulgence of endlessly perpetu-
ated, inner-directed pain.

At the same time, we feel, and are meant to feel, pity
and revulsion in equal measure as we encounter this out-

cast fragment of humanity with his irritating little folksy tune, droning on and on. Look at Georges de La Tour's picture of a blind hurdy-gurdy player and the same mix of feelings is engaged.

Our compassion is complex, and what ultimately complicates it is the fear that this lonely, squalid figure could be us. There but for the grace of God go you or I or anyone else. We are repelled and we are drawn in; we resist, but also admire the fortitude of one who can carry on in such circumstances. Could we do the same? The poem can only have struck a particular chord in Schubert, because he too was a musician. As he told his friend Eduard Bauernfeld in 1827: "I already see you as a Court Councillor and as a famous writer of comedies! But I! What's to become of a poor musician like me? I expect I shall have to slink up to doors in my old age, like Goethe's harper, and beg for bread!"

THE FUGITIVE AND SUPERNUMERARY clue to Schubert's intense personal investment with the figure of the hurdy-gurdy player is that phrase "Dreht er, was er kann"—He grinds away, as best he can. It reminds us of the wanderer's wry "Zittr' ich, was ich zittern kann"— I tremble (as much as I can)—from the song about the falling leaf. It also reminds us of another one of Schubert's

nicknames among his circle, "Kanevas"—in other words,
"What can he do?" or "Is he good for something?":
Schubert's inevitable question when someone new was
brought along to the party. Can he write a poem, play a
violin, sing, dance the polka, whatever? Kanevas, *kann
er was?,* and the hurdy-gurdy player plays "was er kann,"
as much or as well as he can—which is probably not very
well at all.

Schubert's importance as a composer lies, in the end,
in the irreducible magnificence and humanity of his
music. Historically, he is crucial as the first of the canonical "great" composers to have made his living solely
in the marketplace, without a patron, a position in the
court or church, or a musical sinecure of any sort. He
led a bohemian life, financially up and down. His friends
later remarked on his generosity to them when he was
flush—he was their Croesus. He was by no means the
unsuccessful unknown of legend. He made plenty of
money from his compositions. He was proud when he did.
But his position was perilous. Insecurity was woven into
his existence.

There had long been something disreputable about
being a musician. During the Middle Ages, instrumentalists had been viewed as incompetent in many legal matters: unable to be judges, witnesses, or jurors; ineligible
for land tenure; unable to serve as guardians or to hold

civic office; not accepted by the trade guilds; with no right to normal damages as plaintiffs in a civil case. Laws changed but the stigma remained, allied to the deep-rooted suspicion of the rootless and of those whose musical activities verged on the mystical, the magical, and the shamanic-demonic—the tale of the Pied Piper of Hamelin cast a long shadow. The Franconian penal code of 1746 introduced stern measures against "thieves, robbers, gypsies, swindlers, the propertyless and other beggar types," including those disguised as "players, drummers, fiddlers, lute players and singers of songs." A Swabian charter of 1742 warns against the itinerant, among whom are "barrel organists, bagpipers and dulcimer players."

Schubert's own awareness of his liminal status—half genius, half hired hand—can only have been intensified by the novelty of his situation. He was nobody's lackey; at the same time, he was a creature of the marketplace. Two intense outbursts reveal aspects of his frustration. In a letter to his parents regarding the publication of his settings of Sir Walter Scott he wrote: "If only once I could make some fair terms with publishers; but in that matter the wise and beneficent management of the Government has taken care that the artist shall remain for ever the slave of miserable hucksters." That outing to Grinzing with Lachner and Bauernfeld to taste the *Heurige* or new

wine—the occasion commemorated in Schwind's drawing reproduced earlier—ended a few hours later in a pub
in the Viennese suburbs, with Schubert in what Bauernfeld called "an elated state." Two celebrated players from
the opera house orchestra came in, complimented the
famous composer profusely, and asked him to write them
a piece. "No," he replied. "For you I shall write nothing."
"Why?—we are just as much artists as you are"—a reply
which elicited a furious tirade from Schubert:

Artists? Musical hacks are what you are! Nothing else!
One of you bites at the brass mouthpiece of his wooden
stick and the other blows out his cheeks on the horn!
Do you call that art? It's a trade, a knack that earns
money, and nothing more!—You, artists! Don't you
know what the great Lessing says?—How can anyone
spend his whole life doing nothing but biting on a piece
of wood with holes in it! . . . You call yourselves artists?
Blowers and fiddlers are what you are, the whole lot of
you! I am an artist, I! I am Schubert, Franz Schubert,
whom everybody knows and recognises! Who has
written great things and beautiful things, that you
don't begin to understand . . . I am Schubert! Franz
Schubert! And don't you forget it! And if the word art
is mentioned, it is *me* they are talking about, not you
worms and insects . . . you crawling, gnawing worms

that ought to be crushed under my foot—the foot of
the man who is reaching to the stars.

The authenticity of this anecdote, recorded by Bauernfeld, is sometimes doubted; the coruscating anger, the
violent fury, seem on the contrary a true reflection of the
Schubert who could, for example, introduce passages of
such sudden and extraordinary violence into his piano
pieces.

Müller's hurdy-gurdy player, then, must have made an
especial appeal to a composer and musician living on the
threshold of modernity, all too conscious of the dangers
of falling into the terrifying state of indigence that the old
man represents. Schubert's awareness of his own progno-
sis, the terrifying fate of the syphilitic, subject to inevitable physical and mental deterioration, can only have
intensified these fears.

IN UNPACKING THE MEANINGS of Schubert's fifth song,
"Der Lindenbaum" (The Linden Tree), I wanted to avoid
an undue stress upon death as the inviting whisperer—
which is not to deny the undeniable, that death, unnamed
and unnameable, is part of the associative aura of that
song. Death draws nearer towards the end of the cycle,
but equivocally. The graveyard has no place for our

wanderer, though he longs to rest there, and he strides
out of it with his trusty wandering staff and sings a loud
ditty to banish gloomy thoughts; his last words before the
arrival of the hurdy-gurdy man are that he would be better off if the sun set for him forever. It is unsurprising that
many have seen the hurdy-gurdy man as a figure of death,
only encouraged in this by the strong sixteenth-century
iconographic association between the two in the dance-
of-death, or *Totentanz*, genre. Here is Holbein's vision of
Death playing Adam and Eve out of the garden of Eden
to the strains of the hurdy-gurdy:

In so many of these *Totentanz* cycles, however, it is music that is to the fore rather than any particular instrument: music as an ironic accompaniment to the skeletal invitation, the joyous all muddled up with the macabre. A dance of death needs a band, after all. In one of the most extraordinary examples of the genre, Wilhelm Werner von Zimmern's *Vergänglichkeitsbuch* (Book of Mortality), illustrated between 1540 and 1550 and now in the Württembergische Landesbibliothek, a whole succession of instruments is illustrated in Death's hands, from the trumpet to the drum, from the portative organ to the *Dudelsack* or bagpipe.

It is much more fruitful, I would contend, to focus on the change in the terms of narrative engagement which occurs in this last song. Up until now, *Winterreise* has been a "monodrama." Everything has been presented to us by the poetic voice, the wanderer; and neither Müller nor Schubert has played sophisticated games by suggesting shiftiness in such narration as there is. The story may be incomplete, even reticent, perhaps teasing, but the narrator is not unreliable. No gulf opens up between the wandering voice and the poetic puppetmaster, composer, or poet. The complex music in the piano may often be distinct from or even at odds with that of the singing voice, may sometimes provide commentary or represent the outside world, human or natural; but it is not an indepen-

dent entity. Everything is filtered through the wanderer's
subjectivity, even if the harmonic transformations of the
piano part sometimes seem to reflect more the unconscious
than the conscious mind. The central ego does not consequently fragment, and at no point does the pianist become
a separate protagonist. So it seems to me; and it is a high-
falutin theoretical point which was confirmed practically
in our efforts to film the cycle with the director David
Alden in the late 1990s. Recognising the crucial role of
the piano in any performance of *Winterreise*—so crucial
that it seems almost idiotic to have to say it—and wanting
to reflect the equality of interest which a chamber-music
conception of the piece implies (this is not just a singer
with accompaniment), we tried to include the piano in the
visual story we told. It didn't work, and the pianist, Julius
Drake, remained largely invisible throughout the film
(though he played a large role in the documentary made to
accompany it).

In this last song, however, we do hear the piano as
separate for the first time. A notional source of alternative subjectivity, however pinched and etiolated, presents
itself: the hurdy-gurdy player. And so what is achieved,
in the end, is both a wonderful circularity, the musical-
poetical serpent biting its own tail; and the tantalising
offer of narrative closure and an explanation for what has
been going on. Up until now, the audience has experi-

enced the cycle as a monodrama, but now we see the possibility that the hurdy-gurdy player may have been there all along, and have been the very occasion for the wanderer singing his woes. "Will you play your hurdy-gurdy to my songs?" the wanderer asks. If the answer were to be a sturdy yes, then the crazy but logical procedure would be to go right back to the beginning of the whole cycle and start all over again, either with a notion of eternal recurrence in mind—we are trapped in the endless repetition of this existential lament (and remember that sense we had in the first song that this music had been going on forever)—or interpreting the first sing-through as being that monodrama with pianistic imaginarium we all experienced, but giving the second, and subsequent, performances to the accompaniment of the hurdy-gurdy. There is, in fact, a haunting and extraordinary recorded version of *Winterreise* to be found, realised for voice and hurdy-gurdy by the master player Matthias Loibner—a standing refutation, by the way, of the notion that the *Leiermann* is necessarily a deskilled or artless musician.

A momentary swell of passion in the hurdy-gurdy, just as the voice ceases—empathy between two outcasts in their pain?—is succeeded by diminution to pianissimo and a final cadence which in its open-endedness allows us the freedom to choose our own ending.

AFTERMATH

*W*HAT HAPPENS AFTER a performance of *Winterreise* is a little mysterious but usually follows a pattern. Silence emerges as the last hurdy-gurdy phrase dissipates into the hall, a silence which is often extended and forms part of the shared experience of the piece; a silence performed as much by the audience as it is by singer and pianist. A mute, stunned applause usually follows, which can swell into noisier acclaim.

Acclaim? Acclaim for what? For the composer? For the music? For the performance? Is applause, and the performers' acceptance of it, somehow impertinent? It sometimes, indeed often, feels that way. The normal rules of the song recital are in abeyance. No encores are prepared or expected and, however enthusiastically the audience respond, none will be forthcoming. There is a sense of seriousness, of having encountered something above and beyond, something ineffable and untouchable.

There can also be a sense of embarrassment or awkwardness between audience and performers, which the applause does its best, eventually, to eradicate. A song cycle such as *Winterreise* is not rooted in aspects of sung or musical performance which tend to create a certain awe-struck distance. Virtuosity is concealed, vocalism does not unduly draw attention to itself—even ironises itself—and the audience member must almost feel that he or she too is singing, and hence is implicated in the subjectivity which is being projected. The audience identifies with the persona constructed on stage, embodied in sound by piano and voice, but inhabited and projected by the singer. So, having gone so deeply into difficult places, having confronted each other across the footlights and opened up our vulner-abilities over what, at seventy minutes, is a considerable time span, a return to normality can feel unapproachable. End-of-concert rituals can help or they can impede. Some-times it feels impossible to do the customary things—meet friends, have a drink, eat a meal. Solitude may beckon.

| 487

THAT NOTION OF A SHARED EXPOSURE brings me to two myths which need deconstructing. The ideal of humility—of serving the music, of serving the com-poser—is a crucial part of the balancing act in classical performance. The discipline of classical music—the score and its demands—creates an objective space in which the dangers of self-indulgence can be held at bay. Self-expression can move outwards and trace something less solipsistic. At the same time, this can only be achieved, paradoxically, through utter immersion in the work and a merging between the composer's work and the performer's personality. Erasure in the music and the projection of subjectivity through it. Sublimation. But there is no neutral way of presenting this music, and it cannot be impersonal. The performer has to access and transform private aspects of his or her own self (just as, I would argue, the composer does). What the theorists call "performativity" is definitively in play, as much as, if not more than, for the great performers of the popular tradition—a Billie Holiday, a Bob Dylan, or an Amy Winehouse.

Schubert was the first performer of this work, accompanying himself at the piano. He was performing for friends, in a domestic setting, and he was neither a great pianist nor much of a singer. That nonperformance is, of all the performances that could have ever been, the one we would all like to have experienced. The thought of it can inform us, and it can feed our imaginations. At the same time, it cannot be our model.

THE OTHER MYTH is that which denies the relevance of the personal to the creation of this music; the feeling that

talking about the life of the creative artist is a vulgar distraction from the thing itself, from Art with a capital A.
Many writers on music, and on the other arts, decry
the practice of biographical criticism and would claim to
eschew it. It has, nonetheless, an insidious capacity to
creep back in despite analyses of the intentional fallacy
or declarations of the death of the author. Is this no more
than the natural inclination to relish gossip, even rarefied
gossip?

    It is undoubtedly true that there is no clear and pre-
scriptive relationship between life and art or art and life.
To put it at its most crass, Schubert wrote jolly music
when he was gloomy and gloomy music when he was
jolly. But the relationship between artistic expression and
lived experience works over a broader span. It is not just
a matter of the mood of the moment, and it also encom-
passes matters of personal character or predisposition as
well as intellectual presuppositions. Art is created in history, by living, feeling, thinking human beings; we cannot
understand it without grappling with its associations to
and grounding in worlds of emotion, ideology, or practical
constraint. Art is made from the collision between life and
form; it does not exist in some sort of idealised vacuum.
Only by investigating the personal and the political, in
their broadest sense (and this is especially true of Romantic art), can we properly assess the more formal aspects.

This book has not set out to do anything so systematic; it is no more than a small part of a continuing exploration of the complex and beautiful web of meanings—musical and literary, textual and metatextual—within which this *Winter Journey* works its spell.

BIBLIOGRAPHY

A., G., *Robert Schumann: Tagebücher*. Bd. I: 1827–1838 by Georg Eismann, review in *Music & Letters* 54, no. 1 (Jan. 1973), pp. 76–79.

Agawu, Kofi, "Schubert's Sexuality: A Prescription for Analysis?," *19th-Century Music* 17, no. 1, *Schubert: Music, Sexuality, Culture* (Summer 1993), pp. 79–82.

Applegate, Celia, "How German is it? Nationalism and the idea of serious music in the early nineteenth century," *19th-Century Music* 21 (Spring 1998), pp. 274–96.

Ashliman, D. L., "The Novel of Western Adventure in Nineteenth-Century Germany," *Western American Literature* 3 (1968), p. 2.

Auster, Paul, *Winter Journal* (2012).

Barba, Preston, "Cooper in Germany," *Indiana University Studies* 12, no. 5 (1914).

Baumann, Cecilia C., *Wilhelm Müller, the poet of the Schubert song cycles: His life and works* (1981).

Baumann, Cecilia C., and Luetgert, M. J., "*Die Winterreise:* The Secret of the Cycle's Appeal," *Mosaic* 15, no. 1 (Winter 1982), pp. 41–52.

Baxandall, Michael, *The Limewood Sculptors of Renaissance Germany* (1980).

Beckett, Samuel, *Texts for Nothing and other shorter prose, 1950–1976*, ed. Mark Nixon (2010).

Beebe, Barton Carl, "The Search for a Fatherland: James Fenimore Cooper in Germany," Princeton Ph.D. thesis (1998).

Behringer, Wolfgang, "Communications Revolutions: A Historiographical Concept," *German History* 24, no. 3 (2006), pp. 333–374.

———, *A Cultural History of Climate* (2010).

Beyrer, Klaus, "The Mail-Coach Revolution: Landmarks in Travel in Germany Between the Seventeenth and Nineteenth Centuries," *German History* 24, no. 3 (2006), pp. 375–386.

Biba, Otto, "Schubert's position in Viennese musical life," *19th-Century Music* 3, no. 2 (Nov. 1979), pp. 106–113.

Bilson, Malcolm, "Triplet Assimilation in the Music of Schubert," *Historical Performance* 31 (Spring 1994), pp. 27–31.

Bindra, Dalbir, "Weeping: A problem of many facets," *Bulletin of the British Psychological Society* 25, no. 89 (Oct. 1972), pp. 281–284.

Black, Leo, *Franz Schubert: Music and belief* (2003).

Blaicher, Günther, "Wilhelm Müller and the political reception of Byron in nineteenth-century Germany," *Archiv für das Studium der neueren Sprachen und Literaturen* 138. Jg., 223. Bd., 1. Halbjahresbd. Braunschweig (1986), pp. 1–16.

Blum, Jerome, "Transportation and Industry in Austria, 1815–1848," *Journal of Modern History* 15, no. 1 (Mar. 1943), pp. 24–38.

Borries, Erika von, *Wilhelm Müller, der Dichter der "Winterreise": Eine biographie* (2007).

Börsch-Supan, Helmut, "Caspar David Friedrich's Landscapes with Self-Portraits," *Burlington Magazine* 114, no. 834 (Sept. 1972), pp. 620–630.

Brendel, Alfred, *On Music* (2001).

Brentano, Clemens, *Godwi oder das steinerne Bild der Mutter—Ein verwilderten Roman* (1800–09).

Brinkmann, Reinhold, "Musikalische Lyrik, politische Allegorie und die 'heil'ge Kunst': Zur Landschaft von Schuberts *Winterreise*," *Archiv für Musikwissenschaft* 62. Jahrg., H. 2. (2005), pp. 75–97.

———, *Franz Schubert, Lindenbäume und deutsch-nationale Identität—Interpretation eines Liedes* (2004).

Brown, Maurice, *Schubert: A critical biography* (1961).

Brown, Maurice J. E., "The Therese Grob Collection of Songs by Schubert," *Music & Letters* 49, no. 2 (Apr. 1968), pp. 122–134.

Burnham, Scott, "Schubert and the Sound of Memory," *Musical Quarterly* 84, no. 4 (Winter 2000).

Byrne, Lorraine, "Schubert, Goethe and the Singspiel: An Elective Affinity," at http://www.ucd.ie/pages/99/articles/byrne.pdf

Cairns-Smith, A. G., *Seven Clues to the Origin of Life* (1985).

Cameron, Dorothy, "Goethe—Discoverer of the Ice Age," *Glaciology* 5 (1965), pp. 751–753.

Cho, Sung Ki, et al., "Regulation of floral organ abscission in Arabidopsis thaliana," *Proceedings of the National Academy of Sciences* 105.40 (2008), pp. 15629-15634.

Clark, Christopher, "The Wars of Liberation in Prussian Memory: Reflections on the Memorialization of War in Early Nineteenth-Century Germany," *Journal of Modern History* 68, no. 3 (Sept. 1996), pp. 550–576.

Clark, Suzannah, *Analyzing Schubert* (2011).

Clive, Peter, *Schubert and his World: A biographical dictionary* (1997).

Cocker, Mark, *Crow Country* (2007).

Coetzee, J. M., *Summertime* (2009).

Cole, Laurence, review of *Habsburgs Diener in Post und Politik: Das "Haus" Thurn und Taxis zwischen 1745 und 1867* by Siegfried Grillmeyer; Philipp von Zabern in *Central European History* 42, no. 4 (Dec. 2009), pp. 763–766.

Cook, Nicholas, *Music, Imagination, and Culture* (1992).

Cooper, James Fenimore, *The Last of the Mohicans* (1826).

Cottrell, Alan P., *Wilhelm Müller's Lyrical Song-Cycles: Interpretations and texts* (1970).

Craig, Gordon A., *The Germans* (1982). | 493

Cunliffe, W. Gordon, "Cousin Joachim's Steel Helmet: *Der Zauberberg* and the War," *Monatshefte* 68, no. 4 (Winter 1976), pp. 409–417.

Deutsch, Otto Erich, *Schubert: A documentary biography* (1946).

———, *Schubert: Memoirs by his friends* (1958).

Dixon, Thomas, "History in British Tears: Some Reflections on the Anatomy of Modern Emotions," lecture delivered at the annual conference of the Netherlands Historical Association, Koninklijke Bibliotheek Den Haag, 4 November 2011, at http://emotionsblog.history.qmul.ac.uk/wp-content/uploads/2012/03/History-in-British-Tears.pdf

Dortmann, Andrea, *Winter Facets: traces and tropes of the cold* (2007).

Dürhammer, Ilija, *Geheime Botschaften: Homoerotische Subkulturen im Schubert-Kreis, bei Hugo von Hofmannsthal und Thomas Bernhard* (2006).

Dürr, Walther, et al. (eds.), *Schubert Liedlexicon* (2012).

Dürr, Walther, "Schubert and Johann Michael Vogl: A Reappraisal," *19th-Century Music* 3, no. 2 (Nov. 1979), pp. 126–140.

Dwight, Henry Edwin, *Travels in the North of Germany in the Years 1825 and 1826* (1829).

Egger, Irmgard, "Cooper and German Readers," paper presented at the 5th Cooper Seminar, *"James Fenimore Cooper: His Country and His Art,"* at the State University of New York at Oneonta, July 1984, at http://www.oneonta.edu/~cooper/articles/suny/1984suny-egger1.html

Elfenbein, Andrew, *Byron and the Victorians* (1995).

English, Charlie, *The Snow Tourist: A search for the world's purest, deepest snowfall* (2008).

Erickson, Raymond (ed.), *Schubert's Vienna* (1997).

Fagan, Brian, *The Little Ice Age: How climate made history 1300–1850* (2000).

Feil, Arnold, *Fran*₇ *Schubert: "Die schöne Müllerin," "Winterreise"* (1988).

Feurzeig, Lisa, "Heroines in Perversity: Marie Schmith, Animal Magnetism, and the Schubert Circle," *19th-Century Music* 21, no. 2, *Fran*₇ *Schubert: Bicentenary Essays* (Autumn 1997), pp. 223–243.

Fischer-Dieskau, Dietrich, *Echoes of a Lifetime: Memories and Thoughts* (1989).

Fisk, Charles, "Schubert Recollects Himself: The Piano Sonata in C Minor, D. 958," *Musical Quarterly* 84, no. 4 (Winter 2000), pp. 635–654.

Frisch, Walter (ed.), *Schubert: Critical and analytical studies* (1986).

Galt, Anthony H., "The Good Cousins' Domain of Belonging: Tropes in Southern Italian Secret Society Symbol and Ritual, 1810–1821," *Man*, New Series 29, no. 4 (Dec. 1994), pp. 785–807.

Georgiades, Thrasybulos G., *Schubert: Musik und Lyrik* (1967).

Giarusso, Richard, "Beyond the Leiermann: Disorder, reality, and the power of imagination in the final songs of Schubert's *Winterreise*" in *The Unknown Schubert*, ed. Barbara M. Reul and Lorraine Byrne Bodley (2008).

Gibbs, Christopher H. (ed.), *The Cambridge Companion to Schubert* (1997).

Gibbs, Christopher H., *The Life of Schubert* (2000).

Goehr, Linda, *The Imaginary Museum of Musical Works: An essay in the philosophy of music* (2007).

Goethe, Johann Wolfgang von, *Faust*, trans. Walter Kaufmann (1961).

———, *The Sorrows of Young Werther*, trans. David Constantine (2012).

———, *Wilhelm Meister*, trans. H. M. Waidson (2011).

Gopnik, Adam, *Winter: Five Windows on the Season* (2012).

Gouk, Penelope, "Music as a means of social control: some examples of practice and theory in early modern Europe," unpublished paper.

Gouk, Penelope, and Hills, Helen (eds.), *Representing emotions: New connections in the history of art, music, and medicine* (2005).

Gramit, David, "Between 'Täuschung' and 'Seligkeit': Situating Schubert's Dances," *Musical Quarterly* 84, no. 2 (Summer 2000), pp. 221–237.

———, "Constructing a Victorian Schubert: Music, Biography, and Cultural Values," *19th-Century Music* 17, no. 1, *Schubert: Music, Sexuality, Culture* (Summer 1993), pp. 65–78.

———, "Schubert and the Biedermeier: The Aesthetics of Johann Mayrhofer's 'Heliopolis,'" *Music & Letters* 74, no. 3 (Aug. 1993), pp. 355–382.

———, "Schubert's Wanderers and the Autonomous Lied," *Journal of Musicological Research* 14 (1995), pp. 147–168.

————, *Cultivating Music: The aspirations, interests, and limits of German musical culture, 1770–1848* (2002).

Green, Robert A., *The Hurdy-Gurdy in Eighteenth-Century France* (1995).

Gross, Nachum T., "Industrialisation in Austria in the Nineteenth Century," Berkeley Ph.D. dissertation (1966).

Hacking, Ian, *The Taming of Chance* (1990).

Hallmark, Rufus (ed.), *German Lieder in the Nineteenth Century* (1996).

Hanson, Alice M., *Musical Life in Biedermeier Vienna* (1985).

Heimann, Heinz-Dieter, review of *Neue Perspektiven für die Geschichte der Post. Zur Methode der Postgeschichte und ihrem operativen Verhältnis zur allgemeinen Geschichtswissenschaft in Verbindung mit einem Literaturbericht zum Postjubilaum 1490–1990*, *Historische Zeitschrift*, Bd. 253, H. 3 (Dec. 1991), pp. 661–674.

Heine, Heinrich, *Deutschland: A Winter's Tale*, ed. with trans. by T. J. Reed (1997).

Hetenyi, G., "The terminal illness of Franz Schubert and the treatment of syphilis in Vienna in the eighteen hundred and twenties," *Canadian Bulletin of Medical History* 3, no. 1 (Summer 1986), pp. 51–64.

Hilmar, Ernst, *Franz Schubert in His Time* (1988).

Hoeckner, Berthold, "Schumann and Romantic Distance," *Journal of the American Musicological Society* 50, no. 1 (Spring 1997), pp. 55–132.

Hook, Julian, "How to perform impossible rhythms," *Music Theory Online* 17, no. 4 (Dec. 2011), at http://www.mtosmt.org/issues/mto.11.17.4 /mto.11.17.4.hook.html

Iurascu, Ilinca, "German Realism in the Postal Office: Mail-Traffic, Violence, and Nostalgia in Theodor Storm's *Hans und Heinz Kirch* and Wilhelm Raabe's *Stopfkuchen*," *German Studies Review* 32, no. 1 (Feb. 2009), pp. 148–164.

Jarvis, Robin, "The Glory of Motion: De Quincey, Travel, and Romanticism," *Yearbook of English Studies* 34 (2004), pp. 74–87.

Jelinek, J. E., "Sudden Whitening of the Hair," *Bulletin of the New York Academy of Medicine* 48, no. 8 (Sept. 1972).

Kater, Michael H., *The Twisted Muse: Musicians and their music in the Third Reich* (1997).

Katzenstein, Peter J., *Disjoined Parties: Austria and Germany since 1815* (1976).

Kinderman, William, "Wandering Archetypes in Schubert's Instrumental Music," *19th-Century Music* 21, no. 2, *Franz Schubert: Bicentenary Essays* (Autumn 1997), pp. 208–222.

Koerner, Joseph Leo, *Caspar David Friedrich and the Subject of Landscape* (2nd ed., 2009).

Kramer, Lawrence, *Why Classical Music Still Matters* (2007).

Lawley, Paul, "'The Grim Journey': Beckett Listens to Schubert," *Samuel Beckett Today/Aujourd'hui* 11 (2001).

Lindley, Mark, "Marx and Engels on Music," at http://mrzine.monthly review.org/2010/lindley180810.html

Lutz, Tom, *Crying: The natural and cultural history of tears* (1999).

MacDonald, Hugh, "Schubert's Volcanic Temper," *Musical Times* 119, no. 1629 (Nov. 1978), pp. 949–952.

Maier, Franz Michael, "The Idea of Melodic Connection in Samuel Beckett," *Journal of the American Musicological Society* 61, no. 2 (Summer 2008), pp. 373–410.

Mann, Alfred, "Schubert's Lesson with Sechter," *19th-Century Music* 6, no. 2 (Autumn 1982), pp. 159–165.

Mann, Thomas, *The Magic Mountain*, trans. John E. Woods (1995).

Marzluff, John M., and Angell, Tony, *In the Company of Crows and Ravens* (2005).

Matthews, John A., and Briffa, Keith R., "The 'Little Ice Age': Re-Evaluation of an Evolving Concept," *Geografiska Annaler.* Series A, Physical Geography 87, no. 1, Special Issue: *Climate Change and Variability* (2005), pp. 17–36.

McClary, Susan, "Music and Sexuality: On the Steblin/Solomon Debate," *19th-Century Music* 17, no. 1, *Schubert: Music, Sexuality, Culture* (Summer 1993), pp. 83–88.

McKay, Elizabeth Norman, *Franz Schubert: A Biography* (1996).

Messing, Scott, *Schubert in the European Imagination*, 2 vols. (2007).

Montgomery, David, "Triplet Assimilation in the Music of Schubert: Challenging the Ideal," *Historical Performance* (Fall 1993), pp. 79–97.

Moore, Gerald, *The Schubert Song Cycles, with thoughts on performance* (1975).

Müller, F. Max, *Chips from a German Workshop*, vol. 3 (1889).

Müller, Wilhelm, *Rom, Römer und Römerinnen* (1991 edition).

Muxfeldt, Kristina, "Political Crimes and Liberty, or Why Would Schubert Eat a Peacock?," *19th-Century Music* 17, no. 1 (Summer 1993), pp. 47–64.

———, "Schubert, Platen, and the Myth of Narcissus," *Journal of the American Musicological Society* 49, no. 3 (Autumn 1996), pp. 480–523, 525–527.

———, *Vanishing Sensibilities: Schubert, Beethoven, Schumann* (2011).

Nemoianu, Virgil, *The Taming of Romanticism: European literature and the age of Biedermeier* (1984).

Nettheim, Nigel, "Accompanying Schubert's 'Lindenbaum,'" *Piano Journal* 18, no. 52 (February 1997), pp. 15–21.

Newbould, Brian, *Schubert: The music and the man* (1997).

Newbould, Brian (ed.), *Schubert Studies* (1998).

Newsom, John, "Hans Pfitzner, Thomas Mann and *The Magic Mountain*," *Music & Letters* 55, no. 2 (Apr. 1974), pp. 136–150.

Nollen, John Scholte, "Heine and Wilhelm Müller," *Modern Language Notes* 17, no. 4 (Apr. 1902), pp. 103–110.

Oeser, Hans-Christian, "Ice as a Metaphor for Political Stagnation: Some Cultural Parallels between Germany after 1815 and West Germany after 1972," *Maynooth Review/Revieú Mhá Nuad* 11 (Dec. 1984), pp. 60–75.

Ozment, Steven, *A Mighty Fortress: a new history of the German people* (2004). | 497

Peake, Luise Eitel, "Kreutzer's *Wanderlieder*: The Other *Winterreise*," *Musical Quarterly* 65 (1979), pp. 83–102.

Penny, H. Glenn, *Kindred by Choice: Germans and American Indians since 1800* (2013).

Pesic, Peter, "Schubert's Dream," *19th-Century Music* 23, no. 2 (Autumn 1999), pp. 136–144.

Porter, Peter, "Lament Addressed to the People," *London Review of Books* 20, no. 10 (May 1998).

Rath, R. John, "The Carbonari: Their Origins, Initiation Rites, and Aims," *American Historical Review* 69, no. 2 (Jan. 1964), pp. 353–370.

Reade, J. B., "On the Scientific Explanation of Parhelia," *Mathematical Gazette* 87, no. 509 (Jul. 2003), pp. 243–49.

Reed, John, *Schubert: The Final Years* (1972).

———, *The Schubert Song Companion* (1985).

Reed, T. J., "Thomas Mann: The Writer as Historian of His Time," *Modern Language Review* 71, no. 1 (Jan. 1976), pp. 82–96.

Reininghaus, Frieder, *Schubert und das Wirtshaus: Musik unter Metternich* (1979).

Reul, Barbara M., and Bodley, Lorraine Byrne (eds.), *The Unknown Schubert* (2008).

Richards, Robert J., *The Romantic Conception of Life: Science and philosophy in the age of Goethe* (2002).

Robinson, Peter, "Ice and snow in paintings of Little Ice Age winters," *Weather* 60, no. 2 (February 2005).

Rosen, Charles, *Freedom and the Arts: Essays on music and literature* (2012).

———, *Music and Sentiment* (2010).

———, *The Romantic Generation* (1995).

Rosenwein, Barbara H., "Worrying about Emotions in History," *American Historical Review* 107, no. 3 (June 2002), pp. 821–845.

Rousseau, Jean-Jacques, *Reveries of the Solitary Walker,* trans. Russell Goulbourne (2011).

Sadoff, Robert L., "On the nature of crying and weeping," *Psychiatric Quarterly* 40, issue 1-4 (1966), pp. 490–503.

Said, Edward W., *Musical Elaborations* (1992).

Sams, Eric, "Schubert's Illness Re-Examined," *Musical Times* 121, no. 1643 (1980), pp. 15–22.

Schneider, Eva Maria, "Herkunft und Verbreitungsformen der 'Deutschen Nationaltracht der Befreiungskriege' als Ausdruck politischer Gesinnung," Ph.D. dissertation Universität Bonn, Philosophische Fakultät (2002).

Schroeder, David, *Our Schubert: His enduring legacy* (2009).

Schroeder, David P., "Schubert's 'Einsamkeit' and Haslinger's Winterreise," *Music & Letters* 71, no. 3 (1990), pp. 352–360.

Schubert, Franz, *Die Winterreise: Faksimile-Widergabe nach der Originalhandschrift* (1955).

———, *Neue Ausgabe sämtlicher Werke: Lieder Band 4,* ed. Walther Dürr (1979).

Schulze, Hagen, *The Course of German Nationalism: from Frederick the Great to Bismarck* (1991).

Sealsfield, Charles, *Austria as it is, or, Sketches of continental courts, by an eyewitness* (1828).

Shields, David, *Reality Hunger: A Manifesto* (2010).

Siegel, Linda, *Music in German Romantic Literature* (1983).

Smeed, J. W., "The Fifth Song of *Winterreise:* 'Volksgut und Meisterwerk Zugleich,'" *Forum for Modern Language Studies* 37, no. 1 (Jan. 2001), pp. 50–57.

Solomon, Maynard, "Franz Schubert and the Peacocks of Benvenuto Cellini," *19th-Century Music* 12, no. 3 (Spring 1989), pp. 193–206.

———, "Schubert: Family Matters," *19th-Century Music* 28, no. 1 (Summer 2004), pp. 3–14.

———, "Schubert: Some Consequences of Nostalgia," *19th-Century Music* 17, no. 1 (Summer 1993), pp. 34–46.

Steblin, Rita, "In Defense of Scholarship and Archival Research: Why Schubert's Brothers Were Allowed to Marry," *Current Musicology* 62 (1998), pp. 7–17.

————, "Schubert's 'Nina' and the True Peacocks," *Musical Times* 138, no. 1849 (Mar. 1997), pp. 13–19.

————, "Schubert's Pepi: His Love Affair with the Chambermaid Josepha Pöcklhofer and Her Surprising Fate," *Musical Times* 149, no. 1903 (Summer 2008), pp. 47–69.

————, "The Peacock's Tale: Schubert's sexuality reconsidered," *19th-Century Music* 17, no. 1 (Summer 1993), pp. 5–33.

————, "Therese Grob: New documentary research," *Schubert durch die Brille* 28 (2002), pp. 55–100.

Stokes, Richard, *The Book of Lieder: The original texts of over 1000 songs* (2005).

Taruskin, Richard, *The Oxford History of Western Music*, 6 vols. (2005).

Tassel, Eric van, " 'Something utterly new': Listening to Schubert Lieder," *Early Music* (November 1997), pp. 703–714.

Tellenbach, Marie-Elisabeth, "Franz Schubert and Benvenuto Cellini: One Man's Meat," *Musical Times* 141, no. 1870 (Spring 2000), pp. 50–52.

Tunbridge, Laura, *The Song Cycle* (2010).

Turnbull, Peter Evan, *Austria* (London, 1840).

Vaget, Hans Rudolf, " 'Politically Suspect': Music in *The Magic Mountain*," in Vaget (ed.), *Thomas Mann's "The Magic Mountain": A casebook* (2008).

Vaughan, William, *Friedrich* (2004).

Walton, James, "Charcoal Burners' Huts," *Gwerin* 2, issue 2 (1958), pp. 58–67.

————, "Music, Pathology, Sexuality, Beethoven, Schubert," *19th-Century Music* 17, no. 1, *Schubert: Music, Sexuality, Culture* (Summer 1993), pp. 89–93.

Wellbery, David E. (ed.), *A New History of German Literature* (2004).

Wigmore, Richard, *Schubert: The complete song texts* (1988).

Williamson, George S., "What Killed August von Kotzebue? The Temptations of Virtue and the Political Theology of German Nationalism, 1789–1819," *Journal of Modern History* 72, no. 4 (Dec. 2000), pp. 890–943.

Wilson, Eric G., *The Spiritual History of Ice: Romanticism, science, and the imagination* (2003).

Winter, Robert S., "Whose Schubert?," *19th-Century Music* 17, no. 1, *Schubert: Music, Sexuality, Culture* (Summer 1993), pp. 94–101.

Winternitz, Emanuel, "Bagpipes and Hurdy-Gurdies in Their Social Setting," *Metropolitan Museum of Art Bulletin*, New Series 2, no. 1 (Summer 1943), pp. 56–83.

Wolf, Norbert, *Caspar David Friedrich, 1774–1840: The painter of stillness* (2003).

Wolf, Werner, " 'Willst zu meinen Liedern deine Leier drehn?' Intermedial Metatextuality in Schubert's 'Der Leiermann' as a Motivation for Song and Accompaniment and a Contribution to the Unity of *Die Winterreise*," in Walter Bernhart and Werner Wolf (eds.), *Word and Music Studies 3: Essays on the Song Cycle and on Defining the Field* (2001), pp. 121–140.

Wright, C. J., "The 'Spectre' of Science: The Study of Optical Phenomena and the Romantic Imagination," *Journal of the Warburg and Courtauld Institutes* 43 (1980), pp. 186–200.

Youens, Susan, "Schubert, Mahler and the Weight of the Past: *Lieder eines fahrenden Gesellen* and *Winterreise*," *Music & Letters* 67, no. 3 (Jul. 1986), pp. 256–68.

———, *Heinrich Heine and the Lied* (2007).

———, *Retracing a Winter's Journey: Schubert's "Winterreise"* (1991).

———, *Schubert's Late Lieder: Beyond the Song-Cycles* (2002).

Zerubavel, Eviatar, "The Standardization of Time: A Sociohistorical Perspective," *American Journal of Sociology* 88, no. 1 (Jul. 1982), pp. 1–23.

Žižek, Slavoj, "Lenin as a Listener of Schubert," http://www.marxists.org/reference/subject/philosophy/works/ot/zizek1.htm

ILLUSTRATION CREDITS

Ian Bostridge is universally recognized as one of the greatest lieder interpreters of today. He has made numerous award-winning recordings of opera and song, and gives recitals regularly throughout Europe, North America, and the Far East to outstanding critical acclaim. He read modern history at Oxford and received a D.Phil. in 1990. His book *Witchcraft and Its Transformations, c. 1650–c. 1750* was published in 1997; *A Singer's Notebook* followed in 2011. He is Humanitas Professor of Music at the University of Oxford, 2014–15. A regular contributor to *The Guardian* and the *TLS*, he is married to the writer and critic Lucasta Miller. They live in London with their two children.

This book was set in Fournier, a typeface named for Pierre Simon Fournier *le jeune* (1712–1768), a celebrated French type designer. Coming from a family of typefounders, Fournier was an extraordinarily prolific designer of typefaces and of typographic ornaments. He was also the author of the important Manuel typographique (1764–1766), in which he attempted to work out a system standardizing type measurement in points, a system that is still in use internationally.

Fournier's type is considered transitional in that it drew its inspiration from the old style, yet was ingeniously innovational, providing for an elegant, legible appearance. In 1925 his type was revived by the Monotype Corporation of London.

Composed by North Market Street Graphics, Lancaster, Pennsylvania

Printed and bound by L.E.G.O. S.p.A, Lavis Trento, Italy

Designed by Maggie Hinders